Creative Cognition

Creative Cognition
Theory, Research, and Applications

Ronald A. Finke, Thomas B. Ward, and
Steven M. Smith

A Bradford Book
The MIT Press
Cambridge, Massachusetts
London, England

This book was set in Palatino by DEKR Corporation and was printed and bound in the United States of America.

Library of Congress Cataloging-in-Publication Data

Finke, Ronald A.
    Creative cognition : theory, research, and applications / Ronald
A. Finke, Thomas B. Ward, and Steven M. Smith.
        p.   cm.
    "A Bradford book."
    Includes bibliographical references and index.
    ISBN 0-262-06150-3
    1. Creative thinking. 2. Cognition. 3. Imagery (Psychology)
4. Visualization.   I. Ward, Thomas B.   II. Smith, Steven M.
III. Title.
    BF408.F447   1992
    153.3'5—dc20   92-4600
                                                    CIP

Contents

Acknowledgments

We thank the following people for their helpful contributions to the ideas and experiments presented in this book: Stephen Balfour, Angela Becker, Steven Blankenship, Jeffrey Brown, David Cohen, Sridhar Condoor, Richard Crawford, Janet Davidson, Jennifer Freyd, Arthur Glenberg, Marvin Levine, Donna McKeown, Doug Medin, Janet Metcalfe, Chad Neff, Ulric Neisser, Larry Parsons, David Perkins, Traci Ratliff, Nancy Rhodes, Jay Schumacher, Michael Smith, Jyotsna Vaid, and Eddie Vela. We extend special thanks to Jonathan Schooler for his insightful comments on the manuscript. Finally, we thank Tim Davis and Cindy Mullican of Cartographics for their assistance in preparing the illustrations.

Portions of our research were supported by grants R01MH-39809, R01MH-43356, and R01MH-44730 from the National Institute of Mental Health.

Creative Cognition

1

Introduction to Creative Cognition

Overview

Creativity has long been a topic of interest to educators, artists, and historians of science. Until recently, however, it has not been a subject of serious study among cognitive scientists and experimental psychologists. It has been regarded as largely unresearchable, for two primary reasons. First, the subject of creativity has had unscientific connotations, perhaps resulting from reliance on anecdotal or introspective accounts in previous attempts to describe the creative process. Textbooks on human cognition, if they mention creativity at all, tend to do so in an informal, descriptive way compared with traditional topics, such as attention, memory, and problem solving. Second, it is not at all obvious how one might begin to study creativity under controlled laboratory conditions.

In this book, we present an approach to the study of creativity, called *creative cognition*, which is based on the experimental methods of cognitive science. In this approach, we attempt to identify the specific cognitive processes and structures that contribute to creative acts and products and to develop novel techniques for studying creativity within the context of controlled scientific experiments. We view this approach as providing a foundation for a new, emerging field in cognitive science that will complement previous approaches to creativity.

A central feature of the creative cognition approach is that it ties in with current research in traditional areas of human cognition and cognitive psychology. One of the major themes of this book is that findings of creative cognition research can have important implications for both advancing our understanding of creativity and for extending current methods and ideas in these traditional areas. In fact, research in some of these areas, such as imagery, categorization, and problem solving, has already begun to move in the direction of exploring creative cognitive processes.

The creative cognition approach is unique in many respects. First, we conceive of creativity not as a single unitary process but as a product of many types of mental processes, each of which helps to set the stage for creative insight and discovery. In particular, we distinguish between processes used in the generation of cognitive structures and those used to explore the creative implications of those structures. Among the generative processes we consider to be important are memory retrieval, association, mental synthesis, mental transformation, analogical transfer, and categorical reduction. The exploratory processes we regard as most relevant are attribute finding, conceptual interpretation, functional inference, contextual shifting, hypothesis testing, and searching for limitations. We also consider the manner in which these processes should be employed—for example, whether they should occur in a certain order or be constrained in certain ways throughout the creative act.

Second, we distinguish the cognitive structures used in creative cognition from the processes that give rise to them and contribute to their exploration and interpretation. Of particular importance are those cognitive structures that we call preinventive structures, which are used to represent novel visual patterns, object forms, mental blends, category exemplars, mental models, and verbal combinations. Unlike the final, resulting products of creative cognition, preinventive structures are internal representations that may be largely uninterpreted at the time they are initially constructed.

Third, in creative cognition, we attempt to identify the properties of preinventive structures that are exploited in creative search and exploration, such as novelty, ambiguity, implicit meaningfulness, emergence, incongruity, and divergence. We propose that the same processes can lead to either creative cognitions exhibiting these properties or to noncreative cognitions that fail to exhibit them. For example, people can generate original images that lead to insight and innovation or commonplace images that lead nowhere, depending on the properties of those images. Establishing connections between the underlying processes and the properties of the resulting cognitions can lead to a clearer understanding of creative thought and, as a by-product, to a greater understanding of cognition in general.

Not all creative cognitions will be characterized by all of those properties; rather, these properties form a kind of family resemblance concept. Most creative cognitions will possess most of the properties, but different cognitions will contain different subsets of the properties and, with the possible exception of novelty, no one property is necessary. When viewed in this way, the creativity of a given cognition can be conceived in terms of a graded structure. The more of these properties the cognition contains, the more likely it is that it will result in a creative product. Because of this family resemblance view and because we view creative and noncreative cognitions as resulting from the same types of underlying processes, we consider them as essentially lying along the same continuum. Thus, we avoid trying to define creativity and creative cognitive processes in an explicit, absolute way.

Fourth, we distinguish the creative cognitions that give rise to an idea from the quality or value of the idea itself. This is necessary because the same idea could be arrived at resourcefully or accidentally and be regarded as ingenious in one case and fortuitous in the other. In some approaches to creativity and design, only the final product counts; however, it is crucial to know the cognitive processes and structures that are behind an idea. In creative cognition, one accomplishes this by attempting to relate properties of creative cognitions to those of the final products. Some of the properties of creative products that we consider important are originality, practicality, sensibility, productivity, flexibility, inclusiveness, and insightfulness. Establishing these connections helps one to develop a true, cognitive approach to creativity, as well as new, effective methods for teaching people how to generate creative ideas.

Fifth, in adopting the creative cognition approach, we are more concerned with identifying the conditions under which creative discovery is likely to occur than with trying to predict creative performance in an absolute, determined way. By its very nature, creativity is not entirely predictable, though we believe that people can learn how to think in ways that maximize the opportunity for creative insight. Our approach is in contrast, for example, to approaches often taken in studies on problem solving, where one attempts to uncover procedures or algorithms that guarantee a correct solution.

Finally, in creative cognition we strive to develop global information processing models that relate cognitive processes, emergent cognitions, and the resultant creative products because these models can provide a deeper understanding of how creativity is expressed across widely varied domains. This makes it possible to explain, for example, what artistic, inventive, and scientific creativity have in common. We will propose that one such model, which we call the Geneplore model, provides a possible foundation for a unified account of creative cognition.

The Goals of Creative Cognition

Identifying Creative Cognitive Processes
The primary goal of creative cognition is to provide a more explicit account of the cognitive processes and structures that contribute to creative thinking and discovery. One might ask, from the standpoint of traditional studies in cognitive science, why this is such an important issue.

In contemporary research on human cognition, topics such as retrieving memories, generating images, and solving problems have typically been explored in what are essentially noncreative contexts (Anderson 1990; Glass and Holyoak 1986; Kosslyn 1980; Reed 1982). Being creative is one of the most important things that a person can do, yet there is little one can actually learn about creativity from reading the current cognitive literature. Indeed, if a person were to ask, "What can I do to think more creatively?" few answers could be found in most of the cognitive studies that have been conducted up to now.

Granted, there have been previous attempts to develop cognitive approaches to creativity. Gardner (1982), for example, used a cognitive developmental perspective to explore artistic creativity. The major limitation of this and other similar approaches is that they have generally used cognitive terms and concepts only in a general, descriptive sense. Gardner, for example, describes artistic creativity in terms of computational and compositional schemas without going into much detail about the underlying cognitive processes that those schemas would entail. Although such efforts constitute an important initial step toward trying to develop a theory of creative cognition, eventually one would want to identify the specific kinds of cognitive processes underlying creative performance, as well as the properties of the resulting cognitions that distinguish them as creative.

The same criticism can be made of approaches that have attempted to identify general cognitive heuristics related to creativity. An example is the concept of lateral thinking, introduced by de Bono (1975), which is considered in a descriptive and mostly pragmatic context and is theory driven only in the most general sense. Although such approaches often lead to practical techniques for thinking creatively, they are developed more or less independently of contemporary work in cognitive science. Part of the problem is that the term *thinking* is itself vague, referring potentially to a phenomenon influenced by all aspects of cognition rather than to more specific, identifiable processes. One must first specify the component processes of thinking before terms such as *lateral thinking* can be used in a rigorous theory of creative cognition.

On the other hand, a number of studies, most of them in the field of problem solving, have considered very specific types of cognitive processes. These efforts, however, have been restricted for the most part to traditional "insight" problems and the like, where the solutions are already well known (Kaplan and Simon 1990; Metcalfe 1986a; Newell and Simon 1972). In contrast to general cognitive heuristics, these approaches detail specific processes, but they apply to highly restricted domains rather than to creative functioning in general. We believe that in order to understand the true nature of creativity, cognitive processes must be considered in a much broader perspective, where the problems and solutions are not necessarily restricted or known.

In summary, we are proposing a general approach to the study of creativity in terms of specific cognitive processes and structures. Our approach differs from previous approaches in that we are looking at cognitive processes that can give rise to creative insights of many types, not just those that apply to particular tasks or problems. At the same time, we are concerned with developing formal experimental methods for identifying these processes and for testing explicit theories of creative cognition instead of simply relying on general descriptions or heuristics.

Establishing General Principles
A second goal of creative cognition is to establish general cognitive principles of creativity that apply across many domains. We want to be able to specify how one might go about thinking more creatively in general, as a result of experimental findings in studies on creative cognition.

The view that there are general principles of creative thinking is in contrast to the prevalent view among cognitive psychologists that creativity tends to be restricted to particular domains and depends on having the necessary background knowledge and knowing how to apply it (Perkins 1981; Weisberg 1986). One can point to cases, for example, where creative mathematicians or physicists end up making brilliant contributions in only a single, narrow field of study (Bell 1965). Although such cases could be taken as evidence for a domain-specific view, it should be clear that there are many factors, including motivation and inspiration, that might lead a generally creative individual to express creativity in just one domain.

Although we agree that an important part of being creative is knowing the "rules of the game" and becoming skilled at applying them

(Perkins 1981), we do not believe that this is inconsistent with our claim that there are general principles of creative cognition. There is no reason that cognitive strategies that promote creativity in one domain could not be extended to other domains as long as the strategies are sufficiently flexible to accommodate changes in context or structure and as long as the person could recognize when an idea in the new domain was truly important. We believe that creative people share a basic understanding of how to go about being creative; they can then extend their creative skills into other areas as long as they know something about the relevant issues, methods, and values and are sufficiently motivated to do so.

General principles, of course, should be expressed in terms of measurable cognitive operations; one cannot simply rely on vague generalities or prescriptions. Consider again the notion that lateral thinking can promote creativity. One would want to identify the specific kinds of cognitive processes that give rise to or constitute lateral thinking and then provide an explicit account of how they might be extended across different situations or contexts.

Anticipating Creative Discoveries

Having a general theory of creative cognition does not mean that one should always be able to predict when a creative idea will occur. Rather, the goal should be to establish the probability of emergent creativity under various conditions. Having a better understanding of the underlying cognitive processes will increase the likelihood of predicting when a creative idea will be generated, but there is no guarantee that this will happen in every case. Creativity is often surprising and unexpected, and these characteristics need to be taken into account.

This view is to be contrasted with the focus of many current cognitive models, which tend to be strongly deterministic and seek to account for as much variance as possible in performance on particular tasks. They are more concerned with restricting and controlling the kinds of cognitive processes that are used than with allowing performance to vary in creative ways (Finke 1989). Accordingly, they have tended to concentrate on the more mundane aspects of human cognition and reveal little about the act of human discovery.

It is important, in exploring creative cognition, to structure tasks in such a way that subjects have the opportunity to make genuine discoveries within an experimental context; we believe this can be done without compromising the scientific integrity of the research. In addition, we believe it is much easier to predict when something will be creative than to predict exactly what form the creation will take.

Developing Practical Techniques
Another goal of this approach is to develop practical methods for applying the principles of creative cognition in everyday situations. We believe that most people can learn to think more creatively by using these principles, and throughout this book we report numerous studies in support of this claim.

Demystification of Creativity

Avoiding Circularity in Defining Creativity
Early conceptualizations of creativity were often based on various "mystical" accounts—for example, that creativity results from divine intervention, creative life forces, or cosmic forces (Kneller 1965). Certainly, we wish to avoid such notions in trying to develop a serious cognitive theory, but we must also avoid the problem of circularity— to say that people do creative things simply because they were thinking in creative ways.

Identifying the kinds of cognitive processes and strategies that lead to creative insights can help to demystify creativity while avoiding circularity. Creative performance is not explained simply in terms of "creative thinking"; it is explained with reference to particular kinds of cognitive structures that a person employs and in terms of the properties of those structures. A similar argument can be made for the demystification of related concepts, such as "intuition." In this regard, our approach is related to previous approaches that have attempted to demystify mental imagery in terms of specific, underlying cognitive processes (Kosslyn 1980; Kosslyn et al. 1979).

Avoiding Minimization of the Concept
At the same time, however, we do not want to define creativity out of existence, or minimize it conceptually, because there really is something special about the creative mind—something that will always be surprising and innovative. We believe the most reasonable approach is to seek out general principles of creative thought, expressed in terms of cognitive processes and structures, as opposed to trying to reduce creative cognitions to the level of computational units and algorithms, where one risks achieving demystification at the expense of conceptual sterilization.

Hausman (1984) offers an interesting analysis of the problem of how to demystify creativity without having to dispense with the concept. He rejects both rational, deterministic approaches and those based on irrational, transcendental considerations in favor of an approach based on acceptance of the following paradox: How is it ever possible to conceive of a truly creative idea? If you could anticipate the idea, it would be determined and not creative. If you could not anticipate it, how could you generate the idea? Hausman's solution is to accept the paradox that creativity is in part unknowable and that one must allow oneself to be guided by aesthetic considerations, as in the case of an artist who creates in order to discover what it is he or she wanted to create.

In creative cognition, this issue is dealt with by assuming that the cognitive structures that are generated have emergent properties that can be discovered when those structures are explored, where at least some of the properties could not have been anticipated in advance. In this way it is possible to demystify creativity while allowing for the possibility that one might generate radically new and unexpected ideas. This is not to say that all emergent properties will lead to creative insights but simply that their presence in a structure increases the likelihood that a creative discovery will be made.

Previous Approaches to Creativity

Case Studies
Most case studies of creative people have consisted of introspective reports, interviews, and biographical studies. For example, Ghiselin (1952) collected introspective accounts of the creative process by notable writers, artists, composers, and scientists. In this collection, Einstein describes his famous thought experiment of imagining how the world would look while traveling alongside a beam of light, and Mozart describes his method of composing major works entirely in his head. Other important case studies include Gruber and Barrett's (1974) analysis of the conceptual evolution of Darwin's ideas, based on examinations of his notebooks, Gardner's (1982) study of creative artists, accounts by Miller (1984) and Shepard (1978, 1988) of the use of visualization in scientific creativity, and more recently, the collection of case studies assembled by Wallace and Gruber (1989), which explores the lives of notable creative people in modern times.

One shortcoming of this approach is that introspective reports are notorious for being untrustworthy, and this is no less of a concern when the reports are provided by brilliant, creative people. Indeed, when something comes very naturally to you, it may be much harder to describe exactly how you do it, especially when what you are describing is your own creative process. Research on creative cognition could help to validate the kinds of reports people give in case studies, and such reports could in turn suggest new processes to investigate in future experiments. In chapter 2, we discuss some of the conditions under which introspective reports would be particularly useful in this regard.

Psychoanalytic Approaches
In psychoanalytic theory, creative expression is explained in terms of the sublimation of unconscious conflicts. Perhaps the best example is Freud's analysis of the symbolic content of the works of Leonardo da Vinci (Freud 1916). Koestler (1964) has also suggested that creativity arises out of unconscious conflict, as contrary ideas or patterns of thought are brought together. Experimental support for such accounts has come from studies showing that highly creative people tend to score higher on various measures of psychopathology (Barron 1969).

Kubie (1958), on the other hand, rejected the notion that creativity must be grounded in neurosis or conflict and proposed instead that creative ideas could be generated in a perfectly healthy way, as part of preconscious activity. Unconscious processes may leave their signature or define an artist's style, but true creativity comes from the free play of preconscious symbolic processes. In contrast, unconscious processes tend to fixate or stagnate creative thought. There is thus no reason to fear losing one's creativity if one's neurosis is cured. In defending this view, Kubie points out how seldom creative writers and composers actually succeeded in overcoming mental illness through creative expression alone. A similar point has been made recently by Rothenberg (1990) in his analysis of the role that psychosis plays in creativity. Psychotic tendencies may have given rise to certain themes and elements, but the processes that mold these into creative structures are essentially healthy.

In creative cognition, we similarly reject the notion that the unconscious mind does most of the work in generating creative ideas. Unconscious mental processes may contribute to the aesthetic or symbolic qualities of creative thinking, but we regard the creative discoveries themselves as largely a product of organized cognitive exploration. Even so, we do not want to rule out implicit or unconscious processes entirely. Some aspects of retrieval, for example, are probably automatic, as suggested by studies on priming (Marcel 1980). Additionally, the figurative or creative meaning of a statement can often be understood quickly and without deliberate effort, even when an obvious literal interpretation is available (Glucksberg, Gildea, and Bookin 1982). Thus, whereas active, deliberate exploration may increase the range of possible creative interpretations, new discoveries could still arise through associations that occur at preconscious levels.

There is reason to think, however, that certain types of mental disorders might contribute to the highest levels of creative productivity. For example, Hershman and Lieb (1988) provide a convincing account of the role of manic-depression in the creative lives of Newton, Beethoven, Dickens, and van Gogh. States of mania provide an elevated sense of worth and talent and promote ambition, whereas states of depression cause one to become more introspective, compulsive, and isolated from social distractions. We regard such mental states as contributing to the motivation for engaging in creative cognition, a topic we address in chapter 2.

Psychometric Approaches
The classic psychometric approach to creativity is best represented by the work of Guilford. In his studies on the structure of the intellect, Guilford (1956, 1968) developed various tests (such as the "unusual uses" test) to distinguish what he called "convergent" and "divergent" thinking, the latter being characteristic of the flexible nature of creative thought. He regarded creativity as consisting of a combination of primary abilities: sensitivity to problems, fluency in generating ideas, flexibility and novelty of ideas, and the ability to synthesize and reorganize information (Guilford 1950).

Guilford's work has led to considerable interest in identifying cognitive styles that promote creative thinking. Shouksmith (1970), for example, included creative associating and the use of abstract modes of thought along with divergent thinking as cognitive styles related to creativity. Amabile (1983) considered a variety of cognitive styles, such as breaking mental sets, keeping options open, suspending judgment, using wide rather than narrow categories, and recognizing the importance of new ideas, as relevant to creative performance. Hayes (1989) proposed that creative people tend to be intelligent, devoted to their work, independent, driven to be original, and exhibit flexibility in their thinking. Runco's (1990) recent ideational theory emphasizes metacognitive and evaluative skills, in addition to the ability to generate original ideas.

Such approaches have been widely adopted by educational psychologists for the purpose of improving classroom instruction. For example, McLeod and Cropley (1989) identified various cognitive styles that encourage the development of creative thought in classroom settings, such as detecting discrepancies, discovering analogies, overcoming habitual patterns, accepting change and novelty, and tolerating ambiguity. Torrance and Myers (1970) recommended that teachers encourage children to allow for incompleteness in their thinking and then utilize this lack of completeness in original, creative ways.

As this brief survey indicates, there are a variety of cognitive styles thought to be related to creativity. The value of these approaches for creative cognition is that they emphasize that creativity involves multiple cognitive skills and is not simply a unidimensional process. The findings of creative cognition could contribute to work on cognitive styles by helping to identify the specific cognitive processes and structures that underlie them.

Sociological and Historiometric Approaches
In these approaches, the main concerns are social, environmental, and cultural effects on creativity. Amabile (1983), for example, found that monetary reward usually resulted in reduced creativity, whereas creativity was enhanced when people could choose a task they were interested in. Both expecting that one's performance will be evaluated and having others present during the task undermined creativity. Amabile proposed a theory of creativity in which background knowledge, cognitive style, social factors, and environmental influences all contribute to the creative act.

Simonton (1984, 1990) developed a historiometric approach to studying creativity, based on archival research. Simonton considered historical evidence for the influence of social, political, cultural, and personal factors (such as a person's age and health) on the originality, productivity, and perceived eminence of famous people. His work uncovered a large number of interesting findings—for instance, that productivity is not affected by social reinforcement (such as the number of honors one received) or biological stress but is reduced by the number of competitors in one's field and the number of role models that were available. Eminence is a U-shaped function of life span but an inverted U-shaped function of formal education. These and other studies have helped to establish the conditions that facilitate the development and expression of creative genius.

We regard social, cultural, and environmental factors as relevant to creative cognition in that they could affect the kinds of cognitive processes employed in a particular situation or context. For example, rewarding a person for taking a certain approach to a problem may increase the likelihood that the same cognitive processes are brought to bear on similar problems in the future.

Multiple Components Approaches
Some researchers have tried to to develop comprehensive theories of creativity, combining cognitive and socioenvironmental factors. Sternberg and Lubart (1991), for example, have proposed an "investment" theory of creativity, which consists of six major components: intellectual processes, knowledge structures, intellectual style, personality traits, motivational factors, and environmental context. The first three components are considered cognitive resources. The intellectual processes consist of planning, evaluative, metacognitive, and performance skills for solving problems. The knowledge structures are domain specific, providing background information relevant to creative thinking. The intellectual styles refer to the manner of intellectual "government," global versus local focusing, and conservative versus progressive biases. Creative thinking is a product of appropriate intellectual processes, sufficient knowledge, proper intellectual style, the right emotional and motivational factors, and the availability of the necessary environmental resources.

Creative cognition could help to relate such approaches more directly to mainstream cognitive psychology. For example, in the Sternberg and Lubart model, research on creative cognition could help to identify the specific roles that visualization, categorization, and memory retrieval might play in the various components of the model. Such research could also suggest more explicit ways in which multiple components models could be applied to the general problem of teaching people how to think more creatively.

Pragmatic Approaches
We consider next approaches that have focused on the development of practical creativity techniques. First, there is the technique of attribute listing, where one considers the basic attributes of an object and then explores how those attributes might be modified to improve the object (Crawford 1954). For example, if you were trying to design a better piece of chalk, you would list the major attributes of chalk (its typical size, color, shape, hardness, and so on) and then consider how each attribute might be altered (for example, making the chalk much larger or smaller or using different shapes).

In the technique of morphological synthesis (Allen 1962; Zwicky 1957), one lists the important dimensions of an object and the range of possible attributes for each dimension and then considers various novel combinations of those attributes. For example, if you wanted to come up with a new idea for ice cream, you could list the typical flavors of ice cream, along with the types of fruit or nuts that could be added to it, and then explore novel combinations of these attributes (Davis 1973). You might end up with an idea for chocolate ice cream with walnuts, strawberry ice cream with peaches, and so on. An enormous number of possibilities can be generated using this technique, especially as the number of dimensions increases.

Osborn (1953) developed several popular methods for coming up with creative ideas. The technique of brainstorming is based on the free association of ideas in a group setting; the participants withhold criticism and openly encourage unconventional thinking. Osborn also developed idea checklists, a series of questions that can lead to the consideration of new possibilities. Some examples are questions like, "Why is this necessary?" "What other uses are there?" "What other features could be added?" By going through the idea checklist, one may arrive at creative insights that might otherwise have been overlooked.

In the technique of synectics, analogies serve as catalysts for creative thinking and problem solving (Gordon 1961). As one example, a person might explore whether there are analogies in nature that can help to solve a particular problem. For instance, in attempting to design a new appliance for storing food, one might consider how this is accomplished by various plants or animals. One can also imagine oneself playing a personal role in the analogy. Wish fulfillment can be expressed in these analogies as well, as another way of gaining insights into possible solutions. General reviews of these techniques, considered further in chapters 5 and 8, are provided in Adams (1974) and Davis (1973).

The main benefit of pragmatic approaches is that they show that it is possible to train people to think in more creative ways. Research on creative cognition could lead to the development of new and even more effective creativity techniques by identifying the cognitive processes that are responsible for why they work. Some of these approaches, though, particularly attribute listing and morphological synthesis, are limited in that they consider attributes of objects only as they currently exist. Although the modification and recombination of those attributes can lead to innovations, their very inclusion can also lead to restrictions. For instance, to return to the example of coming up with a better design for chalk, morphological synthesis presumably would not allow one to consider possible innovations such as chalk in a spray can, where the chalk would not have a definite shape. Creative cognition can be used to study more general ways in which attributes might be selected and combined.

Artificial Intelligence Approaches

There has been considerable interest in developing ways of enhancing creativity in artificial intelligence (AI). Langley et al. (1987) have identified various heuristics that can contribute to creative problem solving in computers. Schank (1988a, 1988b) has explored how computers might use and modify "scripts" in simulating creative behavior. Johnson-Laird (1988a, 1988b) described computer programs that could improvise music.

Boden (1991) has recently reviewed computational approaches to creativity and presents examples of programs that can create art, find novel geometric proofs, discover scientific laws and principles, and design new products. These programs can generate outputs that in many cases seem surprisingly creative. Boden argues that such efforts have important implications for the understanding of human creativity, pointing out that computers, like people, can apply various rules or heuristics that can result in creative performance.

AI approaches have much in common with creative cognition; the goal of both is to identify the types of cognitive processes that lead to creative insights and both favor a structured approach to creativity rather than one based on simple or random associations among ideas (Mednick 1962). One way in which creative cognition might contribute to AI approaches stems from its emphasis on trying to identify general cognitive principles of creativity. Such principles could contribute to the development of new forms of creative artificial intelligence that could have more general applications. Programs currently used to compose music, for example, have little in common with those used to generate graphic art. Such limitations could be addressed by incorporating principles of creative cognition that are not restricted to narrow domains or applications. We do not believe it is necessary to express such principles in strictly computational terms, however, in order for them to have important implications for human creativity.

Scope of Creative Cognition

One of the important features of the creative cognition approach is that it ties in with current research in a number of cognitive areas. The areas most relevant to creative cognition are imagery, concept formation, categorization, memory, and problem solving; we devote separate chapters to discussing each. The earlier chapters focus mainly on illustrating the basic methods of creative cognition, whereas later chapters focus more on integrating the findings of creative cognition with those of other cognitive studies.

Creative Visualization
The topic of creative visualization would seem to be a natural place to start, given the large body of anecdotal evidence for the role that imagery plays in creative thinking. In chapter 3, we develop a cognitive, experimental approach to the study of creative visualization, using recently developed techniques for exploring the creative qualities of mental images. These studies demonstrate that people can mentally synthesize simple visual forms to make unexpected, creative discoveries.

Creative Invention
In chapter 4, we consider the cognitive processes that underlie the creation of practical objects and inventions. We show, in particular, how mental images called preinventive forms can give rise to new ideas for inventions within a variety of general object categories. We also show that using preinventive forms to discover inventions is distinct from simply interpreting arbitrary shapes or forms in creative ways, and we explore the kinds of cognitive processes and strategies that are useful in making creative refinements in existing designs.

Conceptual Synthesis
Chapter 5 begins by showing how more abstract types of creative concepts are generated using preinventive forms and then moves on to discuss how creative metaphors are formed and how they can expand conceptual domains—for example, how a metaphor like "She's a diamond" can lead one to insights about both the person and diamonds. More generally, we consider how combining separate concepts can result in emergent features that were not part of the representation of either of the concepts as separate entities and the extent to which such emergent features occur in literal and figurative types of conceptual combination.

Structured Imagination
In chapter 6, we consider the concept of imagination in a more global sense. A key topic in this chapter is how imagination is structured by implicit assumptions and other forms of knowledge. We consider the roles of categories, schemas, mental models, and naive theories in guiding imagination and how to overcome the implicit assumptions that limit imagination. We explore how one generates exemplars for real and hypothetical categories and how findings from studies of exemplar generation can be used as a way of learning more about cognitive structures and processes in general.

Fixation, Incubation, and Insight
In chapter 7, we look at recent work on insight, fixation, tip-of-the-tongue states, incubated reminiscence effects, and the role that context plays in memory retrieval and analogical transfer. This work leads to new understandings of the cognitive processes underlying fixation and other types of mental blocks in free recall, problem solving, and product design.

Creative Strategies for Problem Solving
The types of cognitive processes that facilitate creative problem solving and decision making and which contribute to creative exploration in general are explored in chapter 8. We also consider recent work on intuition, induction, and metacognition in relation to problem solving and discuss the implications of this work for creative cognition.

General Applications of Creative Cognition
The methods developed in studies of creative cognition have a wide range of practical applications that span many different fields. In our concluding chapter, we propose a general creativity training program based on the principles of creative cognition and then suggest applications of these principles for product development, architecture, human-computer interaction, education, psychotherapy, predicting future trends, and creative writing.

Before taking up these topics, in the next chapter we present a general model of creative cognition that will provide the framework for our investigations and discuss various methodological considerations in conducting experiments on creative cognition, including the general problem of how to evaluate creative ideas and products. We also discuss in greater detail the various types of cognitive processes and structures presumed to underlie creative cognition and how these relate to current work in other cognitive areas.

2

Theoretical and Methodological Considerations

A General Model

The model we propose is called Geneplore because it considers both generative and exploratory cognitive processes. It is one example of a general, cognitive model of creativity but not necessarily the best or most complete. Nevertheless, it provides a useful framework within which to describe basic cognitive processes related to creativity. In addition, it can account for many of the findings on creative cognition that we present in this book, and it satisfies the requirement that a general model of creative cognition should account for sufficiently diverse aspects of creative performance in terms of explicit cognitive processes and mechanisms.

Overall Structure of the Geneplore Model

The Geneplore model consists of two distinct processing components: a generative phase, followed by an exploratory phase (figure 2.1). In the initial, generative phase, one constructs mental representations called preinventive structures, having various properties that promote creative discovery. These properties are then exploited during an exploratory phase in which one seeks to interpret the preinventive structures in meaningful ways. These preinventive structures can be thought of as internal precursors to the final, externalized creative products and would be generated, regenerated, and modified throughout the course of creative exploration.

If one's initial explorations result in a satisfactory resolution to the task at hand, the initial preinventive structure may lead directly to a creative product. If these explorations are unsuccessful, one of two procedures would come into play, either of which would involve a return to the generative phase: abandon the initial preinventive structure and generate another that may be more promising or modify the initial structure and then repeat the exploratory phase with this modified structure. By continuing these procedures, one would gradually focus the emergent structure on particular themes or problems or

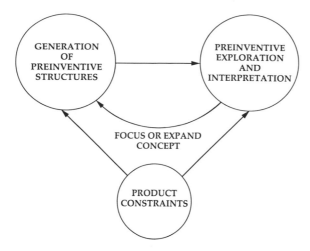

Figure 2.1
The basic structure of the Geneplore model. In the generative phase, one constructs mental representations called preinventive structures. These structures have various emergent properties that are exploited for creative purposes in the exploratory phase. The resulting creative cognitions can be focused or expanded according to task requirements or individual needs by modifying the preinventive structures and repeating the cycle. Constraints on the final product can be imposed at any time during the generative or exploratory phase. Specific examples of generative and exploratory processes, preinventive structures and properties, and product constraints are presented in table 2.1.

expand the structure to explore more general conceptual possibilities. The creative process is therefore cyclic, with the number of cycles being determined by the desired extent of conceptual refinement or expansion.

This cycling between the phases of generation and exploration typically occurs when people engage in creative thinking. For example, a person may retrieve two mental images and combine them in the generation phase to produce a visually interesting form, and then interpret the form as suggesting a new idea for a product. Further examination of the form may lead to the conclusion that the form is incomplete in some respects. A modified form is then generated by retrieving yet another image and mentally combining it with the already existing one. This process may result in a form that represents an improved or more complete design for the product or may lead to completely new and unanticipated interpretations of the form.

There are also cases in which creative discoveries can occur quite rapidly, apparently without repeated generation and exploration—for example, the way people quickly recognize the creative implications of a metaphor. Therefore it is not essential to engage in repetitions of the Geneplore cycle in attempting to make creative discoveries, although this may in fact be necessary in most instances. In addition, in certain experimental situations, it may be desirable to examine the creative products that result from a single generative and exploratory cycle.

The Geneplore model also considers constraints on the creative products and how they affect the underlying cognitive processes. As shown in figure 2.1, these constraints can be imposed during either the generative or the exploratory phase, depending on the nature of the task. Later in this chapter, we consider specific examples of the types of generative and exploratory processes, preinventive structures, and product constraints that contribute to creative cognition.

Most of the cognitive processes that we will consider in the context of the Geneplore model are also central to traditional models in cognitive psychology. Some of these processes are more relevant to the generative phase and others to the exploratory phase. We do not wish to convey the idea, however, that any one process is uniquely associated with one phase or another; the processes are only generally associated with a particular phase. Nor do we wish to convey the idea that all acts of creativity necessarily involve all of these processes. Rather, our attempt to build a general model of creative cognition follows the family resemblance principle: most creative endeavors result from most of these processes, but no one process is necessary and sufficient. One advantage of this characterization is that it allows us to address diverse aspects of creativity, such as artistic creation and scientific discovery, within the same general approach.

Another implication of the Geneplore model is that it allows for the possibility that people can be creative in different ways. Some may be more skilled at generating preinventive structures, for instance, and others may be more skilled at interpreting them. This may help to explain why there are often dramatic individual differences in creative style, as, for example, in the often-noted contrast between Mozart's and Beethoven's styles of composition (Ghiselin 1952; Perkins, 1981). Mozart generated compositions that seemed complete and fully formed in their initial creation; Beethoven often revised his compositions extensively, constantly seeking out new creative possibilities.

The Geneplore model can be applied at many different stages of creative thinking. For instance, it can apply not only to early stages, where one may simply be searching for new ideas in general and where the preinventive structures would be relatively unconstrained, but also to later stages, where one would be close to solving a particular problem or completing a new design and where the preinventive structures would tend to be highly constrained. As preinventive struc-tures evolve, they can be focused more specifically on particular issues or problems or be extended in new directions, depending on the person's interests and intentions.

Generative Processes
Examples of the processes, structures, properties, and constraints that play important roles in the Geneplore model are listed in table 2.1. This list is intended to be representative rather than complete.

The most basic types of generative processes consist of the retrieval of existing structures from memory and the formation of associations among these structures. A particular word or object, for example, could be recalled from memory and then reinterpreted during the exploratory phase. Or several words or objects could be retrieved and then associated in novel ways, resulting in new, simple types of prein-ventive structures. Typically these retrieval and associative processes happen quickly and automatically, but sometimes they are inhibited, resulting in mental blocks and fixation effects.

A richer variety of preinventive structures results from the mental synthesis of component parts and by the mental transformation of the resulting forms. Parts can be mentally rearranged and reassembled, and forms can be rotated or altered in shape to make interesting and potentially useful structures. Single concepts can be combined to form more complex concepts, with the meanings of one or both of the initial

Table 2.1
Examples of Cognitive Processes, Structures, Properties, and Constraints in the Geneplore Model

Generative Processes	Preinventive Structures	Preinventive Properties	Exploratory Processes	Product Constraints
Retrieval	Visual patterns	Novelty	Attribute finding	Product type
Association	Object forms	Ambiguity	Conceptual interpretation	Category
Synthesis	Mental blends	Meaningfulness	Functional inference	Features
Transformation	Category exemplars	Emergence	Contextual shifting	Functions
Analogical transfer	Mental models	Incongruity	Hypothesis testing	Components
Categorical reduction	Verbal combinations	Divergence	Searching for limitations	Resources

concepts being altered as a result. These generative processes, considered at length in chapters 3, 4, and 5, usually yield more intricate creative possibilities than simple retrieval and association.

Another type of generative process is analogical transfer, in which a relationship or set of relationships in one context is transferred to another, resulting in preinventive structures that are analogous to those that are already familiar. For example, early models of the structure of atoms resulted from analogical transfer of the relationships among the sun and planets in the solar system. This process has also been used extensively in the synectics approach. We consider analogical transfer at length in chapters 7 and 8.

Categorical reduction, another important generative process, means mentally reducing objects or elements to more primitive categorical descriptions. One might take a familiar object, such as a house, and conceive of its shape only in terms of basic geometric forms. In this sense, one ends up with a shape that is less loaded categorically and can function more broadly as a preinventive structure. Categorical reduction can involve functional properties as well. For example, one might try to develop a better coffee cup not by considering it as a "cup" but as a container for keeping liquid hot and allowing it to be consumed. This process is considered in chapter 6.

Each of these generative processes has already been explored to some extent in traditional areas within cognitive psychology. For instance, there is a fairly extensive literature on retrieval and associative mechanisms, mental synthesis, conceptual combination, mental transformation, and analogical transfer. We believe that researchers who have been working on these topics have already made a number of implicit contributions to creative cognition. An important feature of creative cognition is that it ties in with current work in other cognitive fields and can inform us about the nature of cognition in general.

As one example, with regard to contemporary research on attentional mechanisms and processing systems in human cognition, we would expect that global, parallel processing is more likely to predominate in the generative phase, particularly when the preinventive structures are initially assembled (McClelland and Rumelhart 1986). As the preinventive structures become more highly developed and refined, however, subsequent generative processes would become more focused and controlled (Schneider and Shiffrin 1977).

Preinventive Structures
The second column in table 2.1 lists examples of the different types of preinventive structures that might be created during the generative phase. The first two examples are visual patterns and object forms.

For instance, one might generate two-dimensional patterns resulting in creative products such as new types of symbols and artistic designs or three-dimensional forms resulting in new inventions and spatial analogies. These preinventive structures, which generally take the form of visual and spatial images, are considered mainly in chapters 3 and 4.

A third type of preinventive structure is a mental blend, a term we use to refer generically to a class of structures that include conceptual combinations, metaphors, and blended mental images. What they have in common is that two distinct entities have been fused to create something new. For example, one might imagine combining a lion with an ostrich to create a new type of animal or blend the concept of furniture with that of household appliances to create a new conceptual category. Mental blends are considered in chapter 5.

Another type of preinventive structure may be created when one generates possible exemplars of unusual or hypothetical categories. The resulting exemplars often have features in common with those of more familiar categories, as well as novel, emergent features that lead to new and unexpected discoveries. For example, in attempting to generate a member of the category "alien creatures that inhabit a planet different from the earth," one might conceive of a creature that resembles earth creatures in some respects but not others. These exemplars suggest that imagination is a highly structured activity; they are discussed in chapter 6.

One can also generate larger-scale preinventive structures, such as mental models, that represent various mechanical or physical systems, as well as global, conceptual systems. Mental models usually start out as structures that are incomplete, unstable, and even unscientific (Gentner and Stevens 1983; Johnson-Laird 1983, 1988a) and are then improved and refined with later exploration and discovery. We consider mental models in chapters 6 and 8.

Finally, preinventive structures can consist of various types of verbal combinations, that is, interesting or suggestive relations among words and phrases that can lead to poetic and other literary explorations. They differ from mental blends in that the elements need not actually be fused, physically or conceptually, in the structure. Examples of these types of preinventive structures are provided in chapters 5 and 7.

This list is not intended to be complete; the domain of preinventive structures could be extended, for example, to include musical forms, action schemas, and other possibilities. What these structures have in common is that they are initially formed without full anticipation of their resulting meaning and interpretation. In addition, they are to be distinguished from the final externalized creative products, which, in contrast, are often fully interpreted and extensively refined.

Although we are treating these structures as internal representations, there is no reason that the structures could not be externalized at any point in the creative act. As we discuss in later chapters, this has the advantage that one could then deal with more complex structures but the disadvantage that it might limit the flexibility in modifying or transforming the structures. Nor do we mean to imply that the preinventive structures can be considered independently of the various generative processes. Rather, we expect that certain types of preinventive structures are more likely to result from particular types of processes. For example, mental blends are more likely to result from mental synthesis than from simple retrieval or association.

Preinventive Properties

Preinventive structures can vary in the extent to which they afford creative outcomes. We consider six properties of preinventive structures that would contribute to creative exploration and discovery. First, and probably most important, is the novelty of the preinventive structures. Although a common, familiar structure might still be interpreted in creative ways, the possibilities for creative discovery should be much greater if the structure is relatively uncommon to begin with.

Second, ambiguity in the structure should also afford greater opportunities for creative exploration and interpretation. Studies on perception, for example, have demonstrated that ambiguous visual patterns can often be interpreted in a variety of original and unexpected ways (Attneave 1971). Ambiguity contributes to discoveries that are made in many types of conceptual combinations as well (Wisniewski and Gentner 1991). For these reasons, one might wish to avoid imposing narrow interpretations onto the preinventive structures when the structures are first being formed.

A third property of preinventive structures that we expect would contribute to creative exploration is implicit meaningfulness—a general, perceived sense of "meaning" in the structure. This sense of meaning, which can be fairly abstract, is related to a preinventive structure's potential for inspiring or eliciting new and unexpected interpretations. As we will show, preinventive structures often seem to have a hidden, underlying meaning to them, which encourages further exploration and search.

A fourth property is that of emergence, which refers to the extent to which unexpected features and relations appear in the preinventive structure. By definition, these features and relations are not anticipated in advance and become apparent only after the preinventive structure is completely formed. This is a common property, for example, of preinventive structures that result from mental synthesis.

Incongruity, a fifth property, refers to the conflict or contrast among elements in a preinventive structure. This often encourages further exploration to uncover deeper meanings and relations in order to reconcile the conflict and reduce the psychological tension it creates. Incongruity has played a major role in previous theories of creativity, such as in Koestler's (1964) theory of bisociation. More recent studies have shown that incongruous components in conceptual combination may result in greater opportunities for originality and discovery than when the components fit together readily (Wisniewski 1991).

Divergence, a further property, is related to ambiguity but refers more specifically to the capacity for finding multiple uses or meanings in the same structure. Something could be relatively unambiguous in terms of its underlying structure but still afford a variety of different interpretations. A hammer, for example, is a relatively unambiguous form but can be used in a variety of different ways—as a tool, a paperweight, a weapon, and so on.

We consider these six properties throughout later chapters, particularly chapter 5, where we explore the question of how these properties might relate to one another and to other features of the preinventive structures. Implicit meaningfulness, for example, may be related to specific structural features such as symmetry or goodness. Incongruity may be related to the infrequency with which certain features occur together in the same structure or to the conceptual distance between the features. Emergence may sometimes be a consequence of ambiguity. These properties are not to be regarded as independent; instead, they are likely to be related in theoretically important ways.

Exploratory Processes

The first example of exploratory processes listed in table 2.1 is attribute finding, the systematic search for emergent features in the preinventive structures. For instance, a person might generate a novel mental image consisting of an unusual combination of parts and then mentally scan the image to determine if any emergent features are present. Attribute finding could also be used to explore emergent features resulting from the creation of conceptual combinations and metaphors. This process is considered mainly in chapters 4 and 5.

Conceptual interpretation refers quite broadly to the process of taking a preinventive structure and finding an abstract, metaphorical, or theoretical interpretation of it. For example, a preinventive structure might be interpreted as representing a new concept in medicine, an idea for the plot of a story, an extension of the theory of relativity, or a theme for a musical composition. More generally, conceptual interpretation can be thought of as the application of world knowledge or naive theories to the task of creative exploration. We consider conceptual interpretations of preinventive structures in chapters 5 and 6.

Functional inference refers to the process of exploring the potential uses or functions of a preinventive structure. One might imagine how a preinventive object form could be used as a particular tool, a piece of furniture, or a device for catching a burglar. This process is often facilitated by imagining oneself actually trying to use the object in various ways. Functional inference is the major exploratory process considered in chapter 4.

Another exploratory process is contextual shifting, or considering a preinventive structure in new or different contexts as a way of gaining insights about other possible uses or meanings of the structure. As will be considered in chapter 7, this process often helps to overcome fixation effects and other obstacles to creative discovery.

Preinventive structures can also be explored in the spirit of hypothesis testing, where one seeks to interpret the structures as representing possible solutions to a problem. For example, a person working on a problem in geometry might generate preinventive structures that represent various solution possibilities and then explore the implications of these structures for solving the problem. In this way, creative solutions to a problem can often be found when more direct methods fail. This type of creative exploration is the subject of chapter 8.

Yet another exploratory process is searching for limitations. Preinventive structures can also provide insights into which ideas will not work or what types of solutions are not feasible. This is often just as important as actually discovering what will work. Discovering limitations can help to restrict future searches and focus creative exploration in more promising directions. For example, when people generate exemplars for novel categories, they often discover that their initial creations are limited in important respects. They might then explore those limitations, leading to the creation of more appropriate exemplars. This exploratory process is considered in chapters 6 and 8.

We assume that these exploratory processes are usually carried out in an organized and systematic way. In terms of conventional research on information-processing mechanisms in human cognition, we would expect that local, serial forms of processing would predominate in the exploratory phase, where the search for creative possibilities would typically occur in a deliberate and controlled manner.

It should be clear that these various exploratory processes could be applied in many different contexts and situations: attempting to develop a scientific theory, improving on an existing design, or finding new meaning in an artistic creation, for example. They could even be shared among groups of people, as in brainstorming, where one person generates a preinventive structure and others try to interpret it.

An individual creative act need not involve all of these processes, nor does any one type of generative or exploratory process best exemplify creative cognition. Rather, we view creativity as resulting from various clusters of these processes, few or none of which may be absolutely essential.

Product Constraints

Constraints on the final creative products could be imposed during either the generative or exploratory phase, depending on the task requirements. We again consider six examples.

First, the particular type of product could be constrained. One could be asked to design a new typewriter or come up with a particular type of solution to a problem. Second, the general category of the product could be restricted, as in inventing a new piece of furniture or conceiving of a new theory in the field of physics.

The particular features that the product must have could be restricted. An appliance, for instance, might have to be a certain size or be portable. A category exemplar may have to include certain necessary or designated features. A related type of constraint concerns the function of the product, restricting its possible uses or performance characteristics. One may have to design a tool that could crush ice, for example, or a jet aircraft that could fly at a certain speed.

There might also be constraints on the particular types of components that can be used in the products—only certain parts may be available—or on the general resources. Certain types of materials might have to be used, or the product may have to be economically feasible.

Later in this chapter, we consider some of the consequences of imposing these restrictions during creativity experiments, as they relate to the generative and exploratory processes.

Function Follows Form

We believe that the Geneplore model provides an attractive alternative to those based exclusively on general descriptions of cognitive influences and styles or, at the opposite extreme, to those based exclusively on highly constrained computational mechanisms. The model represents a healthy middle ground in this respect, in which specific types of cognitive processes can be explored that might contribute to creative performance but in which the processes need not be reduced to the level of strictly computational processes.

In addition, the model allows for an alternative to the normal form-follows-function approach to invention and design, in which one begins by specifying various design parameters and then determines which forms and structures will satisfy those requirements. Whereas creative discovery can, and in most situations probably does, result from this approach, we suggest that a function-follows-form approach, in which one begins by generating nonspecific forms and structures and then explores their possibilities, can also contribute to creative discovery.

In some cases, this new approach may be an even more efficient way of generating creative ideas. For instance, people often end up discovering inventions or concepts that turn out to be much more important than the ones they were contemplating at the very beginning. Researchers in the field of problem solving refer to this as problem finding and consider it an important strategy for creative thinking (Bransford and Stein 1984; Perkins 1981). Problem finding also appears to be an important process in artistic creation. Getzels and Csikszentmihalyi (1976) found that artists produced works of higher rated quality when they did not start with a definite plan in mind but were concerned instead with exploring and discovering emergent structures and forms. This idea is also related to modern principles of freewriting, in which one begins by generating sentences freely and then evaluates the semantic possibilities that emerge (Elbow 1981).

In terms of the Geneplore model, in the more used form-follows-function approach, extensive product constraints would be imposed early in the creative process, during the initial generative phase, which would restrict the types of preinventive structures. It may, however, be optimal to delay imposing these constraints until after the preinventive structures are formed. In chapter 4, for example, we present evidence that people are more likely to make creative discoveries when they generate novel visual images without knowing in advance how the resulting forms will be used.

The Geneplore model is compatible with either approach. In the former case, one generates a form with a specific purpose in mind and then explores its utility for solving a particular problem. In the latter, one generates a form on the basis of aesthetic or other considerations and then explores what problems the form might be useful in solving. In general, the two approaches could be used in conjunction, with one complementing the other.

Creativity and Randomness

We do not believe that randomness is essential or even desirable for creative thinking, although it may contribute to the way in which creative ideas initially take shape (Bateson 1979; Findlay and Lumsden 1988; Johnson-Laird 1988b). The manner in which preinventive structures are constructed and interpreted is not simply a random process, although the structures may be initially conceived without explicit purpose and may be subject to arbitrarily imposed constraints. The resulting insights may be "accidental" in that they can lead to unexpected discoveries, but this is not the same as saying that the insights occur randomly. On the contrary, we believe that exploring new possibilities in preinventive structures is best accomplished in an organized and intelligent manner (Perkins 1981; Weisberg 1986). In this regard, one may distinguish our approach from most so-called brute force methods of generating creative ideas in which random juxtaposition, combination, and association prevail.

Everyday Creativity and Creative Genius

The Geneplore model is intended as a general account of creative cognition; it does not apply merely to instances of profound creative insight. On the contrary, one of the goals of this work is to develop practical techniques that nearly everyone can use when trying to think more creatively.

Creative genius and everyday creativity are regarded as lying along the same continuum and are distinguished by the extent to which creative cognitive processes are employed. This is in the spirit of previous arguments for the demystification of creative genius (Perkins 1981; Weisberg 1986). In terms of the Geneplore model, we suspect that people regarded as creative geniuses are probably able to generate or interpret their preinventive structures more efficiently than others, perhaps by having to go through fewer interpretive steps or refinements of the structures or by being able to generate more useful preinventive structures to begin with.

The Geneplore model may also help to explain the typical lack of strong correlations between measures of creativity and intelligence. Guilford (1968), for example, concluded that people with low IQs tend to be uncreative, whereas people with high IQs can be either creative or uncreative; this is the so-called threshold theory of creativity (Runco and Albert 1986; Simonton 1984; Sternberg 1985). It may be that people with high IQs are better at exploring and interpreting their preinventive structures but not necessarily better at generating them. This idea is also consistent with the findings of various psychometric and componential studies on giftedness in children (Davidson 1986; McLeod and Cropley 1989).

It is probably a mistake to try to learn about creativity by concentrating on creative genius alone. Rather, we believe there is much more to be learned by exploring ways of inspiring creative discovery in ordinary people.

We consider various findings in support of the Geneplore model in chapters 4 through 8 and provide examples of general principles of creative cognition, expressed in terms of specific types of preinventive structures, cognitive processes, and constraints. We do not claim, however, to have tested all aspects of the model or to have established the precise role of all of the proposed structures and processes.

Structuring Creative Opportunities

The basic research strategy in creative cognition is to combine the experimental methods of cognitive science with the opportunity for subjects to make new discoveries. We mean "discoveries" in a literal sense—not just those intended or expected by the researcher. Rather, we allow participants in these studies to generate ideas that neither they nor the researcher may have ever thought of before. This can best be accomplished, we believe, by using a variety of novel methods in combination with standard research techniques.

Structuring the experimental tasks in such a way that creative opportunities are available not only makes it easier to study creative cognition; it also enhances creative performance. If one wishes to examine the relationship between cognitive processes and creative performance, one should encourage as much creativity as possible. Under ordinary situations, baseline levels of creative performance might be expected to be relatively low, and these procedures can be expected to increase those levels.

Predicting Creative Performance

Structuring creative opportunities is a very different approach from that normally taken in cognitive research, where the usual procedure is to generate a set of predictions according to some model or theory and then measure accuracy or response time to verify the predictions (Anderson 1990; Shepard and Cooper 1982). Although these more traditional paradigms have their usefulness, we prefer not to rely on them in creative cognition research. As a rule, we do not attempt to predict exactly the particular responses a person might give or to score the responses according to whether they are "correct" by some criterion. On the contrary, we assume that the most creative responses are the most difficult to predict.

It is useful, therefore, to distinguish between predicting when people are most likely to be creative and predicting the exact nature of the creative products they generate. Creative cognition should be more concerned with the former.

Avoiding Demand Characteristics

Among the advantages of the creative cognition approach is that a researcher can avoid many of the problems associated with demand characteristics, experimenter bias, and the like, since there is seldom a specific answer or response to be expected. Although there may be general demands to think more creatively, these rarely translate into particular expectations for responding in some appropriate way. Creative cognition studies are therefore relatively immune to the most common types of artifacts encountered in cognitive research (Intons-Peterson 1983; Orne 1962; Rosenthal 1976).

Constraining Creative Opportunities

Although it is important to provide for creative opportunities in these experiments, some constraints and controls are needed for a scientific study. One cannot simply tell people to try to be creative in some completely unconstrained way and then claim to have conducted a true experiment. In order to identify the specific cognitive processes that contribute to creative acts, one normally has to constrain the task appropriately and then vary the conditions under which the creative acts occur. Then one can relate these particular conditions, and the cognitive processes that they elicit, to the likelihood that a person will generate a creative idea.

Experimental Procedures and Controls

In choosing the types of methods for the study of creative cognitive processes, the goal is to devise experimental techniques in which the subject has the opportunity to make genuine discoveries but in which the task can be constrained in such a way that it qualifies as a legitimate, scientifically controlled study. The techniques we discuss here are not necessarily unique to creative cognition; most have already been used to some extent in previous cognitive research.

Employing Novel Situations or Tasks

The use of novel situations and tasks is one way to promote creative thinking in that it helps one to avoid approaching or conceptualizing an issue or problem in strictly conventional ways. Most researchers tend to rely on well-worn procedures and paradigms in doing cognitive science, but creative discoveries, in both art and science, often occur in unusual situations, where one is forced to think unconventionally (Getzels and Csikszentmihalyi 1976; Kuhn 1962; Miller 1986; Shepard 1978). One should therefore consider employing unusual tasks and procedures when conducting creative cognition experiments.

Some examples of novel tasks we describe subsequently in this book include the mental synthesis of shapes and forms using unfamiliar sets of parts (chapters 3 and 4), interpreting ambiguous preinventive forms as abstract concepts and metaphors (chapter 5), and generating exemplars for novel and unusual categories (chapter 6). Although not all of the tasks we describe are quite so novel, we have found these more unusual tasks to be especially helpful in studying creative cognition and in enhancing creative performance.

Restricting Elements and Components
Restricting the elements one can use in generating an idea or an invention promotes creative resourcefulness. As a rule, limited resources force one to think in more creative and less conventional ways. Imposing such restrictions therefore helps to stimulate creative thinking in creative cognition experiments.

In traditional studies in cognitive science, of course, researchers usually do constrain the types of stimuli. In creative cognition studies, however, subjects often get to create their own "stimuli," in a manner of speaking, under the restrictions imposed by there experimenter. These restrictions not only promote creativity but also help the researcher to identify the underlying cognitive processes used in dealing with the restrictions.

In the context of the Geneplore model, restricting the components encourages the generation of novel preinventive structures. One is limited in the particular choices of the components but allowed freedom within those choices as to how the components are to be assembled. This technique tends to maximize the novelty and creative potential of the preinventive structures.

In imposing such restrictions, we find that random selection of the elements is a simple method for avoiding conventional combinations. One can then compare such conditions to those in which the restrictions are not imposed. For example, we show in chapter 4 that randomly selecting the parts that can be used to mentally construct preinventive object forms increases the rated creativity of the resulting inventions.

Restricting Domains of Interpretation
Restricting the ways in which creative cognitions are interpreted encourages creative exploration and discovery and further reduces the likelihood that a person will fall back on conventional lines of thought. Restricting the categories, for example, forces people to think about conceptual implications in more atypical ways, which tends to promote creative discovery (Cropley 1967). In addition, restricting the concepts that might be paired in studies of conceptual combination can force one to consider novel interpretations of those concepts.

With regard to the Geneplore model, restricting domains of interpretation encourages deeper explorations of the possible meanings of the preinventive structures. As a result, one often ends up discovering unusual possibilities and implications, which might not have been considered had the person been free to use any interpretive category.

Random selection of interpretive categories is a simple way to accomplish this goal. For example, one can restrict the types of object categories that can be used when interpreting a preinventive object form or the conceptual categories that can be considered in exploring more abstract interpretations. Then one can vary the range of allowable categories or how specifically the categories are defined and see how this affects the creativity of the resulting ideas.

Random choice or combination is not the essential process in creative cognition, however. Even when preinventive structures are constructed using randomly selected parts, they are not put together randomly but in fact, often exhibit deep, structural properties that lead to a variety of inventive possibilities. Nor would we claim that interpreting the preinventive structures is a random process. The use of random constraint in creative cognition studies is simply a methodological convenience.

The idea that restriction can enhance creativity might seem paradoxical; when options are reduced, a person is no longer free to respond in particular ways and might thus be less creative. There are, in fact, certain types of restrictions that clearly inhibit creativity. For example, a person might impose the self-restriction that there is only one solution to a problem, preventing the person from discovering more insightful solutions. It is useful to draw a distinction here between restrictions that encourage new explorations and considerations, and those that tie one to conventional approaches. Whether a particular restriction stimulates or inhibits creativity can be determined empirically.

Suspending Expertise
Another general technique in creative cognition is to suspend or delay the application of expert knowledge. This is done in the spirit of trying to avoid conventional mental sets.

Creativity is often enhanced when one waits before applying expertise (Johnson-Laird 1988b). This seems to be true in a variety of domains, including artistic expression, scientific discovery, and problem solving. Suspending expertise can help to reveal the optimal sequence of cognitive operations that should be employed when trying to generate creative ideas. For example, in terms of the Geneplore model, one can vary when the interpretive categories are specified— in particular, whether this occurs before or after the preinventive structures are generated. One can then determine the effects of "contaminating" the preinventive structures with foreknowledge about the interpretive categories. We present evidence in chapters 4, 5, and 8 that in certain cases expertise is best applied only after the preinventive structures are initially formed.

Encouraging Hypothetical Exploration
Subjects can be encouraged to explore hypothetical possibilities and consequences, in the general spirit of classic studies on divergent thinking (Guilford 1968). For example, subjects could be asked to consider the hypothetical functions of imaginary objects or the characteristics of imaginary creatures. These explorations often lead to creative insights and discoveries and reveal important aspects of the underlying conceptual structures.

A good example of hypothetical exploration of this sort comes from Day (1921), who speculated on the likely traits of "super ants" and "super cats" had they evolved in superior ways instead of simians. Super ants would be compulsive workers, extremely territorial, and free of poverty. Super cats would be solitary thinkers, compulsive cleaners, and superior explorers. They would have no humor, lots of drama, and highly original art without concern for the recognition or appreciation of others.

In chapter 6, we examine various instances of hypothetical exploration in experiments on creative cognition. For example, in studies in which people are asked to imagine and draw new tools, they often create objects that have handles or in some other way require the use of hands. What happens when people must develop tools for the hypothetical case of a very special intelligent creature that has no appendages? Presumably this would require not only hypothetical exploration but also the construction of mental models of the interacting domains of animate and artifact categories.

Creating and Overcoming Mental Blocks
Yet another technique is to deliberately create mental blocks and explore the ways that people overcome them. This allows a researcher to discover what types of cognitive processes help one to avoid fixation effects in creative cognition. In chapter 7, we consider studies in which memory blocks are created by various experimental procedures and tasks as a way of studying creative strategies for retrieving information.

Obtaining Introspective Reports
Introspective reports should not form the sole basis for a theory of creative cognition, but such reports can be useful when they are collected immediately following the creative acts and when there is consensus among the reports. This can help to confirm theoretical assumptions about the contribution of particular cognitive processes and can often lead to new insights for how to restructure creativity experiments.

There is already a growing literature on the use of introspective reports in cognitive research. These include studies on protocol analysis in general problem solving (Ericsson and Simon 1984) and on reports of analogies that experts use when trying to solve scientific problems (Clement 1988, 1989). In creative cognition, we believe it is important to collect self-reports from nonexperts and nonscientists as well, who may sometimes provide better insights into the underlying creative processes.

Assessing Individual Differences
Although we have generally not explored individual differences in our studies of creative cognition, there are a variety of individual difference measures that could be used in conjunction with the techniques described so far. For example, including tests of divergent thinking, attitude and interest inventories, personality inventories, and measures of self-reported creative activities in experiments on creative cognition (Hocevar and Bachelor 1989; Runco in press) would help to reveal whether certain cognitive styles might be related to particular types of creative cognitive processes.

The Geneplore model considers individual differences with respect to the particular ways that preinventive structures are generated and explored. One person may prefer to create preinventive object forms, whereas another may prefer novel verbal structures. Or one may prefer to search for functional properties and another to find creative analogies.

Motivational Factors

Overcoming the Fear of Creativity
We often find in creative cognition research that people are afraid of being creative. In the creative invention studies described in chapter 4, subjects often expressed concern that their initial creations might seem too wild or bizarre. In the exemplar generation studies described in chapter 6, a number of subjects initially protested that they could not draw, and some even seemed embarrassed and turned their drawings face down when leaving the experiment.

Perhaps creativity seems threatening because it is thought to promote disorder, even chaos. Yet real creativity is beautiful and leads to natural harmony and understanding. Indeed, creative insight often enables us to overcome difficult obstacles in surprisingly simple ways.

Experiments on creative cognition should be designed to foster positive attitudes toward creativity, confidence in one's creative potential, and the ability to deal with uncertainty in novel situations (Davis 1973). We find that subjects in these experiments often express considerable surprise at discovering that they can, in fact, think in creative ways, and without fear or trauma.

One effective method for reducing the fear of creativity is to minimize evaluation apprehension. Amabile (1983) found that subjects who expected their performance to be judged showed reduced creativity. It is therefore recommended that subjects not be informed in advance of the particular ways in which their performance will be evaluated in creative cognition tasks.

Creating Intimacy
Levine (1987) introduced the concept of "intimate engagement" as an important prerequisite for successful problem solving. The basic idea is that one needs to become deeply committed to and involved with a problem in order to solve it effectively. One cannot simply treat a problem in a superficial, detached way, allowing oneself to be distracted and unconcerned. This intimacy does not just happen "automatically" or "mindlessly" (Langer 1989); one must be aware of the importance of the problem and realize the need for commitment and involvement.

We think this is also very much true of creativity. One needs to be involved personally in a creative idea in order to sense the full richness of its implications and possibilities. Often this takes the form of "living" within your own creative world, focusing completely on being imaginative (Hilgard 1970) and perhaps even dissociating oneself temporarily from the immediate surroundings (Hilgard 1977). The need for intimate engagement may help to explain why conviction and perseverance are often so important in creative discovery.

This kind of intimacy seems to be lacking in much of the research that is being done in cognitive science. Subjects seldom take a personal interest in their performance, and even when they do, they rarely show the deep level of involvement of the sort that occurs when one actively explores creative possibilities.

In contrast, studies on creative cognition can provide for just this kind of imaginative involvement. After overcoming their initial hesitancy, subjects typically report that they become deeply involved in the experimental tasks and express an interest in continuing to do so even after the experiment is concluded. In addition, the preinventive structures that subjects generate in these experiments are often sufficiently enticing that it becomes difficult for them not to continue to think about them.

Encouraging Playfulness

Many practical techniques for enhancing creativity encourage playful and irrelevant thinking. The contribution of playfulness to creativity is suggested by various anecdotal accounts as well. Einstein, for example, often referred to the importance of "combinational play" in his own creative thinking.

Lieberman (1977) examined the role of various forms of play, including combinational play, in creative thinking. According to Lieberman, playfulness consists of spontaneity, manifest joy, and sense of humor. He found that these playfulness traits were related to various measures of divergent thinking. Such relationships call attention to the importance of "childlike" aspects of creative thought.

Studies on creative cognition should strive to develop paradigms in which participants have the opportunity to engage in combinational play and playful exploration. This is fostered by making the tasks less problem oriented and more open to exploring interesting combinations of elements and ideas.

Inherent Joy of Creative Discovery

Creative cognition is concerned mainly with internal sources of motivation, as opposed to external sources such as reward and pressure for success. In this regard, we believe that the most important motivator for creative thought is the joy of discovery; that people can be inspired by the pleasure of knowing that they are able to discover something new within their own creative thoughts. Perhaps the most serious limitation of artificial intelligence and other strictly computational approaches to creativity is that they regard emotional states as largely irrelevant.

Creative exploration should be fun, and this should be taken into account when designing experiments on creative cognition. People should feel that they can enjoy making discoveries and that there will always be something new to discover, even though they are participating in a scientific study. Getzels and Csikszentmihalyi (1976) reported that artists who felt that they could continue to make new discoveries in their creations—that is, believing that the works were never really "finished"—produced works that were judged to be more creative. To believe in the possibility of continued discovery is vital for motivating creativity.

In the Geneplore model, motivation is seen as affecting creative cognition indirectly, in terms of possibly influencing the selection of particular generative and exploratory processes. This is not to minimize its importance in creative discovery, however. One can feel considerable excitement at having discovered an unexpected, emergent property in a preinventive structure or upon having resolved an apparent incongruity, inspiring further exploration of the structure. In general, intrinsic motivation can arise both prior to the generation of preinventive structures and in response to the properties of those structures.

Evaluating Creative Products

In considering various properties of the final, creative products that might be evaluated in the context of creative cognition experiments, we again favor a family resemblance view, in that not all of the properties will be essential. Some may be more relevant for some types of creativity, but most creative products will possess most of these properties.

Originality

The natural expectation is that a creative idea or product will be original or, at the very least, uncommon. Not surprisingly, measuring the relative frequency of a response is a standard technique for assessing creativity (Torrance 1974). Yet there is a sense in which "frequency" alone is inadequate; several people could come up with the same original idea, and an uncommon idea could also seem unoriginal.

For most purposes, we believe it is adequate to use simple ratings of originality by skilled judges. It does not matter so much whether the judges are always "correct" in regarding something as original; what is more important is that the judges are practiced in making these judgments and apply the same criteria across different experimental conditions. The ideas or inventions need not be original in any absolute sense. Indeed, it is often difficult to know whether anyone else has thought of a particular idea previously.

Boden (1991) draws a distinction between creativity that is relevant to an individual (where a person generates an idea that he or she had never thought of) and creativity that is relevant to history and society as a whole (where the person may never have thought of the idea before but somebody else had). There are practical difficulties with using either criterion as a basis for judging originality, however. For instance, how would you know whether an individual's self-report of originality could be trusted? And whereas judging originality relative to an entire society may be more objective in principle, it is usually quite impractical as a general research method.

One possibility is using experts in a field as judges, and this is in fact the preferred method when evaluating originality in highly restricted domains; however, in studies in which the creative ideas can pertain to any number of categories, as in most of the studies we report in this book, the use of experts as judges becomes much less practical. We therefore prefer to use judges who are not necessarily experts but who are practiced in judging when a product or idea appears to be original across a wide range of categories. In later sections, we take up issues such as the construct validity and reliability of these and related judgments.

Practicality and Sensibility
There is more to creativity than just being novel. Novelty can be arbitrary, as when one simply combines things in a random, unstructured way. In order for creativity to have real substance, it must also be practical or sensible; there must be a sense of value or competence to go along with the originality (Hilgard 1968).

In many creativity studies, people are simply trained to generate a variety of novel ideas without regard to real creative achievement (Perkins 1981). We therefore recommend that in studies on creative cognition, judgments of the general quality of the product, in addition to its originality, need to be included. This normally consists of judging the practicality of an invention or the sensibility of an idea.

The products can then be classified as creative or not in terms of both rated originality and rated practicality or sensibility. This has the advantage that judges need not rate creativity per se, which avoids possible problems associated with the different senses in which people might regard something as being creative (Amabile 1983). For example, what one person means in calling an engineering solution "creative" may be quite different from what another person means in referring to a literary idea as "creative." The first may be focusing more on practicality and the other more on originality and inspirational qualities.

Productivity and Flexibility

One can also measure the productivity of creative ideas, in terms of the number of ideas generated within a particular time period or the time it takes to generate a single idea. Such measures need to be used with care, however, since they tend to confound the process of creative discovery with that of expressing or communicating the ideas. For example, a person might be skilled at generating creative ideas but poor at reporting or describing them.

Additionally, one can measure the range of categories or object types represented by an idea as an indication of the flexibility of the idea. A single invention, for example, might have multiple uses or could function as many different types of objects. A new concept might span many different conceptual categories. Using these measures could help to distinguish between productive thought that merely results in more things of the same type and creative thought that actually results in new types of things.

Marketability and Feasibility

Most successful inventions have to survive a lengthy development and testing phase (Weber and Dixon, 1989), and most creative ideas must undergo a similar process of refinement and critical evaluation (Perkins 1981). Measures of the potential marketability of a creative invention or the potential feasibility of a creative idea might therefore be included. These considerations, though potentially important, are less relevant to a theory of creative cognition. We are more interested in what happens at the front edge of the creative process than in whether the final product will end up being widely accepted. Indeed, many highly creative ideas are initially rejected simply because they are ahead of their time or because the technology needed for their development is not yet available.

Inclusiveness

Inclusiveness is the extent to which old features and structures are represented in the creative products. For example, in trying to improve on an existing design, it is often important to know what features to keep and which ones to eliminate. Similarly, when generating novel exemplars of a category, it is useful to consider the properties of known category exemplars that are retained. For instance, in devising a better coffee cup, what properties of the general category of "cup" tend to be included? What implicit assumptions about the nature of a concept or category serve to structure the individual's imagination?

In chapter 6, we will see that a subject's novel creations are often highly structured by the properties that are characteristic of the categories from which they are generated. Newly generated entities, no matter how novel, still retain some identifiable and predictable structure. Part of the task of creative cognition is to identify that structure and to discover ways to help people overcome the structure if it interferes with their ability to generate creative products.

Insightfulness
An additional property that could be considered in assessing a creative product is insightfulness, defined as the number of different knowledge domains the product contacts. A great insight often has far-reaching consequences, influencing many other fields. The theory of evolution influenced not only biological thinking but also virtually every other aspect of human thought. A particular invention, like the ball bearing or the microchip, can end up having practical implications that extend far beyond the context in which it was originally conceived.

Many other properties could also be considered. In judging artistic creations, one could include the recognizability of a pattern, the craftsmanship of a composition, or the extent to which the work evokes the intended emotional response. In addition, the various product constraints that we listed in table 2.1 could be used to define properties that one might want to consider—for example, how closely the product resembles a particular kind of object or satisfies a particular functional requirement.

We believe that these various product properties could, in principle, be associated with the various types of cognitive processes and structures proposed in the Geneplore model. In addition, some of these properties would follow naturally from specific properties of the preinventive structures. For example, a novel preinventive structure or one rich in emergent features should be more likely to give rise to an invention or idea that would be rated as highly original.

We do not wish to imply that all of these properties need to be assessed in every creative cognition study; some of these properties may be more important for certain studies than others. Our main purpose here has been to consider the range of properties that are potentially useful in creative assessment and how they might be measured. We next consider more general issues related to the assessment of creative performance.

General Issues in Creativity Assessment

Judgment and Classification

Judges may disagree in their ratings because of differences in their backgrounds, experiences, and preferences. What one person regards as original may be regarded as commonplace by another, who has already seen the invention or heard the idea many times before. What one person regards as a practical device may seem confusing to another, who does not understand how it would actually work.

This is why classification must be based on consensus, where most of the judges would have to agree on the ratings. This conservative procedure helps to ensure that ideas or objects classified as creative are more likely actually to be creative. For this reason, the reliability among raters does not have to be high. In fact, except when experts are used and the domains are highly restricted, judges should disagree to some extent, as a reflection of their varying backgrounds and expertise. The resulting classifications are then more likely to be free of idiosyncratic biases.

In the creative invention studies we report, the reliability among raters typically ranged from .5 to .6. These reliabilities are not as high as those in traditional cognitive studies, but they are significant and show that the judges' ratings are not merely arbitrary. In addition, lack of agreement between judges means that any differences between experimental conditions must be rather large in order for statistically significant effects to be observed.

Amabile (1983) distinguishes between consensual and conceptual measures of creativity. Consensual measures are operational, in the sense we have just described, whereas conceptual measures take into account the concepts behind an idea. This raises the question of whether, in experiments on creative cognition, the cognitive processes used to generate an idea should be considered before attempting to classify it.

Our feeling is that judges need not take into account the underlying cognitive processes when they evaluate the creativity of the resulting products. Although it is important, theoretically, to distinguish between cases where a creative idea was generated through the skillful use of creative cognitions and where it was arrived at randomly or arbitrarily, it seems both unnecessary and impractical to do so as part of the evaluative procedure in every creativity experiment.

We recommend, instead, trying to manipulate the cognitive processes through experimental control and then determining the effects of these manipulations on the resultant products. The products, in turn, should then be rated independently of these procedures to minimize experimenter effects and other possible forms of bias. One can then distinguish between structured and accidental creativity in terms of relationships between the creative products and the cognitive processes that gave rise to them.

Manifest and Inspirational Qualities

Real creativity excites; it opens up new directions for future exploration and inspires others to consider interesting possibilities as well. This is an aspect of creativity that most people can come to recognize and appreciate and that goes beyond merely having consensus in evaluative ratings and classifications.

We therefore reject the notion that creative assessment is simply a matter of personal preference or arbitrary convention. This would be like saying that all art or music is equally good; it just depends on what you happen to like. There *is* something special about great art and great music that goes beyond mere agreement or consensus. It also represents or captures something essential about human nature itself.

The same is true of most of the ideas and inventions classified as creative in these studies. We regard them has having construct validity in that they would generally be perceived as creative and inspirational by others. We typically find, in fact, that most people react to these ideas and inventions with surprise and admiration and often comment on how wonderfully creative they seem to be.

Cultural Context

Finally, the cultural and social environment can often influence the perceived creativity of an idea (Csikzentmihalyi 1988; Simonton 1988). What might be considered as preposterous or absurd by one society could be viewed as ingenious by another. If conceptions of what is creative can be biased by society's values, then won't the assessment of creativity always depend on those values?

We have several responses to this potential criticism. First, all studies are carried out within a particular cultural context, and scientific evaluation is always biased to some extent in this way. The ultimate test of creativity is whether a new idea continues to be accepted over time, as society's values change. If the methods of creative cognition do in fact give rise to lasting, innovative ideas, the issue of cultural bias is of relatively little concern. Second, although the content of creative ideas may indeed reflect society's values and concerns to some extent, the cognitive processes that gave rise to those ideas should still apply in any society. Third, many of the ideas that were classified as creative in these studies would seem to transcend specific cultural contexts.

Summary

In this chapter, we have identified various types of cognitive processes and structures that are likely to be important in creative thinking, various methods and techniques that can be useful in creative cognition research, and various ways in which creative products might be evaluated. These have all been considered within the context of the Geneplore model, which is proposed as one example of a general model of creative cognition. In the next chapter, we illustrate how some of these general research methods can be used to develop a scientific approach to the study of creative visualization.

3
Creative Visualization

Mental Synthesis and Transformation

We begin by exploring how creative visualization can be studied using the techniques of creative cognition. We consider in particular how emergent features can be detected in mental images, leading to unexpected visual discoveries, and how images can be mentally synthesized and transformed to provide various creative possibilities. In addition, although more direct support for the Geneplore model will be provided in subsequent chapters, we consider some implications of these findings for several aspects of the model.

Anecdotal Accounts of Visual Thinking
There is considerable evidence that much of our everyday thinking is based on the formation and transformation of visual images (Arnheim 1969; Cooper 1990; Ferguson 1977; Finke 1989; Finke and Shepard 1986; McKim 1980; Pinker 1984; Shepard and Cooper 1982). Moreover, there are many accounts, most of them based on anecdotal reports, of the role that visualization plays in the creative process. For example, many famous scientists have described how mental imagery contributed in an essential way to a key discovery or insight (Koestler 1964; Miller 1984; Shepard 1978, 1988). Perhaps the best known is Einstein's description of having imagined the consequences of traveling at the speed of light, which led him to the concept of special relativity. There are many other examples as well. Kekulé made his fundamental discovery in organic chemistry after having had a dream image in which a snake was coiled in such a way as to represent the molecular structure of benzene. Faraday claimed to have visualized lines of force that emanated from electric and magnetic sources, resulting in the modern conception of electromagnetic fields. Tesla reported that he could determine how well a machine would work by mentally "running" it in his mind. More recently, the physicist Feynman claimed to have used visual images in thinking about interactions among elementary particles, which led to the development of "Feynman diagrams."

There are also numerous accounts of the role that imagery plays in creative literary and artistic achievement. One artist who became blind as an adult claimed to use visualization to paint landscapes by imagining how the overall painting would look (Finke 1986). Skilled writers often comment on the role that imagery plays in giving rise to new ideas for stories (Ghiselin 1952; Koestler 1964). Architects have frequently reported using imagery to explore new ideas for designing buildings and other structures.

Such accounts are suggestive of the importance of visualization in creative thinking and discovery, but a scientific approach to the study of creative cognition needs to be based on more than anecdotes or introspective reports. Empirical methods are needed for studying creative acts under controlled laboratory conditions. Before considering examples of such methods, we review previous attempts to study mental imagery using scientific techniques, which have been applied for the most part in noncreative contexts. These studies have identified the basic characteristics of mental images, many of which are important in creative thinking.

Chronometric Studies of Mental Synthesis and Scanning
There have been a large number of experimental studies on the time it takes to assemble a mental image and to recognize the resulting pattern or form. In classic studies on mental synthesis, subjects are shown the parts of a pattern, are instructed to mentally assemble the parts in specific ways, and are then shown test patterns and have to say whether they recognize the patterns as corresponding to the ones they mentally assembled (Palmer 1977; Thompson and Klatzky 1978). This research has shown that the time needed to complete the mental synthesis increases with the number of parts but that the time needed to recognize the test patterns is independent of the number of mentally synthesized parts or the manner in which the parts were described (Glushko and Cooper 1978). Such findings suggest that people form complete, whole images of a pattern in anticipation of seeing it.

More recently, Kosslyn et al. (1983) found that the time it takes to generate an image depends on both the number of parts that were used in constructing it and the number of meaningful structural units used to organize the parts. As a rule, it takes longer to form images that are more complex in terms of these structural units. This showed that images are assembled piece by piece, in a structurally coherent way (Neisser 1967; Pylyshyn 1973).

Once formed, mental images can be scanned to retrieve the information they contain. Kosslyn, Ball, and Reiser (1978) demonstrated that the time needed to scan between two features in an image increases proportionally to the distance between the features, just as if one were scanning an actual drawing or map. Finke and Pinker (1982) verified these image scanning times in cases where the distances in the imagined pattern could not have been explicitly memorized, which ruled out explanations based on demand characteristics.

These findings on the mental synthesis and scanning of two-dimensional patterns have been extended to three-dimensional forms and structures. Cooper (1990) found that when subjects were given drawings depicting two orthographic views of an object and had to judge whether a third drawing depicted an orthographic view consistent with the first two, they mentally constructed a three-dimensional model of the object and then imagined how it would look from the new perspective. Pinker (1980) found that people could mentally scan a three-dimensional array of objects in depth, in which case the image scanning times were proportional to the three-dimensional distances separating the objects.

Taken together, these findings show that mental images can be inspected in much the same way that one inspects an actual object or pattern. They provide support for the principle of spatial equivalence, which asserts that there is a general correspondence between spatial relations depicted in a mental image and those present in actual surfaces and spaces (Finke 1989). This correspondence can be used to explore novel spatial relations in imagery.

Additional studies reveal that mental images can exhibit a variety of perceptual-like properties, such as the way visual acuity changes as the size of a pattern is varied or as it is displaced into the peripheral visual field (Kosslyn 1975; Finke and Kurtzman 1981). Imagery can also result in perceptual priming, adaptation, and interference (Brooks 1968; Farah 1985; Finke 1979, 1980; Podgorny and Shepard 1978; Segal and Fusella 1970). Such findings support the principle of perceptual equivalence, which asserts that imagery and perception share many of the same types of neural mechanisms (Farah 1988; Finke 1980, 1989). This allows one to explore the perceptual consequences of imagined events.

This work has helped to establish that mental images consist of more than just verbal descriptions or propositions. One of the key debates in imagery research has centered on whether images are more like pictures in the mind or a set of ordered propositions stating various facts and relationships (Anderson 1978; Pylyshyn 1973, 1984; Kosslyn 1980; Kosslyn and Pomerantz 1977). The presence of spatial and perceptual features in mental images provides strong evidence that images resemble pictures in at least some important respects.

Chronometric Studies of Mental Transformation
Other lines of research have explored the time it takes to imagine various transformations of objects and patterns. In their classic experiments on mental rotation, Shepard and Metzler (1971) found that the time required to verify that two perspective drawings depict different views of the same three-dimensional object increases in proportion to the rotational distance between them, suggesting that subjects make these judgments by forming images of the objects and then mentally rotating their images into alignment. Mental rotation can also be used to recognize single, disoriented patterns such as alphanumeric characters; in these experiments, the time it takes to recognize the pattern increases in proportion to the angular distance required for turning the pattern back to its standard, upright position (Cooper and Shepard 1973; Corballis 1988).

Other types of mental transformations have been explored, such as mentally changing the size of an object (Bundesen and Larsen 1975) and the imagined folding of flat patterns to make three-dimensional shapes (Shepard and Feng 1972). More recently Freyd (1987) reported that memories for patterns can undergo spontaneous transformations according to the processes used to construct the patterns. For example, memories for handwritten characters can be distorted in ways that reflect a person's knowledge about the manner in which the characters were generated (Freyd 1983). In addition, memories for an object's final position can be transformed whenever the object is depicted to move in a particular direction, as in demonstrations of representational momentum (Freyd and Finke 1984; Finke and Shyi 1988).

In all of these studies, the typical finding is that the mental transformations resemble corresponding physical transformations. In particular, the mental transformations are carried out in a continuous or analogue fashion, as opposed to a discrete or stepwise manner (Cooper 1976; Freyd and Johnson 1987) and are carried out holistically, with all parts intact, rather than piecemeal, after a person has become sufficiently familiar with the forms (Bethell-Fox and Shepard 1988; Cooper and Podgorny 1976). These findings support the principle of transformational equivalence, which asserts that mental and physical transformations are carried out in corresponding ways and obey many of the same physical laws (Finke 1989). This makes it possible for a person to anticipate changes in a moving object and to mentally test dynamic models of physical systems and processes.

Studies on mental transformation have helped to establish that mental images are not merely static representations, like photographs, but can exhibit motion and change (Shepard and Cooper 1982; Finke

1989; Freyd 1987). Once constructed, a mental image can be manipulated to suit a variety of purposes.

In the Geneplore model, mental synthesis and transformation are considered to be important generative processes. Image scanning falls under the heading of attribute finding and would be considered an exploratory process, serving an important function in the search for unexpected features in an image. As we will demonstrate, these processes also provide some of the basic mechanisms for creative discovery in mental imagery.

Limitations of Chronometric Approaches
Although chronometric studies have uncovered important properties of mental imagery in particular (Shepard and Cooper 1982), and human cognition in general (Posner 1978), the dependent measures used in these studies may be of limited value in creative cognition, for three reasons.

First, as a general rule, chronometric methods are more useful for the study of single cognitive processes in isolation. When used to study a specific process like mental image scanning or mental rotation, for example, these methods can help to reveal the precise manner in which the process is carried out over time. In creative cognition, in contrast, there are usually many kinds of cognitive processes operating in conjunction and with varying rates. For instance, in generating a creative image, one might begin by mentally synthesizing the parts of an object, followed by various mental transformations and rearrangements of the parts, followed, perhaps, by additional syntheses and transformations. To attempt to track all of these processes using chronometric methods would be exceedingly difficult.

A second limitation is that chronometric methods are normally used in tasks that are structured primarily to reduce error variance. In creative cognition, however, the idea is to use experimental methods to discover the unexpected and not simply to elicit an intended response. Indeed, one normally wants to encourage such variation in performance.

Third, much of the chronometric work on mental synthesis, image scanning, and mental transformation has resulted in findings that, although important for establishing an empirical foundation for the scientific study of visualization, might not have seemed very surprising. For example, most people already know how to assemble, scan, and transform their images. They do not necessarily know how to use their images in creative and innovative ways, however. This is why studies on creative cognition can lead to the development of new, effective techniques for training people how to think more creatively.

Emergent Features in Mental Images

Reinterpreting Mental Images
When images are mentally synthesized or transformed, they often end up having properties that are useful in creative discovery. We consider here three of these properties: novelty, ambiguity, and emergence. Images tend to be novel when they are formed using unusual sets of parts or when they are combined in unique ways (Finke and Slayton 1988). Ambiguity is created when an image can be organized in more than one way (Finke, Pinker, and Farah 1989). Of particular importance is emergence. An image displays emergence when its parts or features are combined such that additional, unexpected features result, making it possible to detect new patterns and relations in the image that were not intentionally created (Finke 1991a).

There is an additional principle, structural equivalence, which states that mental images, like physical forms and structures, can be reorganized and reinterpreted (Finke 1989). This principle has particular relevance for creative visualization and goes beyond the previous imagery principles. An image could be spatially distributed, have perceptual characteristics, and be transformed according to the laws of motion and still not yield any new discoveries. The image might continue to represent only what a person intended it to represent at the time the person formed it. In order for new discoveries and insights to occur, the structure of an image must also allow for the detection of unexpected features and relations and, accordingly, the possibility of new interpretations.

In the field of perception, there have been many studies showing that certain patterns can be interpreted in a variety of different ways. For example, some patterns can be seen as representing different kinds of objects (Attneave 1971; Shepard 1990; Shepard and Cermak 1973), while others change their identity when rotated to different orientations (Rock 1973). In such cases, a person must reconceptualize or reorganize the features of the initially construed pattern in order to see it as something different. To explore whether similar kinds of discoveries can also occur in mental imagery, we next consider studies on the detection of emergent patterns.

Evidence for Visual Discoveries in Imagery
Pinker and Finke (1980) used a mental rotation task to explore the recognition of unexpected patterns in mental images. Subjects in their study began by learning the positions of four small objects hung at different depths inside a clear cylinder. The objects were then removed, and the subjects were instructed to rotate the cylinder man-

ually while continuing to imagine the objects rotating along inside of it, until the experimenter told them to stop. The subjects were then asked to report what type of pattern was formed by the four rotated objects, in the same way that constellations of stars can often form recognizable patterns and shapes. The majority of the subjects correctly detected the emergent pattern, which was a parallelogram, although none were able to guess from the initial starting positions that this particular pattern would emerge.

A more comprehensive investigation of the discovery of emergent patterns in images, using mental synthesis in conjunction with mental rotation, was carried out by Finke, Pinker, and Farah (1989). Subjects were given the name of a familiar starting pattern, such as the capital letter B and were then instructed to close their eyes and to imagine changing the pattern according to a sequence of verbally designated transformations, which could involve adding new features or parts, eliminating old ones, or rotating the pattern as a whole—for example, "Start with the letter B, and imagine rotating it 90 degrees to the left, so that the curved part of the letter is at the top. Now imagine attaching an equilateral triangle to the bottom of the rotated B, with the triangle pointing down and having a base equal in width to that of the rotated letter. Now mentally erase the horizontal line at the junction of the rotated B and the triangle. Can you recognize the resulting pattern?" If you had imagined the transformation sequence correctly, you probably would have recognized a heart.

In the experiments of Finke, Pinker, and Farah, subjects participated in similar types of tasks. Examples of some of the transformation sequences are shown in figure 3.1, and the major results are presented in table 3.1, which shows the relative number of pattern recognitions according to how accurately the imagined transformations were carried out. The responses were scored as correct, partially correct (where the reported identification, though different, could still be considered a legitimate alternative interpretation of the emergent pattern), and incorrect. Transformation accuracy was based on drawings that the subjects provided after giving their responses; the transformations were classified as correct, partially correct (with only a minor flaw or error), and incorrect. The transformations were performed correctly on 59.7 percent of the trials, in which case the subjects correctly identified the emergent pattern 58.1 percent of the time. Including valid, alternative interpretations increases this percentage to 69.8 percent. When the transformations were performed incorrectly, however, the subjects never identified the emergent pattern or provided any alternative interpretations of it.

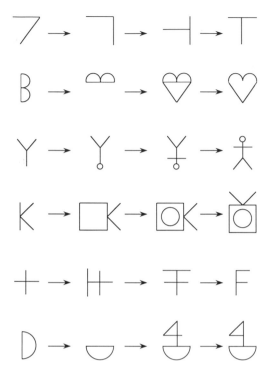

Figure 3.1
Examples of image transformation sequences in experiments on detecting emergent patterns in images. Subjects imagined transforming the initial patterns in specified ways and then attempted to identify the final patterns. (From Finke, Pinker, and Farah 1989.)

Table 3.1
Number of Emergent Patterns Identified According to the Accuracy of the Imagined Transformations

Pattern Identification	Accuracy of Transformation		
	Correct	Partially Correct	Incorrect
Correct	25	2	0
Partially correct	5	5	0
Incorrect	13	8	14

Source: Finke, Pinker, and Farah (1989).
Note: The classifications are based on seventy-two trials.

Controls for Guessing and Expectation
Using a sequence of transformation steps helps to disguise what the emergent pattern will be. In fact, subjects in these experiments were rarely able to guess the emergent pattern after being given the starting pattern. One also needs to ensure that the emergent pattern is sufficiently disguised by the procedures such that it cannot be guessed at any of the later transformation steps as well.

Finke, Pinker, and Farah (1989) included a control experiment in which subjects were explicitly told to try to guess the emergent pattern after each step in the imagery task had been completed. Whereas the emergent patterns were correctly identified, at the end of the transformation sequence, on 47.9 percent of the trials on which the transformations had been carried out accurately, the patterns were correctly anticipated on only 4.2 percent of those trials, which includes guesses that were made on the next-to-last transformation step. Thus, the final recognition of the emergent patterns could not be attributed to guessing strategies that might have been inspired by the nature of the transformations.

Effects of Pattern Goodness
There is considerable evidence that the perceived goodness of the parts of a pattern (i.e., the degree to which the parts seem natural or appear to belong to the pattern) affects how easily the parts can be detected (Palmer 1977) and how effectively they can serve as retrieval cues for the pattern (Bower and Glass 1976). This raises the question of how pattern goodness might also affect the recognition of emergent patterns in imagery.

Reed (1974) showed subjects patterns containing multiple parts and then asked them to try to detect the parts after forming mental images of the patterns. It is easy to see that the pattern shown in figure 3.2 contains four small triangles, two larger, overlapping triangles, two hourglass figures, and a diamond. These constitute "good" parts of the pattern, and they were easy to detect in an image of the pattern. Structurally "poor" parts, however, were much harder to detect in imagery than when actually looking at the pattern. An example is the two parallelograms that are also contained in figure 3.2. Thus, whether an emergent pattern can be detected in imagery may depend on the structure of the pattern and the nature of its parts.

Roskos-Ewoldsen (1991) has explored in greater detail the relationship between pattern goodness and the detection of emergent patterns in images. In a mental synthesis task, she varied the goodness of the component parts used in the mental constructions, as well as the goodness of the overall resulting patterns. Detection of emergent

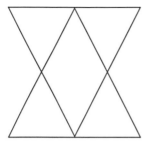

Figure 3.2
An ambiguous pattern whose parts can be organized in a variety of different ways. The
pattern displays structurally "good" and "poor" parts. (From Reed 1974.)

patterns in images was most accurate when the component parts were
structurally good but the overall pattern was structurally poor. This,
in fact, makes sense; it is easier to mentally synthesize "good" parts,
whereas the detection of emergent patterns is facilitated when the
resulting image structure is poorly organized and, hence, easier to
reorganize.

Creative Visual Discoveries

Limitations of Previous Studies
In each of the studies on the detection of emergent patterns, there
were always "right" and "wrong" answers, as defined by the experimenter. But as we indicated in the previous chapter, experiments in
creative cognition should provide opportunities for genuine creative
discovery. One could argue, for example, that the image discoveries
we just reviewed were so contrived that they might never have occurred under any normal conditions, because the subjects always had
to be given explicit instructions for how to mentally combine the parts.
Is it also possible to demonstrate, in the context of an actual experiment, that people can discover unexpected patterns in their images
when not explicitly told how to go about doing so?

Explorations of Creative Visual Synthesis
Finke and Slayton (1988) developed a general procedure for exploring
creative discoveries in mental imagery. In their mental synthesis task,
subjects were given sets of simple pattern parts and were free to
assemble them mentally in any way to make a recognizable shape or
pattern. The parts that were used, consisting of alphanumeric characters and basic geometric patterns, are shown in figure 3.3. At the

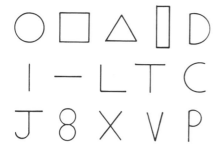

Figure 3.3
Set of stimulus parts used in experiments on creative visual synthesis. Three of the parts were chosen at random at the beginning of each experimental trial. (From Finke and Slayton 1988.)

beginning of each trial, three of the parts were randomly selected with replacement, meaning that the same part could be included more than once. The only constraint was that the simpler parts, shown in the first two rows of figure 3.3, were three times as likely to be selected as the more complex parts, shown in the bottom row. This was done so that these more complex parts would seldom comprise the entire stimulus set. In all, there were 1,135 possible unique sets of parts.

The subjects participated in eight trials each. At the beginning of each trial, the three parts were named by the experimenter, and the subjects were instructed to close their eyes and to imagine assembling the parts to make a recognizable figure, which could be anything at all—letters, numbers, shapes of objects, meaningful symbols, and so on. The only restrictions were that all three parts had to be used, the individual parts could not be deformed, and the resulting patterns had to correspond to something that could be easily recognized and named. Otherwise the subjects were free to mentally combine the parts in any way, which included superimposing, juxtaposing, or rotating them, and varying their relative size.

They were then given two minutes to mentally construct their figure, after which they were instructed to open their eyes and write down on a response sheet the name of the figure, if they had been able to come up with one, and then to draw it as accurately as they could. Once they began to draw the pattern, they could not go back and change the name they had given to it; this ensured that the subjects had recognized the patterns in their images and not in their drawings.

The resulting patterns were scored independently by three judges according to how closely the patterns corresponded to the names they had been given. These correspondence ratings were made using a five-point scale, where ratings of 4 and 5 meant "good" and "very good" correspondence, respectively. The judges were instructed to make these ratings not on the basis of the quality of the drawings but on how well the pattern corresponded to its name—had it been skillfully drawn. In addition, the judges rated which patterns, out of those rated as having good or very good correspondence, seemed to be distinctively creative.

These ratings of correspondence and creativity were used to classify the patterns. Patterns that received an average correspondence rating of at least 4 were considered recognizable. If a recognizable pattern was also judged to be creative by at least two of the judges, it was further classified as a creative pattern. This convention was conservative; in order to be counted as creative, a pattern first had to be rated as easy to recognize.

Finke and Slayton found that subjects were able to come up with a recognizable pattern on 40.5 percent of the trials. Of these, 15.0 percent were classified as creative. These percentages are based on a combined total of 872 trials.

Examples of Creative Visual Patterns
Figure 3.4 contains examples of patterns that were classified as creative in these tasks, together with the sets of parts used in their construction. In these examples, one can see how emergent features resulted from various combinations of the parts. For instance, in the croquet pattern, the rotated letter P and number 8 combine to form two croquet balls in front of a wicket, which are about to be struck by the croquet mallet, depicted by the inverted letter T.

It is worth noting that the subjects were never actually told to try to be creative in any of these experiments. Rather, we had hoped that the structure of the task itself would stimulate creative exploration. Although the parts were familiar, the particular combinations of parts that were selected for the stimulus sets were often unusual. Having to work with unusual sets of parts would tend to promote creative discovery.

An additional finding is that there were never any order or practice effects in these experiments, suggestive of the serendipitous quality of the discoveries. Nor is there any effect of showing subjects examples of creative constructions at the beginning of each trial (Finke and Smith 1989). What seems to be more important is simply having the opportunity to explore interesting possibilities.

Figure 3.5 presents more examples of creative patterns that subjects generated in these tasks. These patterns tended to occur infrequently,

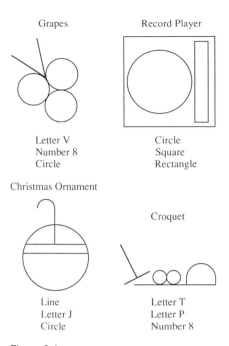

Figure 3.4
Patterns that were classified as creative, together with the sets of parts used in their construction. (From Finke and Slayton 1988.)

in agreement with our expectation that patterns classified as creative should be relatively uncommon. The majority of the creative patterns (69.8 percent) occurred with a relative frequency of 0.5 percent or less.

Controls for Guessing and Experimenter Bias
An important feature of experiments on creative cognition is that they tend to be relatively immune to demand characteristics and other similar artifacts. This is because the most creative products tend to be the most difficult to anticipate. We can demonstrate this empirically, using the creative visual synthesis task.

Finke and Slayton (1988) included control experiments in which both the experimenter and the subjects were encouraged to guess the patterns most likely to result from the mental synthesis. In one experiment, the experimenter generated three guesses for each set of parts; in another, the subjects themselves generated guesses for sets of parts that they would later actually use in the task. Since there were no differences between the accuracy of experimenter and subject pre-

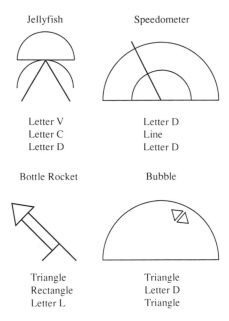

Jellyfish

Letter V
Letter C
Letter D

Speedometer

Letter D
Line
Letter D

Bottle Rocket

Triangle
Rectangle
Letter L

Bubble

Triangle
Letter D
Triangle

Figure 3.5
Additional creative patterns in experiments on creative mental synthesis. (From Finke 1990.)

dictions, we present the combined results in table 3.2. Only 16.5 percent of the recognizable patterns and 13.2 percent of the creative patterns were correctly predicted.

This general finding—that neither the experimenters nor the subjects successfully predicted the emergent patterns in these tasks— provides additional support for our claim that the creative discoveries themselves are for the most part unpredictable. This is not to claim that the discoveries are random or that the likelihood of creative performance cannot be predicted but simply that the particular pathways of creative exploration are often opportunistic and unforeseeable.

Introspective Reports
Finke and Slayton (1988) obtained introspective reports from the subjects to assess the kinds of strategies they had used to perform the task. Although they were never instructed as to how they should go about generating the patterns, nearly three-fourths of the subjects (74.4 percent) reported first combining the parts in their images in a trial-and-error fashion and then exploring possible interpretations of

Table 3.2
Recognizable and Creative Patterns According to Whether They Were
Successfully Predicted

Type of Pattern	Predicted	Not Predicted	Total
Recognizable	40	203	243
Creative	5	33	38

Source: Finke and Slayton (1988).
Note: The classifications are based on 592 trials.

the resulting shapes. This was strongly preferred to various other strategies, including starting out by trying to think of possible patterns that might be associated with the parts. This use of trial-and-error synthesis and exploration is reminiscent of the combinational play so often referred to in anecdotal accounts of the creative process.

Creative Synthesis versus Creative Interpretation
A well-known finding is that one's memory for arbitrary or ambiguous patterns is markedly improved whenever one can think of meaningful or creative interpretations of the patterns (Bower, Karlin, and Dueck 1975). Note in this regard that in the studies on creative mental synthesis, no attempts were made to separate experimentally the mental construction of the patterns from the process of creatively interpreting them. (This distinction is of considerable importance in testing the Geneplore model and is taken up in chapter 4.)

Another limitation of these initial studies is that the classification of patterns as creative was based on direct ratings of perceived creativity. This is potentially troublesome, given the different senses in which something could be regarded as creative. In the research studies considered in subsequent chapters, improved methods are used to assess creativity.

Externalizing the Creative Process

Comparing Mental and Physical Synthesis
A natural question that arises from this work is whether creative performance would be markedly improved if people were actually to draw or manipulate the pattern parts instead of simply imagining the parts and their combinations. To explore this question, Neblett, Finke, and Ginsburg (1989) compared mental and physical synthesis using variations of the methods in the Finke and Slayton study. In the physical synthesis condition, subjects were given transparent overlays

on which the parts were drawn at one of three sizes. They could thus construct their patterns by superimposing and rotating the overlays. The imagery condition was similar to that already described except that the subjects were instructed to use the same size ratios as were used in the physical synthesis condition. In a control condition, subjects were given drawings of the parts that they could inspect and rotate but not superimpose.

Recognizable and creative patterns were scored in the same way as before. Comparisons among the conditions revealed no significant differences in the number of patterns generated in mental and physical synthesis. Recognizable patterns were produced on 51.2 percent of the trials in the physical synthesis condition and on 47.6 percent of the trials in the mental synthesis condition. Of these, 7.0 and 10.0 percent of the patterns, respectively, were classified as creative. Mental and physical synthesis were thus equivalent. Performance was better in each case relative to the control condition, in which the parts could be inspected and manipulated but not actually combined.

Using slightly different procedures, Anderson and Helstrup (1991) compared mental and physical synthesis in the Finke and Slayton task. In their physical synthesis condition, subjects were allowed to draw the patterns as they constructed them. These researchers also found equivalent performance for mental and physical synthesis, with one exception. When told to generate as many patterns as they could on each trial, subjects were able to generate more patterns in the physical synthesis condition. These patterns, however, were no more recognizable or creative than those generated during mental synthesis.

One advantage of using mental synthesis is that it can be carried out with minimal effort, although we would expect that physical synthesis would become easier, relative to mental synthesis, as the number of parts increases, because there are capacity limitations on how many parts and features an image can contain at the same time (Kosslyn 1975, 1980). (In chapter 9, we consider at length these and other potential limitations on creative cognition.)

Strategies for Creative Construction
Exactly how do subjects in these experiments go about constructing patterns? Anderson and Helstrup (1991) explored this issue by examining the drawings that subjects produced in the physical synthesis condition, which revealed the various stages of construction that were used. They found that subjects tended to start out with the more complex parts (such as the letter J) and then tried adding on the simpler parts. This strategy makes sense; the more complex parts lend themselves to a smaller range of possible interpretations, whereas the

simpler parts can be accommodated more easily into an existing structure.

Anderson and Helstrup also compared subjects' ratings of the creativity of their own patterns to those provided by judges and found that the subjects tended to overrate their creativity. A possible explanation is that the subjects were often surprised at what they had discovered in doing the task and thus knew that they did not have those patterns in mind when they started. This recalls the distinction between consensual measures of creativity and conceptual measures, which are based on knowing the manner in which a creative idea was formed. We prefer to use the former in studies on creative cognition, because they tend to be more conservative and objective.

Summary

Theoretical Implications
These studies on creative visualization illustrate some of the advantages of the creative cognition approach. First, they show that it is possible to demonstrate creative performance in controlled laboratory experiments using appropriate tasks and procedures. Subjects were never told to try to be creative, yet the nature of the tasks led them to engage in creative exploration and discovery. On the average, 94.9 percent of the subjects reported at least one recognizable pattern in the experiments, and 30.8 percent were able to come up with at least one creative pattern. This result is all the more significant given that the subjects were not preselected for creative ability and were under severe time restrictions.

The studies also illustrate the importance of combinational play in generating creative ideas, where this was overwhelmingly the preferred strategy in the mental synthesis tasks. Subjects often commented that they started out by trying to think of a specific pattern they could make out of the parts they were given but then soon realized that this was an inefficient strategy because they could rarely get all the parts to fit the original conception. Instead they found it was better to start out by mentally exploring various combinations of the parts, to see what types of interesting patterns could be made, and then to explore meaningful interpretations of the patterns. This strategy takes advantage of the emergent properties of the imagined forms.

The imagined creations evinced a structured quality. The patterns were not randomly assembled but often displayed elegance and beauty. These patterns can be contrasted with purely random forms, such as Rorschach inkblots, to which one might also give creative interpretations. As we establish in chapter 6, real creativity is structured, not random, though it may arise out of randomly chosen elements.

Finally, these studies have implications for contemporary theories of image formation. These theories have focused largely on the manner in which features are retrieved from long-term memory and assembled in a mental image to represent familiar objects and forms (e.g., Kosslyn 1980, 1987; Kosslyn et al. 1983). In creative cognition, one is more concerned with how features are combined in imagery for the purpose of discovering new patterns, relations, and interpretations. We propose that theories of image formation should consider how novel configurations of features are generated and interpreted, in addition to how imagery is used to represent things that are already familiar. In particular, one would want to consider cases in which a person generates an image without knowing in advance what the image is supposed to represent.

Practical Implications
The methods for generating creative images described in this chapter have a number of practical applications, especially in art and visual design. An artist, for example, could randomly select parts of patterns and explore creative ways of combining them in trying to come up with new ideas for a drawing or painting. A designer could use these techniques to invent a new advertising logo. An architect could generate new floor plans for a house or office building by creatively recombining the basic parts of the plan. These techniques, in fact, could be used to explore a wide range of creative possibilities in which ideas can be represented as visual patterns or designs.

The pattern shown in figure 3.6 is one example of how creative visual synthesis can be used to generate and interpret novel symbols. It was mentally constructed by one of the authors using a circle, a

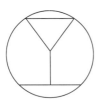

Figure 3.6
A mentally synthesized pattern that can be interpreted as a variety of different kinds of symbols.

triangle, and the letter T as the three parts. The figure could be interpreted as a logo for a swimsuit company, a professional golfers' association, or a wine tasters' club, or as a design for a new kind of highway intersection.

A mentally synthesized pattern does not always have to be associated with a particular interpretation in order to have aesthetic appeal as an art form. Consider the concept of "incomplete" art—where the artist intentionally omits many of the fine details, leaving one's imagination to fill them in. In creative mental synthesis, there are usually many interpretive paths that one can follow.

In the next chapter, we extend these methods to explore the discovery of creative ideas for new inventions and examine in more detail the major features of the Geneplore model. In doing so, we look specifically at the effects of imposing different types of constraints on creative performance.

4

Creative Invention

A Paradigm for Invention

The previous chapter considered some of the basic techniques of creative cognition as applied to the study of creative visualization. In this chapter, we extend these techniques to more general cases in which imagery might be useful in designing or inventing something. The particular aspects of the Geneplore model considered here are the mental synthesis of preinventive object forms, the preinventive properties of ambiguity, meaningfulness, emergence, and divergence, the exploratory processes of attribute finding, functional inference, and contextual shifting, and the effects of imposing constraints on the object category, type, function, and components as they bear on the likelihood that one will generate a creative product. In addition, we propose some general principles of creative cognition that are suggested by these findings.

Creative Mental Synthesis of Real-World Objects

The stimulus sets used in the previous experiments on creative visualization, consisting of flat, two-dimensional forms and alphanumeric characters, were rather limited. The resulting patterns, although often creative, rarely corresponded to practical objects or devices. We now consider the mental synthesis of three-dimensional object parts to form images of whole, solid shapes, which can then be interpreted as new ideas for creative inventions.

Most of the experiments reported in this chapter are taken from Finke (1990). The experiments always began by showing subjects a set of fifteen basic object parts (figure 4.1). In most of the experimental conditions, three parts were randomly selected for each trial, with the random selection subject to the constraint that the simplest parts—the sphere, half-sphere, cube, cone, and cylinder—had a 50 percent chance of being selected; the more specialized parts—the rectangular block, wire, tube, bracket, and flat square—had a 33 percent chance of being selected; and the most specialized parts—the hook, cross,

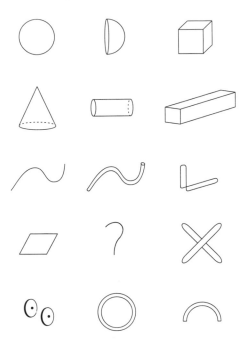

Figure 4.1
Set of object parts in experiments on creative invention. The following names (left to right) were used to designate each of the parts: sphere, half-sphere, cube, cone, cylinder, rectangular block, wire, tube, bracket, flat square, hook, cross, wheels, ring, and handle. (From Finke 1990.)

wheels, ring, and handle—had a 16 percent chance of being selected. As in the previous studies on creative visualization, these constraints reduced the likelihood that the stimulus sets would consist entirely of the most specialized parts.

At the beginning of each trial, the experimenter named the three parts, and the subjects closed their eyes and imagined combining the parts to make a practical object or device. They were never told to try to be creative in doing the task but simply to think of an object that might be useful. All three of the named parts had to be used, even if the same type of part was named more than once. The subjects could vary the size, position, or orientation of any part but could not bend or deform the parts, with the exception of the wire and the tube, which had been defined as bendable. The parts could be put inside one another; they could be hollow or solid and could be made out of any material, including wood, metal, plastic, rubber, or glass, or any combination of these materials.

The objects had to belong to one of the eight general object categories shown in table 4.1, which were chosen to provide a wide range of possible inventions. Depending on the experiment, these categories were specified randomly or could be chosen by the subjects. The subjects were given two minutes to come up with an object using the designated parts; they were then to name the object, draw it, and describe what it did or how its parts functioned. These reports were used in scoring the inventions.

This scoring was accomplished by having judges rate each invention along two dimensions, practicality and originality, using a five-point scale for each, in which ratings of 4 and 5 corresponded, respectively, to practical and very practical or original and very original. These ratings were to be made independently; for example, an object might be practical but not original, original but not practical, or both. In using this procedure, the judges never had to rate creativity per se, an improvement over previous rating techniques. In addition, the judges were instructed to base their ratings not on how well the object was drawn but on the concept represented by the drawing and on the overall design of the object, not on whether it necessarily contained all of the working parts it would actually need. All of the inventions were rated together, in random order and without knowledge of the experimental conditions.

The ratings of practicality and originality were used to classify the objects into invention categories. An object that received an average practicality rating of at least 4.5 was classified as a "practical invention"; a practical invention that received an average originality rating of at least 4.0 was further classified as a "creative invention." These

Table 4.1
Allowable Object Categories in Experiments on Creative Invention

Category	Examples
1. Furniture	Chairs, tables, lamps
2. Personal items	Jewelry, glasses
3. Transportation	Cars, boats
4. Scientific instruments	Measuring devices
5. Appliances	Washing machines, toasters
6. Tools and utensils	Screwdrivers, spoons
7. Weapons	Guns, missiles
8. Toys and games	Baseball bats, dolls

Source: Finke (1990).

conventions ensured that the classifications would reflect consensus among the judges, thus serving to eliminate the effects of idiosyncratic biases in the ratings. Also, the cutoff level for the practicality ratings was set slightly higher than that for the originality ratings, for two reasons. First, on the average, the practicality ratings were higher than the originality ratings, and second, this made the classifications more conservative, emphasizing the practicality of the inventions. We note, however, that the major findings of these studies do not depend on exactly where these cutoffs are made, since they are based on comparisons among the relative numbers of inventions.

An example of an object that was classified as a creative invention is presented in figure 4.2. It is a hip exerciser, assigned to the category "furniture," and was mentally constructed using the half-sphere, the wire, and the rectangular block as the three parts. To use the hip exerciser, you attach the wire to the walls on opposite sides of a room, stand on the base, and then rotate your hips by shifting your weight from side to side while holding the post.

Restricting Object Parts and Categories
The initial experiments tested the idea that creativity would be enhanced whenever one is forced to use unusual sets of parts or to interpret the resulting objects in unconventional ways. This was accomplished by varying whether the parts and the object categories could be freely chosen or were specified using random selection at the beginning of each trial. There were three conditions of interest: (1) the

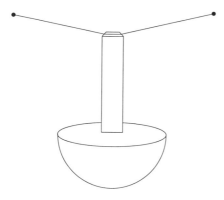

Figure 4.2
The hip exerciser, constructed using the half-sphere, wire, and rectangular block, an example of an object that was classified as a creative invention. By shifting one's weight from side to side while standing on the half-sphere, one can exercise one's hips. (From Finke 1990.)

category was random and the parts were chosen, (2) the category was chosen and the parts were random, and (3) both the category and the parts were random. (The other logical condition, in which both the category and the parts could be freely chosen, was not included, since it would have been trivially unconstrained.) Each subject participated in six trials, and there were sixty subjects per condition.

The major result was that the relative number of creative inventions increased significantly as the task became more highly constrained (table 4.2). In particular, the greatest number of creative inventions was obtained when both the object parts and the interpretive categories were randomly specified at the beginning of the trials. This suggests that the probability of generating a creative invention is enhanced whenever one is forced to think in unconventional ways about possible objects and their uses.

In the most successful condition—where both the parts and the categories were randomly specified—subjects came up with a practical invention on 48.6 percent of the trials and a creative invention on 13.6 percent of the trials. This is quite remarkable, taking into account that the subjects were never told to be creative, that they were not preselected with regard to creative ability, and that they had only two minutes to perform the task.

Examples of Creative Inventions
Among the objects classified as creative inventions in these experiments is the hamburger maker, from the category "tools and utensils" (figure 4.3). This metal object consists of an open half-sphere at one end of the cylinder, which is used to scoop up a measured amount of hamburger meat, and a solid sphere at the opposite end, which is used to roll the meat into a desired shape.

Table 4.2
Number of Inventions According to Whether Object Parts and Categories Were Freely Chosen or Specified Randomly

Type of Invention	Condition		
	Category Random, Parts Chosen	Category Chosen, Parts Random	Category Random, Parts Random
Practical	193	191	175
Creative	17	31	49

Source: Finke (1990).
Note: The categorizations are based on 1,080 trials—360 for each condition.
"Creative" inventions were practical inventions that were rated as original.

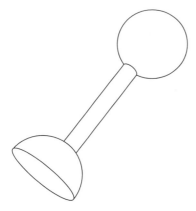

Figure 4.3
A hamburger maker, constructed using the sphere, half-sphere, and cylinder. The opposite ends of the utensil are used to measure the hamburger meat and to roll it into the desired shape. (From Finke 1990.)

The shoestring unlacer (figure 4.4) is from the category "personal items." To untie a knotted shoelace, one inserts the hook into the knot and pulls out one of the loops. The opposite end of the unlacer can be used as a key chain.

The ring wagon (figure 4.5), from the category "toys and games," has a variety of different uses. A child could use it to transport large toys by securing them to the ring. One child could stand on the ring and try to maintain his or her balance while another pulls the wagon. Or a child could place a box of sand on the ring and allow the sand to leak out as the wagon is pulled and rotated, creating patterns and designs.

Virtually all of the creative inventions obtained in these and in the later experiments we will describe were unique. Only rarely was the same invention discovered by different subjects, even when they had used the same sets of parts and were given the same object category.

Table 4.3 provides readers with an opportunity to try the creative invention task. Imagine assembling each set of parts to make a practical object belonging to the designated category. These examples are similar to the kinds of trials that were actually used when the object parts and categories were randomly specified in these experiments.

Restricting Object Types and Functions
The previous experiments show that restricting the object category and the object parts can increase the likelihood of generating a creative invention. We next consider the consequences of restricting the par-

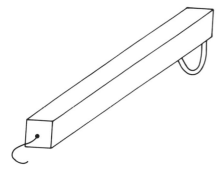

Figure 4.4
The shoestring unlacer, constructed using the rectangular block, hook, and handle. This item can be used to untie a knotted shoelace. (From Finke 1990.)

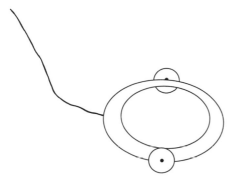

Figure 4.5
The ring wagon, constructed using the ring, wire, and wheels. Children can use this wagon to transport large toys, for example. (From Finke 1990.)

Table 4.3
Examples of Sets of Parts in Experiments on Creative
Invention (Parts and Object Category Specified
Randomly)

Category	Parts
Tools and utensils	Handle Flat square Half-sphere
Weapons	Wire Tube Wheels
Scientific instruments	Hook Cylinder Sphere
Furniture	Ring Sphere Tube
Appliances	Cone Sphere Cylinder
Tools and utensils	Handle Cone Tube
Furniture	Half-sphere Cross Cylinder
Toys and games	Hook Half-sphere Rectangular block
Appliances	Cylinder Cylinder Flat square
Transportation	Sphere Cylinder Tube

Source: Finke (1990).

ticular object types or functions. In one case, we examine the effects of restricting the types of objects within a designated object category. For example, within the category "furniture," a subject might be given "chair" or "table" and have to make that particular type of object out of the three parts. These object types correspond to what are called basic objects in research on concept formation (Rosch et al. 1976). In the other case, we examine the effects of restricting the particular function that an object can have within the category. For example, a subject might be given the description "a piece of furniture that a handicapped person could use" or "a weapon that uses light." These restrictions were balanced between the two experiments such that the particular object categories were represented equally often. The parts were randomly selected, and the general procedures were identical to those in the previous experiments.

Restricting the object types should limit the creative opportunities relative to restricting the object functions because the features contained in a basic object tend to be more specialized (Rosch et al. 1976; Smith and Medin 1981; Smith, Shoben, and Rips 1974), and it may not be possible to always include those features when using parts that are chosen at random. This is less of a problem, however, when only the object functions are specified, since this still allows consideration of a variety of possible features and object types.

These predictions were supported by the results of the experiments (table 4.4). Restricting the object functions resulted in a similar number of creative inventions compared to when just the category had been restricted (see table 4.2), whereas restricting the object types resulted in fewer than half as many creative inventions. Thus, when trying to invent a new device, it might be better not to commit oneself to making the device correspond initially to a particular type of object.

Table 4.4
Number of Inventions According to Whether Object Types or Functions Were Specified Randomly

Type of Invention	Condition	
	Type Random, Parts Random	Function Random, Parts Random
Practical	76	105
Creative	20	51

Source: Finke (1990).
Note: The categorizations are based on 720 trials—360 for each condition. "Creative" inventions were practical inventions rated as original.

Among the creative inventions obtained when the function of the objects was restricted is the doorknob alarm (figure 4.6), generated under the restriction that it had to be "an appliance that could catch a burglar." The half-sphere is used as a doorknob cover, and the smaller spheres attached to the cover are sensitive to heat or motion. The idea is that a burglar cannot open a door without turning or touching the doorknob, thereby setting off an alarm. The snow vacuum shown in figure 4.7 was generated under the restriction that it had to be "a tool for removing snow." A vacuum is created inside the hollow sphere, and snow is sucked into the sphere through the tube. The snow is then allowed to melt, and the water is released back out through the tube, where it can be used as needed.

Introspective Reports
When interviewed, subjects in these experiments reported a preference for using an exploratory strategy in which they began by constructing interesting, suggestive forms and then tried to interpret them, as opposed to starting out with a particular object in mind and then trying to make the available parts conform to that object. The subjects often mentioned that they would try to look for useful properties of the forms they created or to consider ways in which the forms might function as workable devices. Such reports suggest that there may be advantages to allowing functional inference to follow the generation of preinventive object forms, an issue we will explore in the next section.

The subjects seemed genuinely interested in pursuing their ideas, even after the experiment was concluded. They thought that they had learned how they could be more creative as a result of their partici-

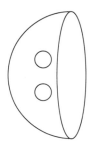

Figure 4.6
A doorknob alarm, constructed using two spheres and the half-sphere, under the restriction that it had to be "an appliance that could catch a burglar." The half-sphere is a cover placed over a doorknob, and the small spheres that are attached to the cover are sensitive to heat or motion. (From Finke 1990.)

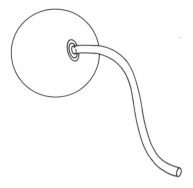

Figure 4.7
A snow vacuum, constructed using the ring, tube, and sphere, under the restriction
that it had to be "a tool for removing snow." A vacuum is created inside the sphere,
which sucks in the snow through the tube. The snow is then allowed to melt, and the
water is released back out through the tube. (From Finke 1990.)

pation. Some even asked whether they were permitted to patent their
inventions, if they indeed turned out to be sufficiently feasible and
original.

Preinventive Forms

Further Support for the Geneplore Model
The findings discussed so far are consistent with some of the basic
concepts behind the Geneplore model. Restricting the types of parts
would encourage the construction of preinventive forms that are novel
and ambiguous and would be more likely to contain unexpected,
emergent properties, whereas restricting the categories would encourage the exploration of deeper implications of the preinventive
forms. Restricting the object types would make the forms conform too
closely to conventional objects, whereas restricting the object functions would avoid this while still allowing for creative exploration.

A more direct test of the Geneplore model requires the experimental
separation of the generative and exploratory phases in order to isolate
the generation of the preinventive forms from the various exploratory
and interpretive processes that might be applied to them. This was
accomplished by having people generate their preinventive forms
before they knew which object category would be selected.

The subjects started by imagining preinventive forms that were not
supposed to represent anything in particular. Rather, the forms were
simply to be interesting and potentially useful in a very general sense.

They were given one minute to mentally synthesize their preinventive forms using the three randomly-specified parts. This turned out to be a relatively easy task; the subjects were able to generate a preinventive form of some sort on virtually every trial.

Examples of these preinventive forms are shown in figure 4.8. After drawing their forms (which they did at this time so that they could not change them later), they were given an object category, selected at random, and were told to interpret the forms as a practical object or device within that category. They had one minute to provide each interpretation.

In this case, the subjects were committed to using their preinventive forms before they knew anything about how they would have to interpret the forms. One of the empirical questions that stems from the Geneplore model is whether the preinventive structures should be relatively free of interpretive bias when they are initially constructed. (This was discussed in chapter 2 in connection with the issue of whether it might sometimes be advantageous to suspend expertise and adopt a function-follows-form approach.)

The results of this experiment are presented in table 4.5, in comparison with those in which the interpretive categories were known in advance. Although the overall number of practical inventions was reduced when the preinventive forms were generated without knowing the object categories, this condition produced the greatest number

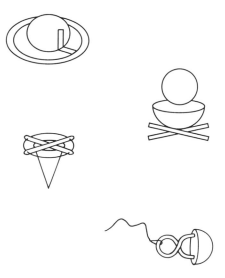

Figure 4.8
Preinventive forms generated without regard to the object categories. (From Finke 1990.)

Table 4.5
Number of Inventions According to Whether the Categories were Chosen in Advance, Specified Randomly in Advance, or Specified Randomly after the Preinventive Forms were Generated

Type of Invention	Condition		
	Category Chosen	Category Random	Preinventive Form
Practical	191	175	120
Creative	31	49	65
Highly creative	11	14	26

Source: Finke (1990).
Note: The categorizations are based on 1,080 trials—360 for each condition. "Creative" inventions were practical inventions rated as original. "Highly creative" inventions received the highest ratings on both originality and practicality.

of creative inventions, the greatest number of inventions that received the very highest ratings, and the highest probability that a practical invention would be classified as a creative invention. Creative inventions were obtained on 18.1 percent of the trials, and two-thirds of the subjects generated at least one creative invention.

In describing the Geneplore model, we proposed that certain properties of the preinventive structures would encourage creative exploration and discovery. Although these properties were not explicitly measured in these experiments, they are apparent from inspection of the preinventive forms. The forms shown in figure 4.8, for example, display a variety of emergent features that resulted from combinations of the object parts. In the first form shown in that figure, the bracket and the ring combine to suggest several possibilities: the bracket might slide around the sphere and underneath the ring, suggestive of a rheostat or similar mechanism; it might support the ring at that point, allowing the ring to flex at the opposite side, or it might allow the ring to pivot at their juncture. These and other possibilities could be explored in the context of trying to interpret the form as a practical device within a specified object category.

The second property that many of the preinventive forms displayed is ambiguity, which allows the forms to be structurally reorganized. For instance, in the second form, the sphere could be seen as separate from the cross and the half-sphere, with the latter two forming the base for the object; or the sphere and the half-sphere could be seen as connected, with the cross free to rotate; or the three parts could be seen as connected together. Exploring the different possible organizations of the forms can lead to many different interpretations.

Perhaps the most intriguing property is the implicit meaningfulness of the forms; they seem to have hidden meanings, inviting one to explore the forms to try to discover those meanings. In the third form in the figure, one is naturally led to wonder what purpose it might have, with its conical base and curious cross-shaped top, perhaps in much the same way that an archeologist might ponder the intended purpose of a curious artifact. Implicit meaningfulness reflects the natural, coherent structure of the forms.

These properties would be especially useful when the interpretive categories are not specified until after the preinventive forms are constructed. In such cases, the forms would need to be explored to a much greater extent, resulting in fewer total discoveries but a greater number of creative discoveries.

Examples of Creative Inventions Based on Preinventive Forms
The form in figure 4.9 was interpreted as a contact lens remover within the category "personal items." To use the remover, one places the rubber cone against the contact lens, covers the back hole with a finger to seal off the air, and lifts the contact off by moving the remover away from the eye. Air pressure keeps the lens on the remover until the finger is lifted.

The preinventive form in figure 4.10 was interpreted as a tension wind vane within the category "scientific instruments." The large, hollow cylinder, which is made of a lightweight material, is attached to the cubical base by the wire. Changes in wind speed and direction

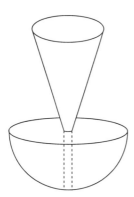

Figure 4.9
The contact lens remover, constructed using the half-sphere, cone, and tube. The user places the rubber cone against the contact lens, covers the back of the tube with a finger, lifts the contact off the eye, and then removes the contact from the cone by releasing the finger from the tube. (From Finke 1990.)

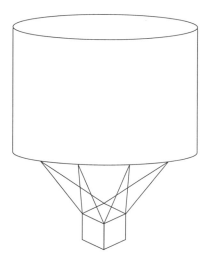

Figure 4.10
The tension wind vane, constructed using the cube, wire, and cylinder. The large, hollow cylinder is made of a lightweight material, and the wire connects the cylinder to the cube. When the wind blows on the cylinder, changes in the wire's tension are recorded and provide a sensitive measure of changes in wind speed and direction. (From Finke 1990.)

are detected by measuring changes in the tension of the wire. The unit can be extremely sensitive to such changes, given the surface area of the cylinder.

A third invention is the universal reacher (figure 4.11), belonging to the category "personal items." This device can be used to retrieve keys and other possessions that fall into hard-to-reach places. The wire is drawn out of the sphere and can be bent and shaped accordingly in order to reach the lost item. The hook allows the device to be secured when both hands are needed to guide the wire.

All of the creative inventions that resulted when subjects interpreted their preinventive forms are listed in table 4.6. These inventions were unique; the subjects never generated the same invention twice, even when using the same sets of parts and object categories. Many of these inventions have at least some potential to be marketed as useful and successful products.

Try to discover your own creative inventions by first generating preinventive forms and then interpreting them. Begin by mentally constructing the preinventive forms using the sets of parts listed in table 4.7, and then draw the forms as soon as you have completed them. Do this before continuing to the next step; it is important that

Figure 4.11
The universal reacher, constructed using the hook, sphere, and wire. The wire is drawn out of the sphere and can be shaped and bent to retrieve things that fall into hard-to-reach places, while the hook allows the device to be secured so that both hands can be used to guide the wire. (From Finke 1990.)

you do not yet know the categories that will be used for interpreting the forms. After you have completed your preinventive forms, refer to table 4.8, which lists the randomly chosen categories to be used in conjunction with each of the forms. Now try to interpret your preinventive forms within the designated categories.

Importance of Generating One's Own Forms
It should be easier to make a creative discovery when one is using one's own preinventive forms. This relates back to our claim that there is more to creative discovery than simply coming up with creative interpretations of randomly assembled or arbitrary structures. In generating a preinventive form, the particular way the parts are arranged reflects the person's sense for which arrangements would be most interesting and potentially most useful. There should thus be an advantage to using self-generated preinventive forms.

To put it another way, there are probably good reasons that a person chose to construct one form rather than another, having to do with the person's background, intuitions, and perhaps aesthetic sense. These may not be shared with anyone else; hence, a preinventive form that can be readily interpreted by one person may not be so easily interpreted by another. To use an analogy, this would be like an artist completing his or her own painting rather than completing one that somebody else had started.

The next experiment used a procedure similar to that of the previous one except that the subjects were given preinventive forms that others had generated instead of constructing the forms themselves. They were given an opportunity to become familiar with the forms, rating them on several measures, such as how well the forms were drawn and how useful they were likely to be, and were then given the object categories at random and instructed to interpret the forms in the same manner as the previous subjects.

Table 4.6
Creative Inventions Resulting from Explorations of
Preinventive Object Forms

Animal shelf	Musical spheres
Automatic plant waterer	Nail puller
Ball catcher	Pastry cooker
Block ball toss	Pie crust poker
Bread warmer	Playground arch
Bug snatcher	Pogo ball
Cone atomizer	Pogo box
Cone buoy	Pogo plop
Conical grater	Portable centrifuge
Conical plant stand	Portable cooler
Contact lens remover	Portable juicer
Covered garden logs	Quarters table
Cross lamp	Ring grenade
Cubical lamp	Ring roller
Depth finder	Rolling ceiling lamp
Diagonal cheese cutter	Rolling magazine rack
Egg holder	Rolling seeder
Expanding vase	Rolling tenderizer
Eyeball raft	Rotating buffer
Fan humidifier	Rotating seed planter
Flexible lamp	Rotating speaker stand
Flexible paperweight	Screw remover
Food transport	Shoe organizer
Food washer	Sink unclogger
Four-way funnel	Sliding hook
Hammer assister	Sliding towel hanger
Hand piercer	Sliding wire noose
Hand plow	Slope gauge
Hanging cutting board	Spherical grinder
Hanging plant holder	Swimmer buoy
Heat sensor	Swing punching bag
Heater cup	Teeter toddler
Hooked bottle opener	Tension wind vane
Humidity detector	Toy equalizer
Jewelry holder	Tree carrier
Juice tenderizer	Tree house suite
Knife cleaner	Tube filter
Laser surveyor	Universal reacher
Lint remover	Vaporizer separator
Locomotive storehouse	Vegetable slicer
Manual dishwasher	Water weigher
Measure mixer	Weed cutter
Melting point indicator	

Source: Finke (1990).

Table 4.7
Sets of Parts for Generating and Interpreting
Preinventive Object Forms

·1. Sphere	6. Flat square
Rectangular block	Flat square
Cone	Wire
2. Half-sphere	7. Cylinder
Sphere	Hook
Tube	Cube
3. Cube	8. Flat square
Ring	Sphere
Cube	Bracket
4. Tube	9. Cube
Wheels	Wire
Hook	Cylinder
5. Cone	10. Wire
Cone	Ring
Rectangular block	Flat square

Source: Finke (1990).
Note: These sets of parts are to be used in
conjunction with the object categories provided
in table 4.8, but only *after* the preinventive forms
are generated.

Table 4.8
Object Categories to Pair Randomly with Sets of Parts in
Table 4.7

1. Personal items	6. Tools and utensils
2. Furniture	7. Scientific instruments
3. Weapons	8. Tools and utensils
4. Furniture	9. Transportation
5. Toys and games	10. Furniture

Source: Finke (1990).
Note: These categories are to be used with the
corresponding sets of parts listed in table 4.7.

Table 4.9
Number of Inventions According to Whether Preinventive Object Forms
Were Generated or Provided

Type of Invention	Condition	
	Preinventive Forms Generated	Preinventive Forms Provided
Practical	120	69
Creative	65	20

Source: Finke (1990).
Note: The categorizations are based on 720 trials—360 for each condition.
"Creative" inventions were practical inventions rated as original.

The subjects were able to come up with far fewer creative inventions compared to those who had generated their own preinventive forms (table 4.9). This result provides further support for our assumption that the preinventive forms are not put together arbitrarily but are structured in a coherent and meaningful way.

One possible criticism is that subjects may have done better in the previous experiment simply because they had been able to practice generating the preinventive forms. Although this was not directly tested, it is an unlikely explanation given the absence of practice effects in any of the creative invention experiments.

The advantage of using self-generated preinventive forms is related to the concept of preparation in creative thinking (Wallas 1926). Perhaps the generation of one's own preinventive forms plays an important role in this preparation stage, where one can begin to acquire a sense for the kinds of potential applications the forms might have or the particular ways in which they might be related to one's own past experiences. A preinventive form that one person constructs may not be so useful or inspiring to others. In fact, one may end up making misleading or irrelevant interpretations when trying to use a preinventive form that belongs to someone else. This may help to explain why misguided decisions often result from "groupthink" situations (Janis 1972), where many people become involved in evaluating a person's initial idea.

There also seems to be a greater degree of personal involvement and commitment when using self-generated preinventive forms. This speaks to the role of intrinsic motivation in these studies. A person is more likely to believe that a self-generated preinventive form will eventually lead to an interesting discovery or insight compared with one that was merely provided, and this leads to greater perseverance, an important aspect of successful creative exploration (Perkins 1981).

Removing Time Restrictions
The findings of experiments on interpreting preinventive forms are even more striking given the severe time restrictions placed on the exploratory phase. When given extended time to explore their preinventive forms, subjects nearly always discover a potentially useful invention or idea. Finke (1990) has reported numerous examples of invention concepts that were generated in this way, with the exploration times ranging from less than a minute to as long as fifteen minutes. Although time restrictions help to make a task empirically manageable, they underestimate the actual potential of these creativity techniques.

Spanning the Object Categories Using a Single Preinventive Form
Another important property of preinventive forms is divergence, which refers to the capacity for the same form to inspire many possible objects and applications. This property is illustrated in figures 4.12 and 4.13, which are based on additional experiments in the Finke (1990) study. Subjects first generated a preinventive form, such as that shown in figure 4.12. They were then given all eight of the object categories, in random order, and had to interpret the form as a practical object or device within each of the categories. There were no time restrictions in this exploratory phase. Examples of inventions for each category based on this particular form are shown in figure 4.13. A single preinventive form can thus give rise to many different types of inventions.

In conducting experiments on preinventive forms, we have often encountered something called the illusion of intentionality (Finke 1990); the preinventive forms appear to have been conceived with the particular inventions in mind, whereas in fact just the opposite happened: the inventions were inferred only after the preinventive forms were constructed. For example, one might think that the examples of

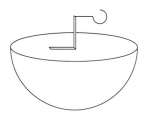

Figure 4.12
A preinventive form in experiments on spanning the object categories, constructed using the bracket, hook, and half-sphere. (From Finke 1990.)

Figure 4.13
Possible interpretations of the preinventive form shown in figure 4.12, spanning the eight object categories as follows (left to right): lawn lounger (furniture), global earrings (personal items), water weigher (scientific instruments), portable agitator (appliances), water sled (transportation), rotating masher (tools and utensils), ring spinner (toys and games), and slasher basher (weapons). (From Finke 1990.)

inventions that were derived from preinventive forms in figures 4.9 through 4.11 were designed in order to satisfy the functional requirements of those inventions. Yet the preinventive forms were constructed without foreknowledge of the category. That the forms appear to have been designed for a specific purpose is an illusion, as is shown particularly by demonstrations of the divergence of the forms.

General Strategies for Interpreting Preinventive Forms
Introspective reports by subjects in these experiments provide insight into the kinds of exploratory strategies that are most useful when attempting to interpret the preinventive forms. The subjects often searched for emergent features in the forms, contemplated their functional properties, imagined themselves actually using the forms, and mentally transformed the context in which the forms might be found.

For example, if a preinventive form were to be interpreted as a tool, a subject might look for suggestive features of the tool, explore various functions of the tool, imagine holding it in his or her hand, and seeing how it might be used in different contexts or situations. Such strategies represent systematic, organized attempts at creative exploration.

A useful analogy is to consider how to go about trying to discover the function of an unusual object or artifact that you happened to come across. Although you might initially have no idea what the object is, you can often gain considerable insight into its possible functions by imagining various ways in which the object might have been used—as a construction tool, a measuring device, a kitchen utensil, and so on. This is similar to the way in which subjects in these experiments went about trying to discover the underlying meaning of their preinventive forms. (We discuss in greater detail these various exploratory strategies in chapters 7 and 8.)

From Preinventive Form to Final Product

Generating a preinventive form and then interpreting it is not all there is to creative invention. The experiments on preinventive forms address only the initial phase of the inventive process. Most inventions have to undergo numerous design modifications before they actually result in workable and marketable products. In terms of the Geneplore model, additional cycles of generation and exploration are often necessary. We have restricted our considerations to a single inventive cycle in these experiments, for two reasons: it helps to identify the cognitive processes and structures that contribute to the initial conception of a creative invention, and it helps to establish the optimal conditions for engaging in creative search and exploration.

Creative Refinement

Creative Modifications of Existing Designs

Most ideas for new inventions come about by considering ways in which existing designs might be improved. By using techniques similar to those for generating preinventive forms, it is possible to investigate creative refinement, where one begins with a common design, mentally attaches or blends in a new shape or part, and then explores the functional implications of the resulting form.

In Finke and Ward (1991), subjects were given the name of a common object, such as *clock* or *table*, together with a randomly chosen part, selected from the same set of parts used in the preinventive form experiments. The subjects were given thirty seconds to mentally combine the object and the part in such a way that the new object would be "interesting to look at." After drawing the object, they were instructed to think of all the ways in which the new design represented an improvement over the original and were given two minutes to do so. (The generation phase in this case was twice as short as in the previous experiments, to limit the opportunity subjects would have to consider the functional implications of the forms while they were still combining the part with the original object.)

Examples of Creative Refinements
On nearly all of the trials, subjects were able to come up with creative refinements of the objects. Figure 4.14 shows a thermometer combined with a bracket, a design with a number of useful features. Instead of having to shake the thermometer repeatedly before use, one simply holds onto the bracket and spins the thermometer around, allowing centrifugal force to push the mercury back down. The bracket makes it easier to insert and remove the thermometer, and it permits the thermometer to be hung in a convenient place when not in use. The object in figure 4.15 is a writing pen combined with a ring. Inserting a finger through the ring results in greater control while writing and less fatigue. An interesting design for a new type of clock is shown in figure 4.16, which resulted when a clock was combined with a ring. The ring surrounds the clock face and is illuminated in such a manner as to substitute for the minute hand. The clock shown in the figure

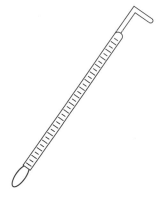

Figure 4.14
Creative refinement of a thermometer by adding a bracket on the end. The resulting design allows one to spin the thermometer instead of having to shake it before use. (From Finke and Ward 1991.)

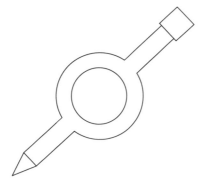

Figure 4.15
Creative refinement of a writing pen by adding a ring in the middle. A person inserts a finger through the ring while using the pen, resulting in greater control and less fatigue. (From Finke and Ward 1991.)

Figure 4.16
Creative refinement of a clock by adding a surrounding ring. The ring is illuminated and replaces the minute hand. (From Finke and Ward 1991.)

displays a time of 12:36. The design could be modified further so that the ring displays different colors after each hour.

We have just begun to explore these and other extensions of the preinventive form experiments. Although these experiments were restricted to a single generative and exploratory phase, in actual practice we would expect that creative refinement would undergo repeated cycles in which the final design gradually takes shape over time.

Summary

Theoretical Implications
The studies examined in this chapter show that it is possible to do controlled experiments in which people generate ideas for new inventions. We can summarize the results of these experiments in terms of four general principles of creative cognition. First, when mentally synthesizing preinventive forms, the likelihood of discovering a creative invention is greater when the component parts are restricted. Second, restricting the interpretive domain increases the likelihood of discovering a creative invention but only up to a point. Whereas it is useful to restrict the object category or the function of the object, restricting the particular type of object makes it less likely that one will discover a creative invention. Third, an invention is more likely to be creative when the preinventive forms are generated before one knows what the interpretive category will be. Fourth, it is better to use preinventive forms that one actually generated. Although these principles were established in cases where people used mental synthesis to generate the forms, we would expect the same principles to apply for other types of preinventive structures and generative processes.

The findings provide support for many aspects of the Geneplore model. They show, for example, that preinventive object forms can give rise to a variety of creative insights for new inventions. These forms are structured in meaningful ways, exhibit emergence and divergence, and invite curiosity and exploration. Interpretation of the forms involves searching for emergent properties and inferring possible new functions. These exploratory processes are governed by the various constraints that the experimental conditions impose on the interpretive categories.

Most important, however, the results of these studies demonstrate the value of a function-follows-form approach to invention and design, which in the Geneplore model corresponds to the case where product constraints are not imposed until after the preinventive form is generated. Creativity was enhanced when the invention task was formally structured so that the preinventive forms were generated without knowing how they would be interpreted. Thus, the studies reveal an important alternative to the more usual form-follows-function approach, in which constraints on design are imposed at the very outset.

Another implication of these findings concerns the distinction between being original and being innovative. One can always take an existing design and change a feature here or there to come up with something new. True innovation, however, has a more visionary or revolutionary quality, and this is something that preinventive forms can often inspire. There is an enormous difference between gimmicky or makeshift ways of improving on something and ideas that have real creative impact.

The preinventive forms generated in these studies represented only the initial phase of the creative process. Ordinarily a considerable amount of refinement and restructuring is needed in order to transform an inventive concept into a real working prototype (Finke 1991b; Goldschmidt in press; Finke in press). As the concept matures, the preinventive forms become more specialized, and the possible directions for further exploration and refinement become more restricted.

Practical Implications
The methods developed in this chapter have a number of practical implications, especially for inventors and engineers. They suggest new ways in which to go about trying to come up with novel concepts for an invention or device. Because preinventive forms are assembled in a natural, intuitive way, there is beauty and coherence to their structure, which can often translate into inventions that are aesthetically appealing and innovative, resulting in products that are more likely to have considerable popular appeal.

The function-follows-form approach considered in this chapter could be useful in complementing current approaches to invention and design. Most design engineers and inventors probably approach their day-to-day activities with specific problems or functions in mind and then generate forms and structures with the intent of solving those problems or satisfying those functions. We suggest that it may be helpful to consider an alternative approach in these efforts: exploring new problems and functions that are suggested by particular forms and structures.

5

Conceptual Synthesis

Creative Concepts

We have seen how the generation and interpretation of preinventive forms can give rise to creative insights for new inventions and designs; now we turn to interpretive processes and preinventive structures that are more abstract. We focus on subjects' interpretations of preinventive object forms in terms of abstract ideas or concepts and consider more complex preinventive structures such as mental blends, schemas, and mental models. We also focus on conceptual combinations and metaphors as two kinds of abstract mental blends and consider their emergent properties, and we examine how properties of mental blends such as ambiguity and incongruity can be viewed as general properties of conceptual combinations and metaphors and how those properties relate to the emergence of unexpected features.

We examine, in addition, the major cognitive theories used to explain people's understanding of conceptual combinations and metaphors, particularly in terms of their ability to predict the resultant properties. In the process, we focus primarily on studies that were not explicitly directed at the topic of creative discovery but that nevertheless are critically informative with respect to the creative process. This reflects our belief that the procedures of mainstream cognitive psychology are directly relevant to this fundamental aspect of human functioning.

Conceptual Interpretations of Preinventive Forms
Considering extensions of the preinventive form studies to cases where the forms must be interpreted as representing an abstract concept brings us closer to classic anecdotal accounts of conceptual discoveries that presumably occurred during creative visualization. The experiments in this first section are again taken from Finke (1990).

Instead of using object categories, the subjects were to use subject categories, which are listed, with examples, in table 5.1. After generating their preinventive forms, the subjects were told that they should interpret their forms as representing an abstract idea or concept that pertained to the specified category. In this case, the preinventive forms were now to be considered as symbolic or metaphorical representations of an idea rather than as literal depictions of a concrete object. For example, if the subject category was "physics and astronomy," the preinventive form might be interpreted as a new concept for how atoms are combined or for how the universe was formed. The subjects were told specifically that their preinventive forms need not actually look like any particular object but could simply represent the concept or idea in a general way. In all other respects, the experimental procedure was similar to that used in the previous experiments on interpreting preinventive forms.

The rating procedure was modified slightly. The dimension of practicality was no longer appropriate and was replaced by the dimension of sensibility, for an idea could be sensible without necessarily being practical. The procedure was otherwise identical to that for rating and classifying the creative inventions. If a concept received an average rating of 4.5 on the five-point scale, it was classified as a "sensible concept," and if a sensible concept received an average rating of 4.0 on the originality scale, it was further classified as a "creative concept."

In the first experiment, the subject categories were chosen at random and were given to the subjects only after they had generated their preinventive forms. This turned out to be more difficult than the previous tasks, as one might expect. The subjects came up with sensible concepts on 16.9 percent of the trials and creative concepts on 7.8 percent of the trials, under the same time restrictions as before, showing that it was possible to interpret the preinventive forms in

Table 5.1
Allowable Subject Categories in Experiments on Creative Concepts

Category	Examples
1. Architecture	Concepts in building design
2. Physics and astronomy	Models of the atom, universe
3. Biology	Methods of animal survival
4. Medicine	Mechanisms of infection
5. Psychology	Theories of personality
6. Literature	Writing styles, techniques
7. Music	Composition, instrumentation
8. Political science	Forms of government

Source: Finke (1990).

these more abstract ways as well, though with somewhat less success. Overall, a third of the subjects came up with at least one creative concept.

Examples of Creative Concepts
In figure 5.1, the concept of conceptual distancing, belonging to the category "psychology," is represented using the cylinder and two half-spheres. The idea suggested by the form is that people who think or believe in much the same way often keep a certain distance between them in a relationship.

Figure 5.2 presents the concept of viral cancellation, belonging to the category "medicine," and represented using the tube, cross, and cube. The idea is that two viruses attempting to invade the same cell may cancel one another, curing or preventing the disease.

Figure 5.3 presents the concept of stylistic containment, belonging to the category "literature," and represented using the cube, tube, and sphere. The idea is that a writer might begin a story using a very broad subject, depicted by the large base of the form, then quickly narrow and contain the subject, and then finally broaden it again at the very end of the story.

Restricting Subject Categories
In the next experiment, subjects were allowed to choose any of the eight subject categories after having generated their preinventive forms. In view of the findings of the previous chapter, this should result in fewer creative ideas, since restrictions on the categories, which tend to promote creative exploration, have now been removed. On the other hand, one might expect that even more creative ideas could be generated in this case, since the subjects could select those subject categories in which they would be most knowledgeable. For example, a student majoring in physics would be more likely to inter-

Figure 5.1
The concept of conceptual distancing, represented using the cylinder and two half-spheres. The idea is that people who believe in much the same way often keep a certain distance between them in a relationship. (From Finke 1990.)

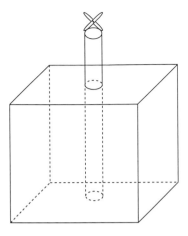

Figure 5.2
The concept of viral cancellation, represented using the tube, cross, and cube. The idea is that two viruses attempting to invade a cell may cancel one another, curing or preventing the disease. (From Finke 1990.)

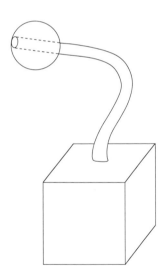

Figure 5.3
The concept of stylistic containment, represented using the cube, tube, and sphere. The idea is that a writer begins with a very broad subject and then quickly narrows and contains it, concentrating on a particular topic, and finally broadens it again at the conclusion. (From Finke 1990.)

pret a preinventive form as representing a concept in physics, compared to someone who knew very little about the subject and was given that category at random.

Table 5.2 presents the results of this experiment in comparison to the previous experiment, where the subject categories had been randomly specified. Over twice as many creative concepts were obtained when the subject categories were restricted, in agreement with the previous findings for restricting the object categories. These techniques thus appear to be most successful when people are forced to interpret their preinventive forms in ways that are less conventional, requiring deeper explorations and considerations.

Suspension of Expertise in Forming Creative Concepts

Naturally, a person is unlikely to make major conceptual contributions to a specialized field of study, such as physics or medicine, without having the necessary expertise. How, then, can one account for the finding that people perform better in these experiments when they cannot choose the subject category?

It is important to distinguish between experimental situations in which subjects are free to choose from among any number of categories after generating their forms and real-life situations in which experts are trying to generate new ideas in a particular, chosen field. If one can arbitrarily select any category whatsoever when interpreting one's forms one is likely to provide interpretations that are superficial and less creative, as suggested by the results of the previous experiment. On the other hand, if one has the expertise that enables one to explore deeper conceptual implications and is already committed to a particular subject one is less likely simply to shift the categories to fit the forms. Instead, he or she would persevere to discover those deeper implications.

Table 5.2
Number of Concepts According to Whether Subject Categories Were Freely Chosen or Specified Randomly

Type of Concept	Condition	
	Subject Category Chosen	Subject Category Random
Sensible	47	61
Creative	13	28

Source: Finke (1990).
Note: The categorizations are based on 720 trials—360 for each condition. "Creative" concepts were sensible concepts rated as original.

Nevertheless, it may be useful to suspend one's expertise when initially generating the preinventive forms. This can be done by generating the forms at times when one is not so preoccupied with an issue or problem, so that the forms can be conceived in a more natural, unbiased way. One can then apply one's expertise later, throughout the exploratory phase. This is not to say that the preinventive forms must be completely independent of expert knowledge and insight but simply that one should not intentionally structure the forms with such knowledge in mind.

Conceptual Combination

Another way in which to explore new conceptual possibilities is to take existing forms or concepts and mentally blend them together. In this section, we consider this process of conceptual combination. The discussion that follows, which is heavily based on Ward and Becker (1991), is focused more on theoretical ideas than on empirical findings. It also differs in that we shift our emphasis from mental imagery to the equally important topics of concept formation and categorization.

We begin by reviewing a portion of the literature that describes work on the basic cognitive processes involved in conceptual combination and show how these processes can contribute to the discovery of creative concepts and how the principles identified in these studies can lead to new advances in research on creative cognition.

Emergent Properties and Creative Exploration

Rather than being limited to representing the world in terms of single concepts (for example, "pets" or "fish"), we are capable of combining concepts to form more restricted or more complex entities (such as "pet fish"). This process of combining concepts allows for enormous flexibility of thought; it allows the development of new concepts from a merging of old ones and affords the possibility of discovering new features of the particular items in the combination as well as of the domains which those items represent. For example, one's original concept of pets may have included the idea that they are warm and cuddly; considering the combined concept of pet fish could lead to a rejection of that idea and new insights about pets in general. Similarly, the combination "pet birds" might include the property "talks," whereas that property is not typical of either component in isolation.

The fact that conceptual combination often results in new categories and emergent features implies that the process can be useful in making creative discoveries. This is not to say that all emergent properties will necessarily be considered creative, however. There is no guarantee that emergent properties will be interesting or useful in their own right; some may reflect simple inferences or the retrieval of known facts. For example, retrieving the property "talks" in the presence of the cue "pet bird" but not in the presence of the separate cues "pet" or "bird" produces an emergent property that would hardly be considered surprising.

Some emergent properties represent more than just the selective retrieval of known facts. For example, the novel compound "hatchet squirrel" might produce a totally novel property, such as "sharp front appendages used for digging holes in trees to bury nuts." This type of emergence points to the importance of considering creative cognitive processes in traditional models of knowledge representation and human cognition.

The elimination and emergence of properties can have consequences that go beyond the simple modification of the initial concepts. For example, one may never have thought about fish as pets before. Considering them as such and noting that pet fish are neither warm nor huggable could spark further consideration of what is truly important or essential about a pet—for example, that it provide a kind of psychological companionship independent of whether it is expressed in the form of licks or hugs. It is in these broad restructurings of entire domains that conceptual combination has its greatest implication for creative discovery.

Although research on conceptual combination has not yet examined the specific role of emergent properties as catalysts for creative exploration, much effort has been devoted to the task of explaining how the properties of the individual components are combined, how some of those properties are eliminated, and how new ones emerge in the combination.

Because they involve a merging of information from two separate concepts, conceptual combinations can be thought of as an example of the preinventive structures that we call mental blends. As we have already noted, preinventive structures can be generated and explored by a variety of processes, and they have certain properties related to their potential for creative discovery. Here we consider different kinds of conceptual combinations and their properties.

Varieties of Conceptual Combination
Conceptual combinations can vary in their novelty, ambiguity, and incongruity, and these properties relate to their usefulness in creative exploration. Some word pairings that exhibit the linguistic form of conceptual combinations, however, may actually be commonly used lexicalized units, such as "traveling salesman" or "county fair." Pre-

sumably, these compounds would be retrieved as whole units rather than created by combining the two concepts. At one point, they may have been understood through a juxtaposition of two separate domains, but they have long since lost the features of ambiguity and incongruity that would ordinarily lead to creative discovery.

In creative cognition, we are more concerned with novel combinations, such as "idea salesman" and "county stair," which may require the more constructive processes of mental synthesis and analogical transfer. Even relatively novel combinations, however, can vary in their degree of ambiguity and incongruity. As an example, because small computers are a recent invention, the concept of "computer table" is also new. But on one's first encounter with the term, there was little doubt about its meaning. In this example, there are few, if any, emergent properties in the "computer table" compound. Similarly, the term "apartment dog" may be new, but its reference to a particular type of real dog is relatively clear.

Now consider a more ambiguous compound, "computer dog." Is it a robotic dog, a real dog that has amazing math abilities, some computer-driven simulation of a dog, a new term for a hacker, or a hot dog prepared in some futuristic computer-controlled device? The lack of a single, clear meaning leads to a search for and possible discovery of emergent features that are not typical of either computers or dogs. In addition, the meanings of either of the individual components or their respective domains might be transformed in the process of interpreting the compound. Importantly, these features and transformations can emerge as a result of the basic process of conceptual combination. Even if people do not deliberately attempt to be creative, the result can still involve the emergence of something novel. In effect, then, research concerned with the basic processes of conceptual combination can often have important implications for creative cognition.

Much research on conceptual combination is concerned with how people are able to determine the "correct" interpretation of a given blend or compound. When approached from this perspective, ambiguity presents a problem for basic language comprehension. When approached from a creative cognition perspective, however, ambiguity may be useful in that it may help to prevent foreclosure on a single obvious meaning. The consequence is that new discoveries and knowledge restructuring can occur.

In terms of the Geneplore model, an initial synthesis of components would result in preinventive structures of varying ambiguity. If the structure is highly ambiguous, initial attempts to understand the compound would not lead to a single satisfactory interpretation. In an attempt to make sense of the compound, exploratory processes such as conceptual interpretation would then come into play. Among other things, this would include the application of world knowledge or "naive" theories to the task of exploring the structure.

In the next section, we consider several models of conceptual combination that deal with different types of combinations: conjunctions (for example, "pets that are also fish"), adjective-noun compounds (for example, "dirty mind"), and noun-noun compounds (such as "car radio"). Because emergence of properties is a central feature of all of these types of combinations, we will be concerned with how these models account for this phenomenon and how their approaches can be related to creative cognition.

The Attribute Inheritance Model

Hampton (1987) presented an attribute inheritance model to explain which attributes of the individual components would be "inherited" by the compound. The model is specific to conjunctions such as "sports that are also games." It suggests that the attributes of the compound will be the union of the attributes of the components, subject to the constraints that the attributes should have sufficient average importance across the components, that any necessary features of either component are inherited, and that no features that are impossible for one of the components will be inherited. Thus, the model characterizes conceptual combination as being largely noncreative in the sense that nothing novel will emerge.

Hampton's model provides a good quantitative fit to the rated importance of attributes for a variety of individual components and conjunctions. There are, however, examples of attributes being listed and rated as important for the compound but not the components, and vice versa. As an example, the conjunction of pets and birds was found to include the attribute "talks," whereas neither of the components included that attribute (Hampton 1987).

Hampton explains the violations of the attribute inheritance model in terms of the application of specific knowledge. For example, in extensional feedback, knowledge about items in the conjunction can be used to attach attributes to the conjunction that are not part of either component. One might, for instance, retrieve a specific known example of a parrot that talks. In doing so, one might then include "talks" as an important attribute of the conjunction "pet birds" even though it would not be listed as an attribute of "pets" or "birds." Interestingly, this leads to the prediction that the more familiar one is with the concepts, the more likely it is that new features will emerge. By this view, unless one already knows something about items in the conjunction, there would be few, if any, emergent properties. The properties of novel conjunctions would consist only of those that were part of the component concepts. Thus, the model explains only the less interesting retrieval-based form of emergence described previously.

Without disputing Hampton's basic premise about familiarity and emergence, we make a distinction between knowing that a familiar compound has properties that are uncharacteristic of its components and discovering that a novel compound has unexpected properties. In the former case, one retrieves factual information about previously known compounds; in the latter case one uses mental synthesis and creative exploration to form a new composite and examine its properties.

Even if emergent properties are the result of retrieving information about known instances, however, they can still perform a creative function. For example, retrieving the fact that pet birds talk could lead one to explore ideas about how other pets, or animals in general, communicate. In effect, the emergent properties of conceptual combinations, if exploited fully, can be a catalyst for conceptual reorganization and further discovery.

The Selective Modification Model

Hampton's attribute inheritance model was designed only to explain conjunctive concepts in which the members of the compound are members of both of the components (as with "pet birds"). Another type of conceptual combination involves the pairing of adjectives and nouns. Emergent properties and unexpected alterations of attributes can also occur in these adjective-noun combinations (Medin and Shoben, 1988; Murphy 1988), and thus they are also of interest in creative cognition.

Smith and Osherson (1984) and Smith et al. (1988) have described a selective modification model to explain the way in which adjectives and nouns interact in adjective-noun compounds. Although the model has certain strengths, it has difficulty accounting for emergent properties. In this model, concepts are represented in terms of attributes and their possible values. For example, the concept "apple" may include the attributes of color, shape, and texture, and the possible values for the attribute of color might be red, green, and brown. Each attribute has a diagnosticity score having to do with the usefulness of that attribute for making category decisions. Each value has a salience score related to its perceived frequency of association with the category.

Noun concepts are complex and include many attributes and values. In contrast, adjectives are simple and can include as few as one attribute and one value. For example, the representation of the adjective "red" might include only the attribute of color and the value red. In conceptual combination, the attribute of the adjective selects and modifies the noun's attributes. This results in an increase in the diagnosticity of the selected attribute, an increase in the salience of the value of the attribute that matches the adjective's value, and a decrease in the salience of the other values.

The selective modification model can explain at least some differences in the typicality of a given instance for simple categories ("apple") and combinations involving adjective-noun compounds ("red apple"), but it has no obvious way of dealing with other types of combinations. In addition, because it treats the attributes as independent of one another, there is no direct means by which it could account for feature interactions of the type described by Medin and Shoben (1988). For example, metal spoons are rated as more typical than wooden spoons for the category "small spoons," whereas the reverse is true for the category "large spoons." This finding implies that size and type of material are not independent in the subjects' representations of the "spoon" concept. Thus, changing a noun by modifying it with a particular adjective can have an impact on the meaning of the noun that is not limited to the specific attribute named by the adjective. In terms of creative exploration, these concomitant and possibly unexpected changes can provide the grounds for new insight and discovery.

Additionally, the selective modification model has no obvious way to account for the fact that subjects judge attributes as being more typical of a compound than of either of its separate components (Murphy 1988). For example, "sticky" is judged to be more true of "dirty bowls" than of either bowls or dirty things. Again, it appears that attributes can emerge from conceptual combinations that are not present (or, at least, are not very salient) in the representations of component concepts.

A problem associated with the selective modification model that may underlie all of these shortcomings is that it does not make reference to world knowledge that exists beyond the concepts involved in the combination. For example, although neither dirty things nor bowls are typically sticky, our general knowledge of cooking can lead to the idea that dirty bowls are sticky. Thus, when we refer to a dirty bowl, invoking this knowledge leads to the inference that "sticky" is a typical attribute. Notice, however, that this involves a different sense of "dirty" than would be invoked in the combinations "dirty car," "dirty deal," "dirty fighter," "dirty dog," and "dirty mind," none of which strongly evokes the property of stickiness. The point is that what emerges may depend on the specific components that are combined, in relation to a person's general knowledge.

The Concept Specialization Model
The concept specialization model (Cohen and Murphy 1984; Murphy 1988) overcomes some of the problems of the selective modification model by including the idea that general knowledge can drive the selection of attributes to be modified. This allows the model to explain how compounds consisting of noun-noun pairings would be interpreted. Consider the combination "apartment dog." Unlike the adjective-noun compound "brown dog," it is not obvious how to determine what attributes to modify in the representation of "dog" without reference to broader knowledge structures. It is plainly nonsensical to modify "dog" with the most salient properties of apartments (their size, materials, number of rooms, function, and so forth). Murphy suggests that the relevant attributes are selected by appeal to general world knowledge. Dogs are not made of wood and plaster board, are not lived in by people, do not contain rooms, and so forth. Apartment dogs are dogs that live in apartments. Thus, general world knowledge helps to narrow the field of possible attributes to "lives in." Note that the selected attributes depend on the specific noun-noun pairing. For example, "a dog that lives in a computer" is an unlikely interpretation for "computer dog."

The concept specialization model adds a second phase of elaboration in which world knowledge is used to infer the existence or nature of other properties. For example, one might use world knowledge to go beyond the conclusion that "apartment dogs live in apartments" to infer other properties, such as the size and temperament of such dogs.

The concept specialization model comes closest to the spirit of the Geneplore model. The initial process of using world knowledge to select attributes and construct a particular combination can be thought of as a specific example of using retrieval and mental synthesis to generate a preinventive form. The elaboration process can be viewed as an example of the exploratory processes of the Geneplore model. These exploratory processes can lead to knowledge restructuring beyond even the type of elaborative inference considered by Murphy (1988). For example, in considering the ideal properties of apartment dogs, one may be led to consider novel selective breeding projects (such as combining a breed of dogs known for its small size with another known for its quiet nature) or novel types of pets (perhaps lizards) that might be better suited to apartments.

Wisniewski and Gentner (1991) have examined subjects' interpretations of novel conceptual combinations and have concluded from some of those interpretations that processes other than selective modification may be operating in conceptual combination. Consider their example of the compound "pony chair." One subject interpreted this to be a small chair. The problem with trying to explain this interpretation in terms of the selective modification model is that the "small" that characterizes horses and ponies would be quite large in the domain of chairs. Thus, the information that would get mapped or transferred in this case must be something on the order of "small in relation to other things in the relevant domain." This kind of relational or structure mapping suggests that the generative process of analogical transfer may also be involved in the initial generation of mental blends. (Analogical transfer is discussed further in chapter 7.)

The Role of Incongruity

Exploring the factors that influence the extent to which emergence occurs in conceptual combination is an important goal for future studies on creative cognition. Another property related to the creative potential of conceptual combinations is incongruity. For example, in describing the process he called bisociation, Koestler (1964) called attention to the general role that conceptual conflict plays in the creative process. Bisociation occurs when previously unrelated levels of experience or frames of reference are suddenly connected. When contrary patterns of thought or behavior interact, one can have collision, resulting in humor; fusion, resulting in new discoveries or intellectual experiences; and confrontation, resulting in aesthetic experiences.

Although no conceptual combination studies have addressed explicitly the relation between incongruity and creative discovery, some suggestive evidence does exist. Wisniewski (1991), for example, had groups of subjects interpret the meanings of conceptual combinations that were composed from similar entities (for example, "skunk squirrel") or dissimilar entities (for example, "hatchet squirrel"). Of most importance, emergent features were found only in the dissimilar combinations. These combinations would have greater incongruity among their components, thereby making creative discovery more likely.

There may be limits on the amount of useful incongruity in conceptual combination. Some components may be so incompatible that no interpretation is possible even after extensive exploration. However, given that people are remarkably resourceful, we suspect that most individuals could eventually achieve some reasonably satisfying interpretation of even the most bizarre combinations.

This is not to say that all individuals will arrive at the same interpretation for a given combination. Indeed, Wisniewski (1991) reported that for some dissimilar pairs, consensus definitions could not be found because each individual provided a somewhat different interpretation. What this points to is that there may be a natural confound between ambiguity and incongruity. Dissimilar pairs, which are incongruous by virtue of the fact that their components come from very different domains, are also ambiguous in the sense that they evoke a multitude of interpretations. Therefore, it may not be possible to separate completely the roles that ambiguity and incongruity play in leading to creative outcomes.

It is also important to consider how to measure the degree of incongruity between the components of a combination. It may be possible to use membership in broad domains (such as artifacts versus natural kinds), as Wisniewski and Gentner (1991) have done, and to regard combinations that cross these domains as incongruous. Such an approach would allow one to distinguish combinations that, on the average, would result in more or fewer emergent properties. However, it would leave unanswered questions such as why "apartment dog" is clear but "computer dog" is ambiguous, although both involve cross-domain combinations. In addition, items within the same domains could differ in their similarity, and these differences might contribute to incongruity and the resulting emergence of novel features.

Literal and Figurative Combinations
Most of the examples of emergent properties that we have described so far involve fairly mundane, literal interpretations of conceptual combinations. Even in these simple cases, however, something that was not part of either of the components appears in their combination. This emergence of something novel is the signature of creative cognition.

Conceptual combinations can lead to figurative as well as literal interpretations. For example, "dirty dog" could refer to an animal that needs a bath, but it is often used figuratively to refer to a person who has just done something we are unhappy with. In addition, "dirty mind" most often refers to a tendency to think bad thoughts rather than the literal idea that the mind has real dirt on it. Nor is "brainwashing" the literal activity of cleaning the dirt off a dirty mind. Presumably these figurative interpretations would allow for even greater creative exploration.

Metaphor

Our discussion of figurative interpretations leads naturally to a consideration of another type of mental blend, metaphor. As used here, metaphor refers to similarity statements of the form "X is Y," in which the speaker attempts to convey some figurative relation between X and Y. For example, in the metaphor "Sally is a diamond," one would most likely by trying to convey in a figurative way some positive information about Sally, not that Sally is literally a particular type of small, hard jewel. For purposes of reference, we will refer to the "X" term as the topic and the "Y" term as the vehicle of the metaphor.

Like conceptual combinations, metaphors involve the mapping or transfer of information from one concept to another. In addition, they allow for the emergence of properties that are not obviously part of either the topic or the vehicle. Thus, like constructing and exploring conceptual combinations, constructing and using a metaphor is by its very nature a creative process.

There are, of course, statements of the form "X is Y" that are intended to convey literal information. For example, "a dog is an animal" is a statement of fact that would not be expected to result in the emergence of any novel properties. Much like the case with conceptual combinations that are lexicalized or have a single obvious interpretation, such literal statements are low in ambiguity and incongruity and would not afford many creative opportunities.

We do not claim, however, that an available literal interpretation will necessarily prevent access to a more figurative or creative meaning, nor do we subscribe to the related position that individuals search for figurative meanings only after a search for a literal meaning fails. Both positions appear to be at odds with existing data (Glucksberg 1991). We do claim that statements with single obvious meanings are less likely to stimulate deliberate, exploratory search than those without such a clear meaning, and we suggest that there may be aspects of retrieval blocking that weigh against creative outcomes, in the sense that a single obvious interpretation may make it more difficult to retrieve and actively consider alternative meanings (an issue we return to in chapter 7).

As is the case with conceptual combination, a variety of models of metaphor comprehension have been proposed. We consider them here with respect to their ability to deal with the issue of emergent properties.

The Salience Imbalance Model

The salience imbalance model (Ortony 1979) is best understood in terms of a contrast between literal similarity statements and metaphors. In a literal similarity statement (such as "cars are like trucks") the properties that match ("wheels," "doors," "used for transportation") are high in salience for both of the items being compared. In metaphors, however (for example, "sermons are like sleeping pills"), properties that are highly salient for the vehicle ("sleep inducing") are not central to the topic. It is the degree of salience imbalance that determines whether the statement would function as a metaphor.

In this model, the features involved in the comparison are only those that are already part of the representation of the vehicle and topic. Much like the selective modification model of conceptual combination, the salience imbalance model has no obvious way to account for the fact that novel features might emerge. Tourangeau and Rips (1991) have recently found, in fact, that features often do emerge in metaphors that were not salient in either the vehicle or the topic. As with conceptual combination, this emergence of something new makes metaphor a natural topic of study within the creative cognition approach.

The Domain Interaction Model

Tourangeau and Rips (1991) argue that the domain interaction model, proposed by Tourangeau and Sternberg (1982), is better able to account for the emergence of features that occurs when a vehicle and topic are combined in a metaphor. In this model, metaphors involve the interaction or juxtaposition of broad domains of knowledge, not just the mapping of isolated features from one single object to another. In effect, the metaphor is understood by a mapping of features that will allow a close alignment of the relative positions of the topic and vehicle within their respective domains. For example, the metaphor "football is the demolition derby of athletics" might be understood by considering features such as "number of collisions" and "damage to competitors." Because the mapping of these features across the domains may not be direct or literal, new properties can emerge. For example, "damage to competitors" could refer to "dents" in a demolition derby and "broken bones" in football, and although one might rate broken bones as a salient feature of the metaphor, one would not necessarily do so for either football or demolition derbies alone.

The most important implication of the domain interaction model for creative cognition is that comprehending a single metaphor can bring about a change in the structure of not just the individual topic and vehicle but also the domains from which the topic and vehicle come. Kelly and Keil (1987) showed that understanding one metaphor can cause other components of potential metaphors involving the same domains to move conceptually closer together. Understanding the "football" metaphor could facilitate an understanding of other metaphors involving the same domains, such as "golf is the antique car show of athletics." This potential for seeing entire domains in a new light is a clear example of creative cognition.

The Class Inclusion Model
An alternative model is Glucksberg and Keysar's (1990) class inclusion model, by which metaphors are understood to mean that both the topic and vehicle are members of the same superordinate category of which the vehicle is a more prototypic member. For example, in the statement "My job is a jail," "jail" serves as a prototypic member of and a label for a category of situations that are confining, unpleasant, and so forth. The metaphor is interpreted as an assertion that "my job" is also a member of that category.

The class inclusion model has in common with Ortony's salience imbalance model the idea that the vehicle and topic share the same features. In that sense, it may also have difficulty accounting for the emergence of novel features in the metaphor. On the other hand, the class inclusion model is in the spirit of creative cognition in the sense that the superordinate category that the vehicle represents need not be preexisting; it may be created on the spot to make sense of the metaphor, in much the same way that other ad hoc categories may be created as needed (Barsalou 1983).

Even when the category already exists, it may not be a dominant one, and its use may involve a restructuring of meaning. For example, with or without a single obvious label, the category "situations that are unpleasant, confining, and so forth" may already be part of an individual's existing knowledge structures. However, we do not typically think of "jail" as a member of that category. Rather, it may be most typical to think of "jail" as a member of the categories "buildings" or "legal sentences." Putting the term in the context of the metaphor "My job is a jail" causes a shift away from these dominant interpretations and toward those that help to make sense of the statement, which allows the possibility of thinking about jails and jobs in an entirely new way. Moreover, by drawing attention to a superordinate category that is not typically thought about, one has the potential to use creative exploration to make discoveries about that domain that would not otherwise have been made. For example, are there other "confining, unpleasant situations" that would be as effective as jail in deterring crime? Considering metaphors in this exploratory way is similar to the use of analogies from different domains to generate solutions to problems (which we discuss in chapters 7 and 8).

Summary

Theoretical Implications
In this chapter, we began by extending the preinventive form studies to cases in which the forms were to be interpreted as representing abstract concepts. These findings demonstrate that preinventive forms can function as catalysts for conceptual exploration and discovery in a variety of abstract domains. In addition, as in the case of creative invention, the likelihood of discovering a creative concept is greater when the interpretive category is specified after the preinventive forms are generated. These findings are consistent with previous findings in support of the Geneplore model.

The most important finding from our consideration of conceptual blends is that when individuals combine two or more concepts, new properties can emerge. This occurs in both conceptual combinations (Murphy 1988) and metaphors (Tourangeau and Rips 1991). In addition, at least for metaphors, there can be considerable restructuring, not just of the meanings of the individual components but also of the domains from which they come (Kelly and Keil 1987). These findings suggest that the merging of concepts is an inherently creative process.

There is also suggestive evidence about the properties of mental blends that relate to their usefulness in creative discovery. For example, incongruity among the components of mental blends seems to result in a greater number of emergent features (Wisniewski 1991). The role of incongruity in metaphors is less clear, although the topic and vehicle must be sufficiently different for the statement to be figurative. At the same time, there must be some limits to incongruity. If items in a metaphor are too discrepant, for example, the result may simply be an anomalous statement (Ortony 1979), with no inherited or emergent properties.

Incongruity of components and the related property of ambiguity may result in more creative cognitions precisely because they do not lead to a single obvious interpretation, as is normally the case with highly congruent and unambiguous combinations. When obvious interpretations are readily available, efforts to construct alternate interpretations by retrieving different aspects of the components may be blocked. (We explore at length retrieval blocking, fixation, and related impediments to creative cognition in chapter 7.)

Much research on conceptual combination and metaphor has been concerned with comprehension rather than production. The processes by which individuals retrieve and synthesize components to generate interesting combinations and metaphors have received less attention and are ripe for study. This focus on comprehension has led to concern with issues such as how people are able to determine the intended meaning of an expression. This is, of course, an important goal for cognitive psychology. An equally important goal is to understand the processes of creative discovery that apply when people generate and explore various types of mental blends. For instance, studies of how people explore the possible meanings of conceptual combinations and metaphors, particularly those that are incongruous or ambiguous, would be highly desirable.

Finally, we believe that basic research on mental blends would have implications for work on dreams and other transitional states in which the blending of features and concepts is fairly common. Dreams, for example, often exhibit blends of familiar elements such as people, places, and themes. Perhaps the extent to which one might discover creative interpretations of a dream could be related to the properties of the blended structures, in much the same way that those properties give rise to creative interpretations in conceptual combinations and metaphors.

Practical Implications

There are many ways in which preinventive forms could be used to enhance conceptual discovery. A physicist might generate a variety of preinventive forms and then try to interpret them as representing new concepts in atomic theory or relativity. A medical researcher could explore preinventive forms to come up with new ideas for how to treat a disease. A writer might try to use these forms to suggest a new theme for a novel. (In chapters 8 and 9, we offer specific suggestions for how one might go about trying to make these and other types of creative discoveries using preinventive structures and forms.)

Several practical suggestions for enhancing creativity follow from studies on conceptual combination. One example is Koberg and Bagnall's (1974) morphological forced connections. In this approach, one attempts to generate new entities by listing typical attributes of an object, generating alternative values for those attributes, and randomly combining those alternative values. One might try to develop a new table, for example, by listing typical attributes such as "four legs," "wooden," and "uniformly flat surface." One could then consider variations on each of those features and combinations of those variations, such as a "six-legged metal table with indentations in the surface."

Morphological forced connections involve combinations of the attributes of a single object rather than combinations of separate objects. Presumably, however, the procedure could be extended to include object combinations. For example, the game of baseball includes wooden bats, hard balls, two teams of nine players, particular dimensions for the playing area, and so forth. A new game might be developed by considering combinations of variants on those objects and entities.

Zwicky developed a related approach called morphological synthesis (Adams 1974; see also chapter 1). In this approach, different dimensions of an object would be considered, and all possible combinations of values on those dimensions would be examined. For example, in developing a new form of transportation, one might consider combinations of values on the dimensions of power source (steam, electricity, gasoline engine), place of operation (air, water, rails), and means of support for a passenger (chair, bed, sling).

Some researchers who study conceptual combination have developed experimental materials using a similar procedure of generating lists of concepts and examining all possible pairings of items from each list (Shoben 1991). Presumably the same technique could be used for creatively exploring the consequences of merging entities from various domains. These approaches could also be adapted to the task of developing innovative concepts or even new areas of research within a particular discipline. Consider the list of adjectives and nouns relevant to the field of psychology that are shown in table 5.3. Might novel areas of research be generated by arbitrarily combining these adjectives and nouns? Certainly many of the pairings would result in well-known concepts and others would be nonsensical, but possibly certain combinations would lead to new insights or, at the very least, new questions about whether such concepts are worth investigating.

In a related way, one might imagine new disciplines that emerge from combining existing ones. Although combined disciplines (as well as research topics) typically grow out of common interests and theoretical developments, perhaps by suggesting nonexistent disciplines and considering what work would be done within them, new insights about solutions to problems could emerge. We do not pretend to know which of these hypothetical, emergent disciplines would be useful, but for purposes of illustration, consider what kinds of work would go on in a department of psychoeconomic engineering.

One advantage of morphological synthesis is that it can be used to generate a large number of preinventive structures for later exploration; however, as we have argued, random combination may not always be the best approach. There may be so many combinations that it would be impossible to search all of them. In addition, the use of random combinations would be sensible only if one knew nothing whatsoever about how creative cognition operates or how it might be influenced by the specific properties of the items in the combinations.

Table 5.3
Common Psychological Terms

Adjectives	Nouns
Perceptual	Memory
Conceptual	Attention
Implicit	Problem solving
Explicit	Perception
Intuitive	Masking
Contingent	Categorization
Conditioned	Recognition
Deliberate	Personality
Affective	Amnesia
Excitatory	Imagery
Inhibitory	Learning
Spatial	Thinking
Visual	Chunking

Note: The adjectives and nouns can be combined to suggest new conceptual categories for psychological research.

These "brute force" methods are essentially uninformed by the principles of creative cognition. For example, rather than randomly combining concepts, one might deliberately combine concepts from different domains, such as natural and artifactual categories, where the resulting ambiguity and incongruity would facilitate creative discovery.

6

Structured Imagination

Imagination

This chapter focuses on the topic of imagination, broadly defined. We consider various ways of characterizing imagination and how imagination differs from but overlaps with mental imagery. Most of the research we describe examines what happens when we ask people to imagine and produce novel entities. We deal with the issue of whether imagination is better thought of as a highly idiosyncratic phenomenon or as something that is predictable and open to investigation by normative experimental procedures. More specifically, we attempt to identify some of the principles by which imagination is structured. This concern with the structure of imagination reflects our belief that the commonalities that exist across creative products are as important to the discipline of creative cognition as are the originality and novelty of those products.

We use findings from traditional approaches to categorization to make predictions about the kinds of principles that may structure imagination, we examine the role of category exemplars, schemas, and mental models in imagination tasks, as well as the general role of constraints in affecting the products of imagination, and we consider the processes of retrieval, mental synthesis, mental transformation, and categorical reduction as they relate to the generation of imaginative entities.

The Concept of Structured Imagination

Imagination has been described in many different ways; there is no single correct definition for the term. The difficulty of specifying the nature of imagination led Murray (1986) to begin by considering what it is not. In Murray's view imagination is not merely generating an image of some known but physically absent person or entity; this is more an example of recalling than of generating something truly novel. McKellar (1957) makes a similar distinction between what he calls "memory images" and "imagination images" but goes on to comment on the potential fuzziness of the distinction. At the same time, imaginative thinking is not merely the experience of something outside the bounds of known reality, as might occur, for example, in hallucinations. For instance, people commonly use expressions such as, "It didn't really happen. You just imagined it." We exclude from consideration this commonsense use of the term.

We propose that imagination involves the generation and experience of ideas and products that go beyond what is currently known; however, we view this property as necessary but not sufficient. We concur with Murray that imagination also involves cognitive activity directed at some goal. In our view, that goal can be well or ill defined. It can be as concrete as devising a better mousetrap, as literary as writing a poem or story, as artistic as producing a painting, as scientific as developing a model or theory, as personal as finding a better life, or as immaterial as generating novel forms for their aesthetic appeal or for the sheer pleasure of doing so. Although fantasy, dreaming, and other cognitive activities may well fit the commonsense notion of imagination, our focus is mainly on activities that result in some tangible product.

As with the general concept of creativity, one might consider imagination to be so highly idiosyncratic and unpredictable that it cannot be investigated readily using experimental approaches. According to this view, we would anticipate that if ten people were given the task of imagining a new animal, they would produce ten very different entities that had little, if anything, in common. Imagination would be a mysterious process through which new ideas spring into being full blown and with no obvious link to existing cognitive structures.

We propose, however, that imagination is influenced by existing knowledge frameworks in the same way that any task involving the use of categories and concepts would be influenced by those frameworks. The term we use to refer to the impact of existing conceptual knowledge on imagined entities is *structured imagination* (Ward 1991a).

There have been previous arguments consistent with the idea that imagination is structured, though these have been based primarily on philosophical considerations. For example, McKellar (1957) argued that all forms of thinking, including imagination, are influenced by prior experiences. Although McKellar described some specific examples of how different types of thought, such as hypnogogic imagery, might be tied to prior experience, little work has been conducted within contemporary cognitive psychology that specifically examines structured imagination.

Much of the work presented in this chapter is concerned with documenting the ways in which imagination is structured and the processes by which that structuring occurs. We do not view the products of imagination as completely determined or predictable, however. Our point is simply that because subjects share similar knowledge structures, their imagined entities will share certain properties that can be inferred from those structures. Within those broad commonalities, much individual variation is still possible.

We also distinguish between imagination and mental imagery. We view imagination as simultaneously a more global and a more restrictive concept than mental imagery. Imagination is the process by which people mentally generate novel objects, settings, events, and so on. It is more global than mental imagery in the sense that although these imagined entities might take of the form of mental images, they need not. Imaginative products can also exist in the form of verbal descriptions. Imagination is also more restrictive than mental imagery in the sense that it must involve the generation of something new, whereas certain manifestations of mental imagery can be purely recollective.

It is also important to distinguish between the process of using one's imagination and how imaginative, innovative, or creative the resulting product might be judged to be. As used here, imagination and imaginative activity are defined as the processes that occur when individuals perform a task in which they must generate some novel entity. "Entity" is used broadly to refer to a new object or design, a modification of an existing object or design, or a new or modified creature, character, event, scene, relation, or complex set of relations. These entities may or may not be judged by external criteria to be "creative;" we are more interested in identifying the common properties that structure the entities.

Our interest in trying to predict the structured properties of imaginative creations is not inconsistent with our earlier claim that creative products are usually unpredictable. Even when the exact form that something will take cannot be predicted, one can still often identify the kinds of features that would structure the creation. Again, we regard creativity as neither a random process nor one that is predetermined but as a highly structured activity that can often result in surprising and unexpected outcomes.

Traditional Approaches to Categorization
It is important to use a principled approach in trying to support the argument that imagination is structured. For example, for any given set of products, one could always think of at least some features that they have in common (that they all took less than one hour to produce,

that they were all drawn on a single sheet of paper, and so on). This would be a trivial demonstration of structured imagination. To provide a more compelling case, one would want to predict in advance what sorts of properties are likely to structure a person's creations. We attempt to do so here by drawing on research from traditional approaches to categorization.

Research on categorization has typically taken one or two general approaches—one concerned with the formation of new categories and the other with judgments about preexisting categories. In the former approach, the experimenter presents the subject with some set of materials and asks that individual to partition the set into subgroups in a manner that seems appropriate to the subject or to learn a particular subgrouping that the experimenter has designated as correct. The stimuli in these studies have been dot patterns (Posner and Keele 1968), descriptions of fictitious diseases (Medin et al. 1982), descriptions of members of particular groups (Wattenmaker et al. 1986), letter strings (Reber 1976), faces (Ward and Scott 1987), and novel animals (Ward et al. 1989).

In the second approach, the subject is asked to make judgments or provide information about known categories—for example, by listing attributes of category members (Rosch et al. 1976; Rosch and Mervis 1975) and judging the typicality or goodness of an exemplar as a category member (Barsalou 1987).

We use the term *traditional* to refer to both of these approaches. This is not intended to be pejorative but rather to contrast with the present focus on tasks that require the subject to generate something truly novel, which we refer to as *generative*. Although consistent with our use of "generative" in the context of the Geneplore model, the term is used here in a somewhat broader sense.

The traditional approaches have been extremely valuable in providing information about how people learn new categories, about the structure of existing categories, and about how category information is accessed and used; however, they are not designed to provide information about the more creative or generative aspects of categorization. Although learning new categories and forming new groupings with novel experimental materials could be thought of as generative, it would be a very limited type of generative activity. Even when people are required to learn new categories, the structure of what is to be learned is most often determined by the experimenter. Similarly, when individuals are allowed to form groups according to their own preferred principles, the possible principles are most often constrained by the way attributes are allowed to vary in the presented materials. In contrast, our concern is with the way in which individuals go beyond existing category information to generate something new, without the constraints imposed by experimenter-devised rules or materials.

There are some traditional tasks that do involve going beyond the information as given. For example, inductive inference requires the subject to extend a known property of one category instance to other instances for which the property has not been explicitly stated. But even inductive inference has the feeling of following a clear path to the most reasonable, single answer. There is a sense in which it is either correct or incorrect. The generative tasks described in this chapter are more open-ended, with few objective criteria as to what constitutes a "correct" response.

The studies we describe are motivated in part by the idea that category structures and processes influence many types of creative activities, including practical endeavors, such as designing new or better products to meet specific needs, and literary or artistic activities such as developing new characters, scenes, or situations for a story. They can even include more purely whimsical activities, such as daydreaming about life on other planets or how life would be different if some event had or had not happened.

Although they are not focused on the creative aspects of categorization, the theoretical and empirical ideas that have emerged from the traditional approaches are important in guiding expectations about what should happen when we ask people to use their imagination. These findings allow direct predictions about how imagined entities should be structured, and as a result they allow an investigation of the concept of structured imagination. In addition, traditional categorization research has led to the development of many models of category structures and processes, including prototype models (Posner and Keele 1968; Reed 1972), featural models (Hayes-Roth and Hayes-Roth 1977), exemplar models (Medin and Schaffer 1978), episodic trace models (Hintzman 1986), connectionist models (Gluck and Bower, 1988), and theory-based models (Murphy and Medin 1985). These models provide alternate ways of conceptualizing how people go about the task of generating a novel exemplar of a known category. Thus, previous theoretical and empirical work can help direct research on the creative uses of categories. At the same time, examining the generative functions of categories can help us to learn more about categorization in general.

One of the most fundamental ideas to emerge from traditional approaches to categorization is that of the basic level (Rosch et al. 1976). Any given object can be represented at many different levels of abstraction. A siamese cat, for example, can be thought of as a siamese, a cat, a mammal, an animal, a living thing, and so on. Despite the multitude of possible levels of representation, most individuals tend to represent objects at what Rosch and her colleagues called the basic level of abstraction, an optimal balance between the breadth of the category and the ease of separating members and nonmembers. For a siamese cat, the basic level would be "cat."

A number of experimental procedures have converged to establish the basic level as a real psychological phenomenon. These include spontaneous labeling of objects, making rapid category decisions, listing the attributes of category members, describing actions taken with respect to objects, and recognizing objects from averaged shapes (Rosch et al. 1976). Because of its central role in human categorization, the basic level has continued to attract considerable research attention (Lassaline, Wisniewski, and Medin in press; Tversky and Hemenway 1984).

The basic level is thus a primary candidate for a structuring principle for imagination. Because it has an impact on many nongenerative aspects of categorization, it would very likely have an impact on the more generative aspects as well. In particular, we will use the idea that the general shape of something is important for making basic level distinctions to predict the properties that are included when people attempt to generate creative exemplars.

Traditional grouping studies have also revealed that certain properties, such as size, are less important in forming categories (Landau, Smith, and Jones 1988; Ward et al. 1989). We will use these observations to make predictions about properties that will be unimportant in structuring creative exemplars.

In addition, traditional approaches have revealed the importance of correlated attributes (Rosch 1978). Rather than co-occurring randomly, attributes of real-world categories tend to occur in distinct clusters. For example, feathers and wings occur much more often together than do fur and wings. Correlated attributes are such a basic part of human cognition that even infants as young as ten months of age appear sensitive to them (Younger and Cohen 1986). Given the fundamental role of correlated features, such correlations may structure the more generative aspects of categorization as well.

Beyond this focus on the properties identified in traditional categorization studies, we also consider the possibility that new properties and principles will emerge from studies on the creative use of categories. These principles can feed back to traditional studies and lead to new predictions about what should be observed in those studies as well.

The Exemplar Generation Paradigm

The paradigm used extensively in the studies to be described is called exemplar generation (Ward 1991a). In this paradigm, subjects are given the task of generating a new member of some known category— for example, an animal that would exist on a planet somewhere else in the universe. Of most concern are the properties that subjects typically include in their drawings and the extent to which those properties are predictable from previous work on categorization. Although the category used in many of these studies was "animals," the exemplar generation paradigm could be used with a wide variety of other categories, including inventions, artifacts, and various types of abstract concepts.

A Planet Like Earth

In the first study, Ward (1991a) gave fifty college students the task of imagining a planet that exists somewhere else in the galaxy but is similar to earth in size, terrain, and climate. They were then asked to imagine and draw an animal that lived on that planet. Because the planet was described as similar to earth, the properties of the exemplars served as a baseline against which to compare exemplars from subsequent studies in which the planet was described as being very different from earth.

In addition to providing the initial drawing of their imagined animal, subjects responded to questions about the diet, habitat, sensory organs, and appendages of the creature. The questions were designed to provide information about nonvisible properties of the creatures and to help to clarify ambiguities in interpreting the visible properties of the drawings. As an example, the subject might have included appendages that a coder would suspect to be arms but statements by the subject helped to clarify that they were indeed intended as arms rather than wings, tentacles, or some other type of structure. The verbal responses also helped to identify the functions of the depicted properties (for example, that the creature's legs were used for walking).

After providing drawings and verbal responses for their initial creations, subjects were asked to draw another member of the same species and subsequently answered questions regarding any differences between the first and second creature that were again designed to clarify any ambiguities. Finally, the subjects were asked to imagine and draw a member of some different species from the same planet and to answer questions about cross-species differences.

The central issue was whether the subjects' creations would exhibit common, predictable structures. Are there commonalities that exist across the subjects' initial creations, or does each subject produce an idiosyncratic creation that has little in common with the creations of others? Do subjects produce the same kinds of similarities and differences across and within species, or is this also idiosyncratic? Most important, are the observed commonalities predictable from known properties of the existing categories and from empirical work in traditional paradigms?

To examine commonalities across the subjects' initial creations, Ward (1991a) considered that the majority of animals with which subjects would be familiar possessed, at a minimum, bilateral symmetry, sensory organs, and functional appendages. These properties would be central to most subjects' representations of the category "animal." Thus, if imagination is structured by known category properties, it should be the case that most subjects' initial creations would possess these properties.

The results showed that large majorities of individuals drew creatures that were bilaterally symmetric (98 percent), had at least one major sense organ (98 percent), and had at least one major type of appendage (92 percent). The most common sense organs were eyes, (92 percent), and the most common appendages were legs (88 percent). Eighty-six percent of the creatures had a mouth. Figure 6.1 shows an example of a creature containing many of these properties. These percentages indicate a great deal of similarity to typical earth animals, a similarity that becomes even more evident when we consider the actual numbers of each type of appendage and sense organ. Figure 6.2 shows the percentage of individuals who drew creatures containing a typical number of legs and arms. Figure 6.3 shows the same type of information for eyes and ears. The vast majority of individuals who included these attributes did so in a way that was highly typical of earth creatures.

In summary, when subjects are asked to imagine an animal from another planet, their creations have a great deal in common with one another and with the properties of typical earth animals. Rather than being idiosyncratic and unpredictable, the use of imagination to generate new exemplars of a category appears to be highly structured by the characteristic attributes of known category members.

Basic Level Contrasts
The principles that organize existing categories might also be expected to structure variations that subjects allow in their creations, both within and between categories. One of the fundamental organizing

Figure 6.1
An imaginary creature created in experiments on exemplar generation. (From Ward
1991a.)

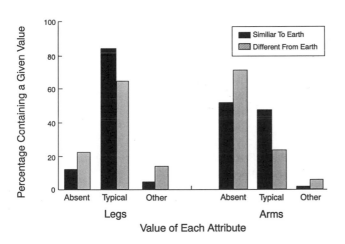

Figure 6.2
Percentage of imaginary creatures that had no legs, two or four legs, or some other
number of legs and that had no arms, two arms, or some other number of arms, when
people imagined a planet similar to earth and a planet completely different from earth.
(From Ward 1991a.)

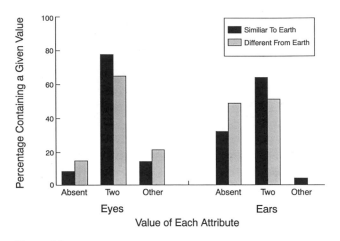

Figure 6.3
Percentage of imaginary creatures that had no eyes or ears, two eyes and ears, or some other number of eyes and ears. (From Ward 1991a.)

principles in this regard is the tendency to categorize at the basic level. In Ward (1991a), the role of the basic level in structuring imagination was examined by comparing the kinds of differences subjects allowed in generating another member of the same species and a member of a different species. On the assumption that the basic level is pervasive enough to influence imaginative endeavors, one would predict that subjects would approach the task of generating a member of a different species as one of generating a member of a different basic level category (for example, producing first a birdlike and then a fishlike species). Because shape is an important feature for differentiating items at the basic level (Tversky and Hemenway 1984), one would also predict that most people would vary shape across but not within species.

The results clearly favored the position that subjects assume basic level differentiation across species. In this case, they were highly likely to vary the overall shape (94 percent), appendages (80 percent), or sense organs (74 percent). But when they produced a member of the same species, they were much less likely to vary shape (20 percent), appendages (20 percent), or sense organs (16 percent). Examples of one subject's same-species and different-species creatures are shown in figure 6.4.

The fact that subjects varied shape and parts only rarely within species and often across species is consistent with earlier findings from studies in which subjects were told to list properties of members

a   b   c

Figure 6.4
One subject's (a) initial creation, (b) same-species variant, and (c) different-species variant. (From Ward 1991a.)

of known biological categories (Tversky and Hemenway 1984). In general, these findings demonstrate that the knowledge underlying attribute listing effects also manifests itself in creative generation tasks.

Research from traditional paradigms can also help in making predictions about the kinds of properties that subjects will allow to vary within species. For example, Ward et al. (1989) presented subjects with the items depicted in figure 6.5 and provided a separate label for each one. The subjects were told that the items were examples of two different types of animals. They were then shown new animals that varied from these examples in shape, size, number of legs, and type of legs and were asked to judge whether the variants were members of one, the other, or neither category. The subjects tended to assign variants to the labeled categories on the basis of overall shape and the number and type of legs. Size had no effect on their category decisions. Similarly Landau, Smith, and Jones (1988) found that when novel labels are used, young children rely on shape for making category decisions and ignore large differences in size. If the same properties influence generative and nongenerative categorization, then we should expect that subjects would be much more likely to vary size than shape or appendages in generating a second member of the same species.

The data confirmed these predictions. In generating a new member of the same species, subjects varied size considerably more often (54 percent) than either shape (20 percent) or appendages (20 percent). In contrast, in generating a member of a different species, subjects varied

Figure 6.5
Items used in studies on category generalization. (From Ward 1990.)

size less often (41 percent) than either shape (94 percent) or appendages (80 percent).

A Planet Different from Earth

The data from the first experiment were originally intended as a baseline against which more variable creations from subsequent studies could be compared. The planet was described as being very similar to earth, so it may not be surprising that the properties of the imagined creatures were highly structured in terms of characteristic properties of typical earth animals.

A second experiment (Ward 1991a) was conducted to determine the extent to which imaginary animals on a planet that was described as being very different from earth would be structured according to the same principles. The most striking aspect of the results was their similarity to those of the first experiment. In fact, the results matched those of the first experiment in every respect but one: subjects were less likely to include typical numbers of appendages and sense organs. Despite this tendency, however, the subjects were just as likely to include sense organs and appendages in their imaginary creatures. These differences and commonalities across the two studies are depicted in figures 6.2 and 6.3.

The results of these two experiments reveal that imagination, at least in the form of imagining some novel exemplar of a known category, is highly structured. This structuring exists in terms of the concrete perceptual features of individual animals, as well as the more abstract relational properties between members of the same and different categories.

Comparing the findings from these two studies allows one to infer what properties subjects believe can differ from those of known category exemplars and what properties cannot. Apparently bilateral symmetry, appendages, and sensory receptors are central to most individuals' concepts about animals and will be present across differing conditions. The specific manifestation of appendages and sense organs is less important and can vary across conditions. Studies on exemplar generation can therefore help to determine which properties are important to category representation and which are not.

Correlated Attributes

Another structuring principle revealed in traditional approaches to categorization is that of correlated attributes. We describe three experiments concerned with the extent to which imagination is structured by these attributes. The first examines the commonly cited correlation among feathers, beaks, and wings (Rosch et al. 1976). The second examines a less cited and more implicit link between intelligence and humanoid structure, and the third examines the idea that age is correlated with the ratio of head size to body size.

In the first experiment, half of the subjects were told that the animal to be generated was feathered, and half were told that it was furry (Ward 1991a). In both cases, the planet was described as being completely different from earth. The most important data from this study are presented in figure 6.6. Subjects in the feathered condition were significantly more likely than those in the furry condition to generate animals that had wings and beaks and significantly less likely to generate animals with ears. Sample drawings are shown in figures 6.7 and 6.8..

The results for wings and beaks are completely consistent with the idea that exemplar generation is structured by knowledge of correlated properties. The link between feathers and an absence of ears is not often discussed in the categorization literature but is quite sensible given the auricular regions that are typical of birds. These findings draw attention to the idea that possible new correlations found in structured imagination studies might also be expected to emerge in traditional categorization studies.

A second study (Ward 1991a) examined the role of correlated attributes in exemplar generation for a more abstract kind of correlation. Half of the subjects were told that the animal was highly intelligent, and half were given no special information about intelligence. The

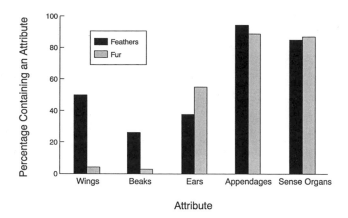

Figure 6.6
Percentage of imaginary creatures that had wings, beaks, ears, at least one major appendage (legs, arms, or wings), and at least one major sense organ (eyes, ears, or a nose). (From Ward 1991a.)

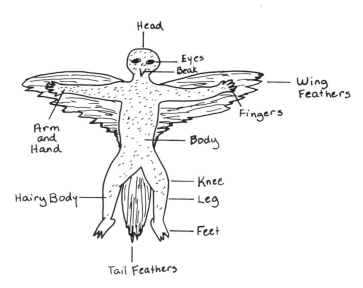

Figure 6.7
An imaginary creature generated under the constraint that it had to possess feathers. (From Ward 1991a.)

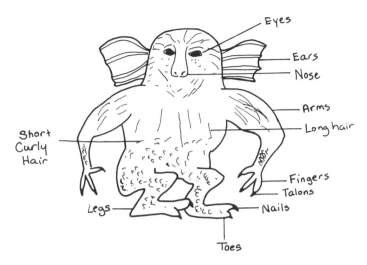

Figure 6.8
An imaginary creature generated under the constraint that it had to possess fur. (From Ward 1991a.)

rationale was that subjects may have the implicit belief that external and internal structures are correlated (see Keil 1989). Thus, they would assume that creatures that have humanlike intelligence would also have humanlike appearance. Indeed, alleged encounters with space-faring extraterrestrials often involve descriptions of humanlike creatures (Malmstrom and Coffman 1979). This suggests that one's category structures may include an implicit correlation between high intelligence and humanoid form.

The most important findings are presented in figure 6.9. Subjects in the "intelligent" condition were significantly more likely to produce creatures that were humanoid, communicated, wore clothing, and interacted with artifacts other than clothing. Sample items from the two conditions are shown in figures 6.10 and 6.11. The results reveal the impact of attribute correlations on exemplar generation that are more abstract than those based simply on perceptual properties. They also reveal interactions between the broad domains of animate and artifact categories and suggest that structured imagination may involve the development of mental models of those interactions.

A final study of correlated properties was concerned with the link between age and head-to-body size ratio. In most species, very young members have a larger head-to-body size ratio than adults. This phenomenon has generated much theoretical speculation about the role this larger ratio might play in evoking caretaking. Our concern, how-

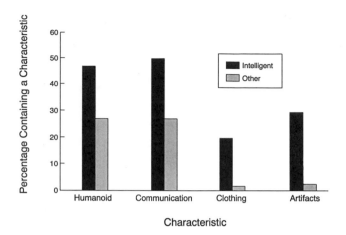

Figure 6.9
Percentage of imaginary creatures that had a humanoid structure, some form of communication, clothing, and other artifacts. (From Ward 1991a.)

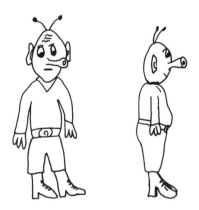

Figure 6.10
An imaginary creature generated under the constraint that it had to be "intelligent." (From Ward 1991a.)

Figure 6.11
An imaginary creature generated without regard to intelligence. (From Ward 1991a.)

ever, is whether this correlation is part of subjects' knowledge structures and whether it manifests itself in imagination.

In this last study, subjects were first asked to generate a member of an intelligent species. They were then asked whether they had intended their drawing to represent a full-grown or young member of the species. Whichever of these possibilities the subjects indicated, they were then instructed to draw the other possibility. When they completed the second drawing, they were asked whether they had consciously tried to make the younger one have a higher head-to-body size ratio. These reports were collected to determine whether the effects might be attributable to having explicit access to this information. Because this particular correlation is more subtle, it would help to alleviate any concerns that the observed structuring effects are the product of demand characteristics that lead subjects to produce obvious correlations. The main findings were straightforward: subjects produced significantly larger head-to-body size ratios in their drawings of young members than of those of adults. This was true regardless of whether they reported deliberately doing so.

Structures and Processes in Structured Imagination

How can we describe or characterize the structured imagination findings in terms of traditional categorization models? Because imagination is clearly influenced by conceptual information, any complete model of categorization must be able to specify how categorical knowledge achieves this impact. More generally, categorization models should be able to deal with the generative as well as nongenerative functions of categories. Thus, in addition to using such models to help in interpreting findings on imagination, we can use imagination to inform us about the usefulness of categorization models.

Simple Categorization Models

Although none of the existing categorization models have been explicitly applied to the question of how a person might imagine new members of a category, the principles used in those models offer some suggestions for how this process would operate. In deciding whether a given entity is a member of some known category, the person presumably evaluates that entity against some stored representation of the category. Depending on the model, that stored representation could have the form of exemplars, abstracted prototypes, feature frequencies, and so on. Although the processes would differ somewhat for the different models, in general category decisions would be based on featural matches and comparisons of similarity between the test item and the stored representation. To extend these notions to describe imaginative activity, rather than using stored information as a standard against which to evaluate a presented entity, the person engaged in exemplar generation would use that same stored information to generate something new. The initial development of a new entity from stored representations, which corresponds to the generative phase of the Geneplore model, can result from the retrieval of single exemplars or other category representations, the synthesis of two or more retrieved representations, and the transformation of retrieved information.

Regardless of which type of representation is stored and accessed, there would be a striking similarity between the stored structures and the initially generated novel product. That is, just as similarity or feature matching plays a central role in deciding category membership, it would presumably play a central role in generating novel products. Unless subjects examined the initial forms in an exploration phase and decided to impose major transformations, their drawings would share many properties with known category members.

Even if the structures were extensively transformed, there may exist certain attributes that are so central to the concept that subjects would almost always include them. Thus, the fact that subjects' initial drawings included characteristic attributes of typical animals could be described using the terminology of most, if not all, of these models. Using an exemplar model, for example, one could argue that subjects perform the task by retrieving some known category exemplar and modifying it to some degree. By this view, the properties in the imagined creatures would be present as a by-product of their presence in the retrieved exemplar. Within a model involving an abstraction of a prototype or a representation of the category in terms of a "best example," presumably that entity would be retrieved. As with the exemplar model, the characteristic features would be present in the new creation because of their association with the retrieved entities. In any case, the important point is that the created entities are not conceived of randomly. Preinventive structures are not completely arbitrary; they exhibit important properties that are determined by underlying knowledge structures.

Some subjects' drawings were highly similar to specific earth creatures, as would be expected if they had simply retrieved and drawn a single known exemplar. Others appeared to be combinations of two or more earth creatures, as would be expected if subjects had retrieved multiple exemplars and had combined them using mental synthesis. Finally, some drawings did not appear similar to any known earth creatures or combination of creatures but exhibited new arrangements of familiar features. This is consistent with the idea that subjects had either retrieved more abstract ideas about what properties constitute an animal, or they retrieved known exemplars and then mentally transformed their parts.

The Importance of Naive Theories
Although they can capture some of the specific features of what is created, exemplar and prototype models may miss some of the richness of the creations because they are concerned solely with the features that are present in the creations and not with the reasons those features are important to the category.

Accordingly, typical categorization models have been justly criticized for their reliance on feature matching and similarity as explanatory constructs (Murphy and Medin 1985). The argument against an explanatory role for similarity is essentially that it may not do any of the difficult theoretical work of explaining many categorization phenomena; objects may appear similar because they are members of the same category, and not vice versa. One can certainly describe a set of features and attribute correlations that category members have in common and note that members are similar in the sense that they tend to share those features. However, this leaves open the question of how those particular features were chosen as the focus of attention to begin with. Of all the possible features and correlations that could be considered, why are some central to the concept and others either more peripheral or not included at all?

One answer involves the idea that categories are embedded within naive theories or belief systems. These broad frameworks are thought to provide coherence to categories. That is, rather than consisting of exemplars, simple collections of feature values, correlated features, prototypic members, or other uninterpreted representations, categories are thought to include (or be included within) broad knowledge structures that provide explanations for observed featural regularities (Murphy and Medin 1985; Keil 1989). These knowledge structures, which are broader than any one category, help people to organize and interpret category information in terms of beliefs about how the world works. For example, the empirically observable correlation between the properties of feathers, wings, pointed beaks, hollow bones, and flight may be favored in internal representations of the category "bird" not simply because those properties often occur together but because people may possess more general ideas about gravity, wind resistance, and movement that provide an organizing framework within which such a correlation makes sense. Many other correlations may be empirically present (such as wings and three-toed feet) but are not noticed because they do not make sense within a person's belief systems.

In terms of traditional approaches, such naive theories help to account for which features and feature correlations will be noticed and incorporated into the category representation. Similarly, accounts of the role of category information in directing imagination may benefit from a focus on naive theories that highlight the importance of certain features or attempt to explain observed correlations. Why are some attributes of the category included in the generated exemplars and others not? Presumably those attributes that are included are part of broader conceptions of life and environmental pressures for survival and adaptation.

Exemplar generation studies may provide hints about a person's implicit theories about animals. For example, most people presumably believe that an animal must have some means of locomotion and therefore must possess appendages. Although not a necessary property, bilateral symmetry may also convey the adaptive advantage of efficient movement (Gardner 1964). In addition, an animal must have some means of extracting information from the world and of taking in nourishment and therefore must possess sensory receptors and a mouth. The greater tendency to include eyes rather than ears may reflect an anthropocentric belief that vision is generally a more important sense than audition. There may be other aspects to a person's beliefs about animals (life span, growth, reproduction, and so on) that could also be expressed in creative exemplars. These attributes are included in imagined animals not simply because they are present in most known exemplars or are part of some abstracted set of typical features but because, in imagining new animals, people invoke broader knowledge structures that serve to organize or provide coherence to the concept of animal.

These implicit theories may also be useful in explaining some of the observed correlations, particularly those that involve attributes that are more abstract than simple perceptual properties. For example, the fact that intelligent creatures tended to be humanoid may reflect the operation of a general belief about the properties of natural categories: similarity of external appearance is linked to similarity of deeper, nonobservable properties. The greater tendency for intelligent creatures to communicate, wear clothing, and interact with artifacts may be based on broad theories about how organisms interact with one another and with their environments. Thus, attributes such as clothing are included not simply because they happen to be stored as part of the category "human" but because of a belief system that includes the idea that intelligent creatures manipulate their environments to create artifacts that meet certain needs (such as protection from elements). For some subjects, the inclusion of clothing could even reflect the operation of a belief system that includes the idea that the primary goal of intelligent creatures is to overcome their baser "animal nature." Thus, just as they provide coherence for existing concepts, implicit theories may provide the glue that binds imagined entities to the categories from which they are generated.

These theories would also help to account for the way in which people respond to constraints. Suppose that we had asked subjects to generate creatures that live on a planet that has many times the gravity of earth. Their initial tendency may be to generate some highly typical earth creature, but in evaluating its viability they might recognize that certain modifications are needed. Of all the attributes present in their initial attempt, which ones should be modified? Access to exemplars, prototypes, or feature frequencies alone would not allow an answer to this type of question. Presumably subjects would need to call on a rich body of physical knowledge to deal with the question. In terms of the Geneplore model, this evaluation would presumably occur in the exploratory phase. For particularly difficult constraints, it may be that subjects would have to repeat several cycles of generation and exploration in order to arrive at an appropriate set of attributes.

Whether people generate novel items by retrieving exemplars or accessing abstract principles may well depend on the conditions of the experiment. In related studies (described more fully in chapter 7), we presented examples of animal and object categories to subjects and examined the extent to which their creations included properties of those examples (Smith, Ward, and Schumacher 1991, Jansson and Smith 1991). Such an approach may be much more likely to induce exemplar retrieval and modification. In other recent work, we have strongly urged subjects not to base their creations on any real or fictional animals they have ever encountered. Such approaches would reduce reliance on specific exemplars, yet they have so far resulted in creations whose properties very closely match those described in previous sections and which very closely resemble real earth creatures.

Bigger Structures: Schemas and Mental Models

Imagination is a much richer phenomenon than we have indicated thus far. Although it clearly applies when people generate a new member of a category, imagination also comes into play when people conceive of more complex entities, such as novel scenes, events, societies, and even whole new worlds. These more complex entities involve not just single categories but also relations among categories. Thus, it is useful to consider the kinds of cognitive structures that might help to direct these more complex imaginings.

Schemas

Schemas are abstract knowledge structures that can include information about multiple objects and the relations among them. We distinguish schemas from categories by suggesting that a category consists of single kinds of objects that share a taxonomic link—for example, chairs, televisions, and paintings. In contrast, schemas specify the relations among several discrete categories, and these often cut across standard taxonomic boundaries. A schema for a living room might contain not only chairs, televisions, paintings, and other discrete categories but also the typical relations among them. Schemas can be organized spatially, as in the case of a living room, or temporally as in the case of "taking a vacation" or "going to a restaurant" (Mandler 1984; Schank and Abelson 1977). The former can be referred to as "scenes" and the latter as "scripts".

Schemas have had an important impact in traditional studies in cognitive psychology (Bartlett 1932). They structure the encoding of new information, the retrieval of old information, and inferences based on that information. Because of their importance in structuring these nongenerative aspects of cognition, it would not be surprising to find that schemas also guide, and perhaps limit, creative generation and imagination. In addition, because people tend to form exception rules for cases that do not fit into an existing schema rather than modify the more general schema (Holland et al. 1986), schemas may be quite resistant to change. It may thus be difficult to overcome their impact on imagination.

Schank (1988a) has highlighted the dangers of script-based thinking. Although scripts may be useful in the sense of facilitating routine tasks, the nearly automatic manner in which they are employed can inhibit imagination and creativity. Schank notes many real-world situations in which mindless adherence to scripts leads to unimaginative solutions to problems. Scripts make our lives easy, and so we continue to do things the way we have always done them, even when better ways might exist.

Although the exemplar generation studies described previously were directed at discrete categories rather than schemas, there is nevertheless evidence that subjects in these studies were accessing schemas. The fact that "intelligent" creatures tended to wear clothing, communicate with one another, and interact with artifacts indicates that subjects were going beyond a discrete animal category.

Mental Models

One problem with schemas is their inflexibility (Holland et al. 1986). Although they are helpful in structuring our understanding of and responses to routine situations, they are not as helpful in unusual situations or when violations of the routine occur. It is unreasonable to think that we have preexisting schemas to handle all possible situations. Schemas may also be unhelpful when violations of the routine must occur in order to solve some problem or develop some novel entity.

For these latter situations, a more useful cognitive structure may be mental models (Gentner and Stevens 1983; Johnson-Laird 1983), dynamic entities whose properties make them particularly useful as preinventive structures. They can be thought of as active constructions that represent the current or desired state of affairs, as well as information about how to get from one state to another. As such, they involve the interplay between many preexisting schemas and categories. Because mental models provide a way of representing the interaction of information from different knowledge domains, it is with these more elaborate and dynamic constructs that we may be able to account for types of imaginative activity that go beyond the generation of single, new exemplars.

Mental models are complex enough that one can use them to describe how imagination operates in complex endeavors such as engineering design and scientific discovery. Engineers, for example, often work with complex and interactive systems, such as automatic transmissions and drive trains. Mental models provide a convenient way of conceptualizing how such physical systems operate. Similarly, scientists must often develop models of intricate physical structures, ranging from the atom to the human brain. Mental models can help to characterize these structures as well.

Mental models are sometimes developed by way of analogy to other complex systems, such as a representation of the atom in terms of the solar system or the mind in terms of a computerlike information processing system. We consider the use of analogy and mental models in more detail in chapter 8. For now, we note that even these elaborate forms of imagination are influenced by existing ideas and technologies that are part of their creator's cultural context, as in the case of computer models of the mind.

In the exemplar generation studies, we did not explicitly give subjects tasks that were complex enough to require elaborate mental models. Subjects may nevertheless have used them. For example, in generating a novel animal, subjects might have considered what kind of environment existed on the planet and what kind of adaptations would be useful for those conditions. Such a process would involve the development of a mental model of the interactions among the concepts of animals, environments, and evolutionary adaptations. Indeed, science fiction writers often describe the activity of developing an alien creature as one that includes a consideration of the characteristics of its planet, society, local environment, and so forth.

As another example, we gave subjects the task of generating tools that might be used by an intelligent species on some other planet. Many of the generated tools had distinct handles. One interpretation of this result is that the subjects performed the task by generating mental models that included the idea that tools are used by intelligent creatures and that those creatures have specific types of appendages, such as hands. Thus, products developed in one domain (tools) can be constrained by assumptions about another domain (intelligent animals).

It might be possible to ensure the use of mental models in future studies by giving subjects more constrained tasks—for example, by suggesting that the animals to be generated exist in bizarre environments such as planets that are completely liquid or gaseous, that have excessive gravity, and so forth. Or one could ask subjects to generate tools for intelligent beings that have special needs (for example, they have no hands or are unable to use their hands). One could also ask for more elaborate creations such as predictions about life in the future or suggestions about a better way of solving complex problems.

The benefits of studying imagination in more elaborate tasks are threefold. First, one can capture aspects of imagination that are more complex and interactive and describe them in the framework of contemporary research on mental models. Second, by examining the interaction of knowledge domains in imagination tasks, we have another window on the general cognitive processes involved in constructing and using mental models. Finally, many practical problems are more complex than generating a single exemplar of a category, and it is important to understand the cognitive processes involved in those more complex situations.

One aspect of mental models that is particularly helpful in understanding imagination is that they can be thought of as active constructions that are used to make predictions or generate expectations (Gentner and Stevens 1983; Holland et al. 1986; Johnson-Laird 1983). In effect, mental models can be tested and modified. Thus, they provide a way of thinking about how one might make new discoveries. For example, in the process of testing a mental model, one might encounter a discrepancy between expected and resulting outcomes. This failure could lead to the discovery that an implicit assumption has been operating and is preventing an adequate solution to some problem. In terms of the Geneplore model, this discrepancy would be discovered in the exploratory phase and would result, ultimately, in the generation of a new, and presumably more adequate, model.

Mental models also provide a way of thinking about an interesting paradox that arises from the concept of structured imagination. If imagination is structured by existing knowledge, how are originality and innovation possible? We suggest that although individual categories and schemas alone might result in strongly normative creations, when those structures are combined in the development of a more comprehensive mental model, discoveries can be made and properties can emerge that would not have been predictable from an analysis of those individual component concepts. The integrative, combinatory, and transformative possibilities of mental models provide a framework within which originality can emerge.

Structured Imagination in Highly Creative Works

Because the subjects in Ward's (1991a) exemplar generation studies were beginning-level college students, a legitimate concern could be raised about just how imaginative these individuals truly are. Perhaps the striking commonalities across the drawings and the strong adherence to characteristic properties of typical earth species are more indicative of the nature of this restricted population than of the operation of imagination in general. Taking into account empirical and anecdotal observations that indicate that an adherence to known properties is a more general phenomenon, we then consider the idea that adherence to certain principles may not always be a bad thing. Part of the task of increasing inventiveness may involve distinguishing those properties of existing structures that should be maintained and those that should be eliminated. In the context of discussing these issues, we will also consider how external constraints might operate to influence the outcome of imaginative endeavors.

Imaginative Creatures in Movies
Ward (1991b) examined the properties of alien creatures in the three movies in the "Star Wars" series. The now-famous bar scene in the first movie was touted as depicting a highly creative collection of exotic and imaginative creatures. By a consensual definition, these creatures would certainly be considered imaginative and creative. Nevertheless, the vast majority of these creatures were bilaterally symmetric, had appendages, and displayed various types of sense organs. Thus, even these highly innovative products of imagination were structured by the same sorts of characteristic properties that structure the exemplars generated by college students.

The "Star Wars" creatures may also reveal the operation of other kinds of constraints or pressures. For example, to produce a movie that will appeal to a wide audience, it may be necessary to develop creatures that the audience can relate to at some level. Violating too many characteristic properties might make the creatures completely uninteresting to most viewers, no matter how creative they may be. Thus, factors other than beliefs about what life may have been like a long time ago in another galaxy may have influenced the development of these creatures.

Mythical Beings and Transformations
In a somewhat different but related vein, Kelly and Keil (1985) examined the kinds of transformations that are described in Ovid's *Metamorpheses* and the Grimm Brothers' *Fairy Tales*. They found that these transformations were not randomly distributed across the different types of creations. Rather, they were influenced by ontological boundaries (for example, between animals and plants) and by other organizing principles of category structure. For example, in both sources, conscious beings were considerably more likely to be transformed into other animals than into plants. As Kelly and Keil point out, these transformations could reflect the operation of constraints such as maintaining reader interest. On the other hand, they may reflect a deliberate attempt on the part of the authors to generate comprehensible stories that are easily incorporated into the conceptual structures of readers. Finally, they could reflect a more implicit adherence to category structuring principles.

Knowledge about the correlation between age and the ratio of head-to-body size has also been shown to influence the creations of professional artists. Pittenger (1990) measured the head-to-body ratio in drawings of fictional, anthropomorphized animals in children's books. He examined pairs of illustrations in which the members of the pair were of the same species and for which it was clear which member was the older one. Pittenger found that for ninety-three out of one hundred pairs, the older member had a smaller ratio of head size to body size. Like the Kelly and Keil results, it could be that illustrators consciously and deliberately vary this ratio—or it could be that such knowledge is not consciously accessed and influences their creations implicitly, as in the case of our college students' creations.

Overcoming Influences of Unwanted Attributes

There are two ways to think about the phenomenon of structured imagination. On the positive side, one can think of existing cognitive structures as usefully directing or guiding the development of new ideas along sensible lines. If certain attributes have proved useful in dealing with past problems, they may well be useful in the future. On the negative side, one can think of these structures as constraining or limiting imagination. Which perspective is more appropriate depends on which attributes are maintained and their role in the overall functioning of the new creation. Here we consider ways of overcoming the structuring influence of existing knowledge frameworks in cases where such structuring can be inhibitory.

One possibility is to attempt to make implicit assumptions explicit or raise them to consciousness (Schank, 1988a). For example, if one becomes aware through exploration that an implicit assumption that animals need to be bilaterally symmetric has influenced the generation of an initial form for a novel creature, one can deliberately overcome that assumption. An important question, however, is how to become aware of the operation of implicit assumptions.

Several popular techniques for enhancing creativity bear an interesting relation to this issue. For example, the attribute listing and morphological synthesis approaches encourage the listing of the attributes of an object and then considering modifications on those attributes. Using these techniques, one might list "wooden handle" as one of the attributes of a hammer and then consider the implications of changing that attribute to some other property, such as a rubber handle. These techniques certainly make one aware of implicit assumptions about an object's features, but unless one also considered "no handle" as a variant on that attribute, one would implicitly include a handle in the ultimate configuration, even when it might not be useful (for example, for beings without appendages).

Another procedure for overcoming unwanted attributes is the generative process that we have called categorical reduction, a shift from categorizing an object at the basic level to categorizing it more abstractly in terms of its underlying or constituent properties. Rather than representing a chair as a "chair," for example, one might represent it in terms of properties such as "stable" and "elevated flat surface," with the consequence that it would then be seen as useful for standing on to change a lightbulb.

Categorical reduction is most effective when an innovator has to consider the properties of objects in terms of the exact goals that must be met by a new product. For example, rather than specifying that the task is to design a better coffee cup, we could specify that the task is to develop a container to keep liquid hot and to allow someone to consume that liquid. The former specification would call attention to aspects of coffee cups that might be irrelevant and perhaps interfering (Jansson and Smith 1991), whereas the latter might activate only those properties most relevant to the goal. In other words, in contrast to making the problem solver consciously aware of interfering attributes, categorical reduction would have the virtue of not activating those attributes in the first place. This idea about the value of specifying the functions that a new object must satisfy is consistent with studies described in chapter 4, in which specifying an object's function led to more creative outcomes than specifying an object's type. (We return to these issues in chapter 7 in discussing the topic of design fixation.)

Related to this is the importance of failure. For example, when the running of a mental model leads to a prediction that is not confirmed or to outcomes that are contrary to those expected, one can often modify the rules that make up the model (Holland et al. 1986). These modifications can then lead to better rules in the future. Several authors have mentioned the potentially stimulating effect of failure (Holland et al. 1986; Murray 1986; Schank 1988a) and, in particular, the importance of the individual's response to that failure. When viewed as an opportunity to revise old ways of representing the world, failure can help one to overcome implicit assumptions.

Summary

Theoretical Implications
This chapter has focused on how existing conceptual frameworks and belief systems can both constrain or inhibit and structure or direct imagination. Basic category knowledge, as well as more elaborate forms of knowledge such as implicit theories, schemas, and mental

models, can influence the outcome of tasks involving the use of imagination. We therefore think of imagination as being more similar to ordinary nonimaginative thinking than it is different in that both are structured by many of the same principles.

Two important implications follow from these conclusions. First, imagination can be readily addressed within the existing framework of contemporary cognitive psychology. Second, using a creative cognition approach, the study of imagination may allow new insights about the nature of category structures and processes. For example, properties that have not yet been observed in standard categorization tasks may consistently emerge in novel creations. The approach may then lead to new questions about the role that emergent properties might play in traditional categorization studies. In effect, we can use empirical and theoretical work on categorization to aid in the study of imagination and use imagination as a process to learn more about the nature of categorization.

Although we have excluded hallucinations, delusions, and dreams from consideration, these too may be structured by existing knowledge frameworks (McKellar 1957). It may thus be fruitful to examine the commonalities and differences in structuring principles across the continuum that ranges from rational to delusional thought. As with the study of imagination, this can lead to insights regarding the nature of thought in general.

Much work remains to be done on the study of imagination. We must still specify the properties that are most critical in determining the nature and extent of structuring and consider the conditions under which people generate imaginative products by retrieving and modifying exemplars and by accessing knowledge structures with their attendant implicit assumptions and beliefs. In addition, we must consider a wider range of imaginative phenomena, including painting, film making, and creative writing. Finally, we must try to identify the best ways of helping people to retain those attributes that really are helpful in arriving at new solutions and to overcome those attributes that tend to interfere.

Practical Implications
Research on structured imagination can have practical implications as well. As one example, Lorenz (1974) cited the case of development of train cars. When they were first produced, they included running boards, a feature of their predecessors, the horse-drawn carriage. Only later was the running board replaced by a central aisle through which a conductor could walk more safely. This is a striking case of including a characteristic property of typical members of a known category in

generating some new product, even when that property may be useless or harmful.

Jansson and Smith (1991) have provided a more experimentally controlled version of this same phenomenon. They had engineers develop products after viewing examples of other products designed to meet the same need. The engineers included properties of the examples in their own designs, even when explicitly instructed not to do so.

One way to view the inclusion of unnecessary attributes in inventions and designs is that people are not thinking as imaginatively as they might be able to. Thus, a person might learn to become more imaginative by eliminating those attributes from their creations. There are several ways in which this might be accomplished. First, the inclusion of any given attribute may result from implicit rather than explicit processes. In this case, one might be able to be more creative by examining as many properties of a generated form as possible and asking whether each is necessary and, if so, why. More generally, one could systematically explore the consequences of removing or altering each of the attributes to reveal the nature of any interfering, implicit assumptions.

In a related ways, it may be that unwanted attributes are included in a new form because they happen to be tied to familiar, known exemplars. Presumably these exemplars will tend to be central to the category and thus contain a large number of characteristic attributes. In this case, a possible strategy for becoming more imaginative would be to deliberately retrieve atypical exemplars. This would require familiarity with the extent to which attributes can vary within a category. For example, in trying to generate a new alien creature, one might deliberately exclude any creature that seems familiar or contains a typical set of features.

7

Insight, Fixation, and Incubation

Memory Mechanisms in Creative Cognition

We have developed the idea that much of creative cognition is structured, in that existing knowledge bases guide and often restrict the form that imagined creations can take. Now we consider the specific kinds of memory mechanisms that might operate in creative cognition when information is retrieved from those knowledge bases, particularly retrieval processes that can facilitate or inhibit creative performance and how one might exploit or overcome them. We discuss these processes primarily in the context of generating exemplars and solving specific types of problems; more general issues concerning creative strategies for problem solving are addressed in chapter 8.

The topics in this chapter include whether traditional insight problems are solved by way of a sudden restructuring of the problem or the incremental retrieval of problem-specific information from memory, tip-of-the-tongue retrieval failures and their resolution, fixation and incubation in problem-solving and creative generation tasks, whether spreading activation may underlie incubation effects, and the conditions under which analogical transfer can occur. These topics will be related to various aspects of the Geneplore model.

Theoretical and empirical studies of human memory have provided one of the foundations of modern cognitive psychology (Anderson 1990; Anderson and Bower 1973). It would seem as if this large body of knowledge would be of obvious relevance for those interested in the dynamics of creativity, but it is seldom referred to in the creativity literature. Moreover, those who study human memory have published only sporadically on the topic of creativity (Campbell 1960; Stein 1989). As was the case with traditional work in categorization, we believe that studies on creative cognition can have important implications for traditional work in human memory, and vice versa.

Retrieval Versus Restructuring

Historically, there have been two schools of thought on the nature of memory mechanisms involved in problem solving. The stimulus-response school endorsed a trial-and-error, incremental approach to problem solving, citing studies of rats solving mazes and cats emerging from puzzle boxes (Thorndike 1898). The Gestalt school proposed that problems were solved through a process of insight. Once the insight was realized, the problem solver could quickly implement the solution. Early demonstrations of insight came from Kohler's (1927) work with chimpanzees and Wertheimer's (1959) studies on learning mathematical principles.

More recently, controversy has erupted over how insight problems are solved, with the "memory" position stating that ideas are retrieved incrementally as problem solving progresses (Weisberg and Alba 1981, 1982) and the "restructuring" position stating that insights are discontinuous, beyond awareness, and involve a rapid cognitive restructuring of the problem (Metcalfe 1986a, 1986b; Metcalfe and Wiebe 1987). This modern controversy centers on the observation and logical interpretation of both naturalistic and laboratory experiences. Are creative ideas realized in sudden flashes of insight, or are the putative insights simply misinterpretations of what are actually step-by-step retrieval processes?

Classic Reports of Insight

There are many anecdotal reports of insight in which scientists, philosophers, or mathematicians suddenly realized important solutions to problems after initial solution attempts had failed. Much significance has been attached to these sudden insights, not only because of their subsequent influence on human knowledge but because of the mysterious ways in which they seem to have occurred: precipitously, full blown, and originating beyond awareness.

Perhaps the most dramatic case was the insight achieved by Archimedes, the third-century B.C. philosopher, mathematician, and inventor. His relative, King Hiero of Syracuse, was concerned that a gold crown that he had commissioned had been alloyed with cheaper silver by an unscrupulous goldsmith. Knowing the densities of both gold and silver and able to find the weight of the crown, he had only to determine the crown's volume. Although there were known methods for computing the volumes of various regular solids, the crown was irregularly shaped, and its volume could be determined only by melting it down into a simpler form, a highly undesirable approach.

Initially thwarted in his attempts to solve the problem, Archimedes noticed the water he displaced when getting into a bath. Suddenly realizing that the problem could be solved using displacement, he leaped from his bath and ran back to his home without bothering to clothe himself, shouting "Eureka!"

Other well-known cases of sudden insights include Kekulé's realization that the benzene molecule was configured as a ring rather than a chain and the mathematician Poincaré's unanticipated discovery of an expression for Fuchsian functions, which dawned on him as he stepped onto a bus. A more recent example is the discovery of PCR (polymerase chain reaction), a powerful technique used for producing vast amounts of DNA from tiny samples. The idea for PCR reportedly flashed into the mind of biochemist Kary Mullis in 1983 during a midnight drive through the mountains of northern California. The insight was so clear and so surprising that Mullis pulled his car off the road to admire the idea.

Anecdotal accounts of sudden insight are sufficiently numerous and detailed to credit their existence. These testimonials can be quite discouraging, however, because the descriptions imply no method for producing insights; one must simply wait for divine inspiration. Furthermore, Archimedes, Kekulé, Poincaré, and Mullis were not necessarily great introspectionists, and their descriptions of their insights may not have accurately reflected the true underlying cognitive processes. As we have argued, the methods of creative cognition can help to demystify those processes and avoid reliance on purely introspective reports.

Early Laboratory Demonstrations
The Gestalt psychologists were particularly interested in insight. Kohler (1927), for example, placed chimpanzees in a large cage with a bunch of bananas hanging out of reach from the ceiling. After initially failing to reach the bananas using simple solutions (by jumping or throwing sticks), the chimps often seemed to give up. Suddenly some of the chimps would stack boxes under the bananas and climb atop the boxes to reach their goal. In another version of this task, chimpanzees had apparent insights about using sticks found in the cage as rakes, allowing them to reach bananas that were placed outside the cage. The suddenness of the solutions and the lack of problem-oriented behavior immediately prior to the solutions led Kohler to conclude that the chimpanzees were using insight rather than trial-and-error methods.

Reinterpretations of Insight

Weisberg and his colleagues have attempted to debunk some of the myths about creativity by recasting terms like *creative genius, divergent thinking,* and *insight* as popular misconceptions. In particular, Weisberg (1986) has attacked the Gestalt claims about the role that insight plays in problem solving. For example, he cites studies by Birch (1975) showing that chimpanzees with no prior relevant experience do not solve Kohler's rake problem, implying that successful performance on insight problems depends more on the retrieval of specific past experiences than on any special form of cognitive restructuring. A similar point—that many alleged instances of creative insight may be due instead simply to retrieving relevant information—has been made by Perkins (1981).

Weisberg and Alba (1981) extended the same line of reasoning to other types of insight problems. Challenging the view that such problems are initially not solved because subjects make inappropriate assumptions about the problems, they argued that if this view were correct, then simply informing subjects about the need to shed these assumptions should lead to prompt solutions. On the other hand, if retrieving prior experiences is what is important for solving these problems, then merely overcoming these assumptions would not necessarily yield the solutions.

To test this hypothesis, Weisberg and Alba had subjects perform the nine-dot problem. The task is to connect all nine dots, arranged in three rows of three dots each, with four straight lines without lifting the pen. The top two examples in figure 7.1 show failed solution attempts in which the lines are confined to an imaginary square created by the nine dots. According to Gestalt psychologists, subjects make the unwarranted assumption that the lines must be confined to this square, which prevents them from seeing the correct solution. Weisberg and Alba reasoned that telling the subjects that the correct solution required that they go outside the square should eliminate this assumption and pave the way for insight. They found, however, that this produced not insight but rather trial-and-error strategies; the subjects generated failed solutions that went outside the square, as shown in bottom left example in the figure. They concluded that solving these and other types of insight problems occurs only when problem-specific knowledge is drawn from memory.

Is it really the case that "insight" is simply a popular misconception? The question has been at the center of a number of recent debates in cognitive psychology (Dominowski 1981; Ellen 1982; Metcalfe 1986a, 1986b; Weisberg and Alba 1982). We next consider evidence that in-

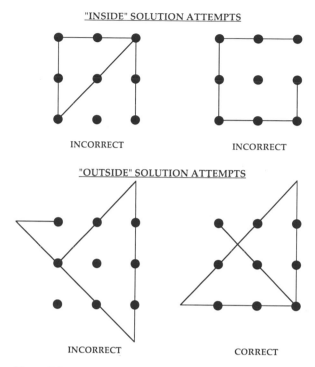

Figure 7.1
Incorrect solutions on the nine-dot problem that stay inside the perimeter of an imaginary square, an incorrect solution that goes outside the perimeter of the square, and the correct solution.

sight is, in fact, a useful concept that can play an important role in creative cognition.

The Catastrophic Nature of Insight
Metcalfe has taken up a position counter to the memory hypothesis, reporting a number of experiments that support the idea that problem solving can be insightful (Metcalfe 1986a, 1986b; Metcalfe and Wiebe 1987). Metcalfe reasoned that if solving insight problems relied heavily on the retrieval of prior knowledge, then subjects' predicted success on these problems should be similar to their predicted success on noninsight problems. On the other hand, if the solution of insight problems relies on a sudden, "catastrophic" restructuring process, then predictions of success for the two types of problems should show a very different pattern.

In one set of experiments, Metcalfe (1986a) tested predictions of success in the course of working on insight problems like the one shown in figure 7.2 and compared these predictions to those for success on answering trivia questions. Metcalfe found that the subjects accurately predicted success for the trivia questions but not the insight problems, which is consistent with the insight hypothesis but not the memory hypothesis.

In another set of experiments (Metcalfe 1986b), subjects gave "warmth" ratings, indicating how close they were to an impending solution, every ten seconds in the course of working on insight problems. Metcalfe found that these feelings of warmth did not rise until the last ten-second interval prior to the solution and were more likely to predict impending failures than impending successes. Again, awareness of impending success increased suddenly rather than incrementally.

In a third set of experiments, Metcalfe and Weibe (1987) compared warmth ratings for insight and noninsight (algebra) problems. Although the ratings rose incrementally prior to solutions of the algebra problems, there was again a sudden, catastrophic rise in warmth for the insight problems. Metcalfe and Weibe concluded that insight was a genuine phenomenon that could not be explained simply in terms of ordinary retrieval mechanisms.

Geneplore and the Memory Hypothesis
Even if one adheres to the idea that there is no such thing as insight, the untenable position that creative discoveries or solutions are simply retrieved from memory does not have to follow. Weisberg and Alba (1981), for example, differentiate their position from more traditional associationist views, stating that a problem can cue information in memory, which can then provide the basis for generating creative strategies for solving the problem.

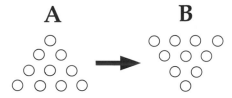

Figure 7.2
An insight problem used in studies on predicting eventual success. The task is to make pattern A change to pattern B by moving only three dots. (From Metcalfe 1986b.)

The Geneplore model is in essential agreement with this statement of the memory hypothesis, holding that information in memory can provide useful clues and critical information for solving a problem. This information can then provide a basis for generating interesting possibilities and exploring their implications. For example, many of the strategies that subjects employed in the creative invention studies in chapter 4 were no doubt inspired by initial associations to the features of their preinventive forms.

However, the Geneplore model is in disagreement with Weisberg's conclusions about the uselessness of the concept of insight. Insights may occur, for example, when novel properties emerge unexpectedly from combinations of elements drawn from memory, when retrieved information is transformed or modified, or when a coherence or systematic reclassification is discovered among pieces of information retrieved from memory. Similarly, the related concept of "fixation," which will be considered in the following sections and which has also been subject to criticism, can be described as occurring when material generated from memory diverts thinking away from ultimately useful solutions. Rather than throwing such concepts away, we believe that a reexamination of the concepts is a more useful approach.

Incubation, Fixation, and Recovery

Incubation refers to cases in which a problem is set aside temporarily after an initial impasse is reached. The problem can then be solved more easily when attention is returned to it, or a solution may suddenly burst into the problem solver's awareness even without intentionally returning to the problem.

Incubation has served as a useful metaphor for the sudden realization of ideas that people often report after having failed in their initial attempts to solve a problem. Unfortunately, the metaphor suggests that these insights arise as the result of "unconscious work," where the ideas are left to be passively discovered in a flash of awareness. There are, however, sensible alternatives to the unconscious work hypothesis (Perkins 1981).

An Alternative Approach to Incubation

Instead of relating the concept of incubation to the amount of work that is unconsciously devoted to a problem, consider the idea that incubation simply occurs whenever fixation dissipates. Thinking may be "stuck" when information searches continue to produce the same incorrect or inappropriate material, thus preventing retrieval of correct or appropriate material. The inappropriate information is then more likely to be retrieved with each successive attempt, making the situation worse. When one stops thinking about a problem, fixation decreases, resulting in a greater likelihood of retrieving the appropriate information.

Fixation is a very general phenomenon and can occur in a wide variety of cognitive domains, including output interference in retrieval (Rundus 1973), the tip-of-the-tongue phenomenon (Brown and McNeill 1966), the use of algorithms in problem solving (Luchins and Luchins 1959), and creative idea generation (Smith, Ward, and Schumacher 1991).

Fixation in Traditional Cognitive Tasks
Interference created by fixation, and recovery from that interference, have been examined by a number of memory researchers, including Briggs (1954), Barnes and Underwood (1959), Brown (1976), and Mensink and Raaijmakers (1988). In a typical task, two paired-associate lists are learned: an A-B list (for example, chair-lake, tree-gold), followed by an A-C list (chair-head, tree-book). As the A-C list is learned, the C response increases in accessibility while the competing B response decreases. Thinking of B as the correct target and C as the distractor, this situation results in a retrieval block, the mnemonic equivalent of fixation in idea generation. Over time, the B response regains accessibility, which represents recovery from fixation.

In the course of free recall, retrieval of already recalled information may thus prevent the retrieval of new unrecalled material. One explanation is that the retrieved items are incremented in strength and replaced within the current search set (Shiffrin 1970). Subsequent retrieval attempts are then biased toward re-retrieving already-recalled items, which leads to fixation. This account of output interference can explain inhibition of retrieval from semantic memory (Brown 1981), fan effects (Anderson 1983), and the counterintuitive, negative effects of part-set cuing (Slamecka 1968).

The tip-of-the-tongue (TOT) phenomenon has also been described as falling into the general category of fixation effects. When trying to recall a person's name, for example, retrieval of incorrect names may inhibit the retrieval of the correct name. A "cognitive diary" study by Reason and Lucas (1984) indicated that 53 percent of the reported naturally occurring TOT experiences were the result of an incorrect word or name coming to mind and blocking retrieval of the correct word or name. An experimental study by Jones and Langford (1987) found that negative priming using "blocking words" increased the occurrence of TOT states; this occurred when phonologically similar words were presented during the retrieval task. Similar findings of increased TOT levels resulting from blocking words have been reported by Jones (1989), Maylor (1990), and Smith (1991).

When fixation occurs during problem solving, the interfering agent is often an inappropriate approach or solution. Luchins and Luchins (1959) found that an algorithm discovered early in problem-solving trials could inhibit performance on later trials, when the algorithm was no longer appropriate. Smith and Blankenship's (1989) subjects performed more poorly on picture-word problems (rebuses) when those problems were accompanied by misleading hints that diverted thinking away from the correct answers. Examples of these problems and their solutions are shown in figure 7.3 and table 7.1. In a related study, performance on the Remote Associates Test was disrupted by presenting misleading clues or by having subjects memorize the clues in advance (Smith and Blankenship 1991). Table 7.2 presents example problems and solutions that were used in this study. These findings point to the importance of overcoming fixation in discovering new solutions to a problem.

Fixation in Creative Idea Generation
In attacking supposed myths about creativity, Weisberg (1986) also challenged the idea that fixation inhibits problem solving, claiming that most real life problems do not involve the kinds of hidden tricks that fixation studies often employ. However, it is difficult to imagine that engineering designers at the National Aeronautics and Space

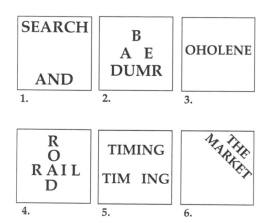

Figure 7.3
Examples of rebus problems in studies on fixation in which misleading clues were given. The misleading clues and solutions for these problems are listed in table 7.1. (From Smith and Blankenship 1989.)

Table 7.1
Clues and Solutions to Rebuses, figure 7.3

Misleading Clues	Correct Solutions
1. Destroy	Search high and low
2. Dumb bear	Bermuda triangle
3. Chemical	Hole in one
4. Tracks	Railroad crossing
5. Late	Split-second timing
6. Stock	Corner the market

Table 7.2
Examples of Problems, Misleading Clues, and Solutions for the Remote
Associates Test

Problem			Solution
TYPE style	GHOST goblin	STORY tale	writer
WHEEL tire	ELECTRIC cord	HIGH low	chair
CAT nap	SLEEP night	BOARD wood	walk
SHIP ocean	OUTER inner	CRAWL floor	space
FAMILY mother	APPLE pie	HOUSE home	tree
WORM bug	SCOTCH whiskey	RED green	tape
ARM leg	COAL furnace	PEACH pear	pit

Source: Smith and Blankenship (1991).
Note: Test items are shown in uppercase, misleading clues are shown
beneath each item in lowercase, and solutions are shown to the right of the
problems.

Administration, federal investigators unraveling a case, or medical researchers working to cure or prevent an unknown disease would agree with Weisberg's assurances that hidden tricks and pitfalls are nothing to worry about. Moreover, not all creative problem-solving tasks that have been used in these studies are tricky.

Smith, Ward, and Schumacher (1991) tested the effects of providing fixating examples on idea generation in a creative production task in which there was not a specific, hidden solution. This task was a variant of the exemplar generation task discussed in chapter 6. Subjects generated designs for as many different toys or imaginary creatures as they could in twenty minutes. Examples of designs were shown to half the subjects in advance; it was hypothesized that these subjects' designs would be more likely to contain the specific attributes depicted in the examples, assuming that the examples served to fixate creative generation. In this "fixation" condition, three designs were shown to each subject that had three attributes in common. Each example toy had a ball as part of the design, involved a high level of physical activity, and used electronic devices. Each example creature had four legs, antennae, and a tail. Subjects were given a minute to view the examples, but they were never told to make their own creatures and toys like the examples. In the control condition, the task was identical except that the subjects were never shown any examples.

The results are summarized in table 7.3. Although the two groups generated approximately the same average number of designs, subjects in the group that had seen the examples were far more likely to generate ideas that contained the features of the examples. The examples, therefore, had a fixating effect in the sense that they constrained the range of ideas that were produced by the subjects who had viewed them. A sample creature shown to subjects in the fixation condition and examples of subjects' creations in the fixation and control conditions are shown in figures 7.4 and 7.5, respectively.

It is particularly revealing to examine some of the toys that were generated in these tasks. Figure 7.6 presents a toy that was shown to subjects in the fixation condition. This was "tether tennis", a game in which a person bounces the ball between the two rackets, and a counter records electronically the number of successful hits. One subject who viewed this fixating example conceived of the idea of an "auto pitcher," in which a person can practice hitting a baseball that is electronically guided along a particular path (figure 7.7). All three of the major features depicted in the fixating example—used electronics, included a ball, and involved a high degree of physical activity—were incorporated in this design. In contrast is the toy shown in figure 7.8, "water jets," created by a subject who did not view any of the fixating

Table 7.3
Percentages of Generated Ideas Containing Features of Previous Examples

| | Condition | |
Feature	Fixation	Control
Creatures		
Antennae	17	5
Tail	37	15
Four legs	19	14
Toys		
Ball	31	11
Physical activity	39	23
Electronic device	35	30

Source: Smith, Ward, and Schumacher (1991).
Note: Subjects were shown example items in the fixation condition, such as those in figures 7.4 and 7.6, but not in the control condition.

EXAMPLE

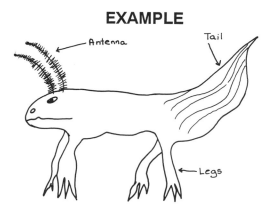

Figure 7.4
An imaginary creature shown to subjects in studies on fixation in creative idea generation. All example creatures had four legs, a tail, and antennae. (From Smith, Ward, and Schumacher 1991.)

FIXATED   **NON-FIXATED**

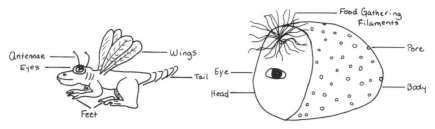

Figure 7.5
Imaginary creatures that subjects generated after viewing the creature shown in figure
7.4 (left), and in the control condition (right), in which no examples were shown. (From
Smith, Ward, and Schumacher 1991.)

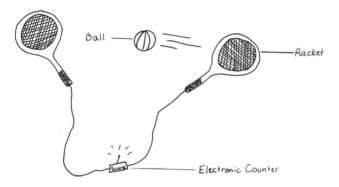

Figure 7.6
A novel toy shown to subjects in studies on fixation in creative idea generation. All
example toys contained electronic devices, used a ball, and involved a high degree of
physical activity. In this toy, tether tennis, a person bounces the ball between the rackets,
and the number of successful hits is automatically recorded by an electronic counter.
(From Smith, Ward, and Schumacher 1991.)

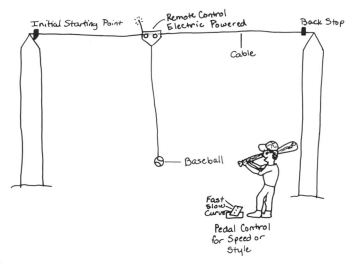

Figure 7.7
A toy generated by a subject after viewing the toy shown in figure 7.6. This toy, called an "auto pitcher," allows one to practice hitting a baseball, which is guided electronically along a cable. The design contains all three of the major features contained in the previous example. (From Smith, Ward, and Schumacher 1991.)

examples. The toy is attached to a faucet, and as water goes up the pipe, toy airplanes are launched at regular intervals. This design bears very little resemblance to that shown in figure 7.6.

It is possible that demand characteristics led subjects to believe that their creations should conform to these examples. To test this possibility, Smith et al. asked one group of subjects to make their designs as different as possible from the examples and another group to conform closely to the examples. Although fixation increased when subjects were asked to conform, it was not reduced when subjects were explicitly told to generate designs different from the examples. Therefore, demand characteristics could not have been responsible for the previous fixation effects.

Would the same constraining effects be found for a more realistic engineering design task? Jansson and Smith (1991) tested what they referred to as *design fixation* in college engineering students. The subjects had an hour to generate as many varied designs as possible for a given problem; each design was drawn, verbally labeled, and explained. In the fixation condition, the subjects were shown an example design that was relevant to their problem. One problem had students generate designs for a bicycle rack, a second required ideas

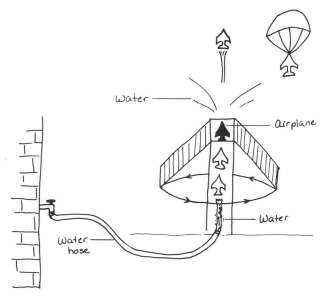

Figure 7.8
A toy generated by a subject who was not shown any example toys. The toy is called "water jets"; one hooks the hose to a faucet, and toy airplanes are launched at regular intervals. This design bears very little resemblance to that shown in figure 7.6. (From Smith, Ward, and Schumacher 1991.)

for a measuring cup for blind people, and a third required designs for a disposable spillproof coffee cup. No examples were shown to a control group.

The results of the experiment were similar to the previous results. Although the control and fixation groups generated an equal number of designs, subjects in the fixation group generated a narrower range of ideas, which displayed a close adherence to the sample designs they had viewed (table 7.4). For example, only 6 percent of the control subjects designed bike racks with suction cups, but the fixation subjects, who had seen an example with suction cups, generated 54 percent of their designs with suction cups. Additional measures showed that the designs of the control subjects were both more original and more flexible than those of the fixation subjects.

Would the subjects' designs also show fixation effects with regard to features that were missing in the examples? Engineering students were given a sample measuring cup for the blind that lacked two important features: an overflow device and a way of making infinitely

Table 7.4
Percentages of Designs Containing Features of Previous Examples

	Condition	
Feature	Fixation	Control
Bicycle rack		
Top mounted	71	59
Suction cups	54	6
Tire railways	48	15
Measuring cup for the blind		
Noninfinitely variable	78	57
No overflow device	54	17
Disposable spillproof cup		
Mouthpiece	39	10
Straw	17	1
Leaky design	39	30

Source: Jansson and Smith (1991).
Note: Subjects were shown example designs in the fixation condition but not in the control condition.

variable measurements. Far more designs generated by the fixation group contained these flaws, as compared with the control group.

In a related experiment, subjects were explicitly told not to incorporate straws or mouthpieces in their designs for a disposable spillproof cup. Nonetheless, subjects who had seen examples with these features were far more likely than control subjects to generate designs with straws and mouthpieces. This finding further addressed the possible problem of demand characteristics in these studies.

Perhaps the limited experience of engineering design students made them more susceptible than professional engineers to design fixation. Jansson and Smith (1991) explored this possibility by testing a group of professional engineering designers from the structural design department of a major corporation. The problem was to design an apparatus that could take samples from and measure speed and pressure in various places in a human intestine with minimum discomfort to the patient. Professionals in the fixation group were far more likely than those in the control group to conform to the sample design, even though it contained a number of detrimental features.

These findings appear to contradict Weisberg's (1986) contention that fixation interferes with creative problem solving only in trick situations. In these engineering design problems, the tasks were well defined, and many solutions were possible, yet fixation still occurred.

A Positive Use of Forgetting
Why is this maladaptive phenomenon of fixation so ubiquitous? One possibility is that it is often advantageous to adhere to retrieval strategies that have worked successfully in the past. When those strategies become inappropriate, however, it is time to forget them.

The word *forget* usually has a negative connotation, indicating that some needed or important information has been lost. People who study memory are often concerned primarily with memory enhancement, working to reduce the amount of forgetting. Subjects in memory experiments are generally regarded as performing better the more they remember.

In cases where recalling information leads to fixation, however, there will be decrements in performance as memory impedes thinking. The solution is to allow the information to be forgotten, by displacement, interference, decay, repression, or other related processes. This enables more useful information to become accessible. This increase in accessibility can serve as a memory mechanism for recovery, reminiscence in episodic recall, and, most important for our discussion, incubation.

Consider the phenomenon of reminiscence—the finding that additional items from a memory list are recalled as time passes. Although few explanations have been offered for why reminiscence occurs, one reasonable account was proposed by Roediger and Thorpe (1978). Given that output interference builds up as more items are initially recalled, reminiscence may result from a release from output interference over time. It then becomes more likely that new items in memory will be sampled. In this sense, reminiscence occurs because output interference is "forgotten."

Evidence in support of this theory was provided by Smith and Vela (1991). Subjects were shown a list of fifty pictures of common objects and were given two successive recall tests without any intervening exposure to the original list. Of interest was the amount of reminiscence (as measured by the number of items recalled on the retest that were not recalled on the first test) as a function of the incubation interval, defined as the time between the two recall tests. Smith and Vela reasoned that the output interference that built up during the first test would have more time to dissipate if the incubation interval was increased. This would result in new types of memory searches and a greater chance of recalling items not retrieved in the initial search. In agreement with this prediction, Smith and Vela found greater reminiscence on a delayed retest than an immediate retest. This incubated reminiscence effect was concentrated in the first minute or two of the retest.

To relate incubation in problem solving to that in reminiscence, Smith and Blankenship (1989, 1991) treated problem-solving tasks as analogous to recall tests in traditional reminiscence studies. They reasoned that fixation, like output interference, should occur on the initial test but should then be dissipated following an incubation interval. In other words, insight into the solution should be more likely once the problem has been put aside and initially misleading information has become less accessible. In several experiments, they found evidence for incubation effects in problem solving, with subjects having greater success at completing unsolved problems if the retest was delayed. Although incubation is popularly referred to in introductory psychology textbooks, few experiments found replicated incubation effects prior to the Smith and Blankenship studies (Olton 1979).

The "forgetting" approach to fixation and incubation is similar to approaches that have been recommended by others (Anderson 1975; Posner 1973; Woodworth and Schlosberg 1954). Although this approach is supported by the studies considered in this section, much remains to be investigated. For instance, Bjork (1989) has advanced a theory concerned with the adaptive significance of retrieval failure and retrieval inhibition. He maintains that these are adaptive mechanisms, useful for losing out-of-date information. We propose that creative cognition should be concerned with extending the idea of the adaptive significance of forgetting to include fixation and related impediments to creative retrieval, problem solving, and design.

Spreading Activation as a Mechanism for Incubation

Another approach to studying memory mechanisms in incubation was suggested by Yaniv and Meyer (1987); they were concerned with the question of how a solution or an approach to a solution can increase in accessibility over time before the critical information reaches awareness. In attempting to answer this question, they invoked the notion of spreading activation, a popular theoretical construct based on the common finding that knowledge is more accessible if it has been used (or retrieved) recently and that the activation then spreads to other forms of knowledge closely related to it. In this way, information critical to a solution may receive activation from related material, even if the critical information has not been consciously retrieved.

To test the notion that activation could spread after an initial failed retrieval attempt, Yaniv and Meyer presented subjects with definitions of rare words, asking them to retrieve the words from memory. This task is known to produce tip-of-the-tongue experiences. They hypothesized that subjective reports of feelings of knowing might indicate that a word was activated in memory and could be recognized, even if it was not yet successfully retrieved. In support of this prediction, Yaniv and Meyer found that unrecalled words for which higher feelings of knowing had been given were better recognized than those for which lower ratings had been given, suggesting that spreading activation might serve as an underlying memory mechanism in incubation.

Connor, Balota, and Neely (1990), however, suggested an alternative explanation of these results. They hypothesized that general familiarity with a topic might affect the subject's feeling-of-knowing ratings for words in that topic area. For example, a subject who is knowledgeable about music might give a high feeling-of-knowing rating for the definition of an unusual musical term, which the subject would then be more likely to recognize in any event. To test this idea, after first replicating Yaniv and Meyer's results, Connor, Balota, and Neely then reversed the order of events in the basic procedure. The subjects were first given the word recognition task and a week later received the rare word definitions task. Spreading activation from the definitions, therefore, could not affect word recognition. Nonetheless, the results again showed a relation between feeling-of-knowing judgments and word recognition, contradicting the spreading activation interpretation. Thus, the precise role that spreading activation might play in incubation remains to be determined.

Contextual Cues and the Use of Analogy

Analogies retrieved from memory can also be useful in solving problems. The question of how analogical reasoning maps relations from one domain to another will be taken up in chapter 8. Here we consider the more basic question of how one selects a particular analogy to assist the discovery of creative solutions.

Spontaneous Analogical Transfer

In a classic study, Duncker (1945) had subjects read a story about a general who sent contingents of his army simultaneously down converging roads to capture a fortress. He then posed the following problem: You have a patient who has an inoperable stomach tumor. There are some rays that, at sufficient intensity, destroy organic tissue. How can you free the patient of the tumor without destroying the healthy tissue surrounding it? The subjects who solved the problem used analogical transfer; they related the story of converging attacks on the fortress to the idea that low-level rays could converge on the tumor from many different directions at once. This paradigm has since been used as the prototype for studying analogical transfer in many different situations (Gick and Holyoak 1980; Perfetto, Bransford, and Franks 1983).

Although it is important to know that one can use certain analogies to solve a problem, it is in fact very unlikely that one will spontaneously recall and use a particular analogy, without hints or directions from the experimenter. Gick and Holyoak (1980) found that only 30 percent of the subjects used the converging rays strategy after reading the military story without hints, whereas hinting to the subjects to use the story increased discovery of the converging rays solution to 70 percent.

Most explanations for this low rate of spontaneous analogical transfer have centered around the idea that novices in a knowledge domain tend to represent analogies according to surface features such as perceptual characteristics, making appropriate analogical transfer difficult (Novick 1988). Experts, on the other hand, include a deeper, more meaningful representation of the problem and are therefore more able to transfer an appropriate analogy.

Novick (1988) listed the primary cognitive processes that underlie analogical transfer as problem representation, search and retrieval, mapping, and procedure adaptation. The present discussion will focus on search and retrieval processes; the other processes are considered in chapter 8. Two well-known factors that influence memory retrieval are time and context; memory searches are most likely to access recent and contextually similar material. Yet simple recency does not appear to induce spontaneous analogical transfer, as shown by studies in which analogies are presented just prior to the critical transfer problems (Gick and Holyoak 1980; Perfetto, Bransford, and Franks 1983). Therefore, our attention will focus on contextual factors that may influence the search for and retrieval of analogies.

Context-Dependent Memory
One of the oldest and best-known memory principles is that greater similarity between learning and test conditions will lead to better memory (McGeoch and Irion 1952). The extent to which successful remembering depends on this similarity reflects the context dependence of the memory. Many types of contextual conditions have been found to affect memory, among them physical surroundings or background music (Smith 1979, 1985, 1988), verbal cues (Tulving and Thomson 1973), and mood and drug states (Eich 1980). In addition, interest has grown recently in what is called transfer-appropriate processing, the principle that the greater the overlap is between the

cognitive operations performed during learning and recall the better one's memory will be (Blaxton 1989).

One relevant finding is that indirect measures of memory, in which memories are tested without explicitly referring to the targets (Richardson-Klavehn and Bjork 1988; Schacter 1987), appear to be reliably influenced by incidental manipulations of the memory context (Smith, Vela, and Heath 1990). For example, a subject who hears "bair" is likely to think of the high-frequency spelling of the homophone *bear*. However, if one has recently read the word *bare*, then the homophone is more likely to be interpreted as *bare*, the low-frequency spelling. Smith, Vela, and Heath (1990) found that this effect was stronger for subjects whose initial learning context was reinstated than for those tested in a different context. Context-dependent memory effects have also been found using other indirect memory measures (Vela 1991).

Contextual Cues and Analogical Transfer
If we regard the amount of analogical transfer as another indirect memory measure, then we might expect such transfer to also show a context-dependent pattern. Spencer and Weisberg (1986) gave subjects analogies to read in one context, followed by Duncker's radiation problem, which was presented in either the same context or a different one. Although all subjects could use the analogies in solving the problem when they were explicitly directed to do so, spontaneous analogical transfer was context dependent. Those tested in the context in which the analogy had been studied were more likely than those tested in an altered context to use the analogy spontaneously to solve the problem.

A study reported by Needham and Begg (1991) tested the importance of transfer-appropriate processing on spontaneous analogical transfer. Analogies to the test problems were presented in either problem-oriented or memory-oriented ways. Memory-oriented subjects were told to study the passages in preparation for a subsequent recall test, whereas problem-oriented subjects were asked to explain the solutions used in the analogies. Needham and Begg found that more target problems were solved by subjects in the problem-oriented condition, although memory-oriented subjects performed better on a recall test. Thus, analogical transfer is enhanced when the same types of cognitive processes are activated during initial exposure to an analogy and the subsequent presentation of a problem.

Although considerable research is still needed, it appears that spontaneous analogical transfer can be cued by contextual factors. As Spencer and Weisberg (1986) point out, however, the fact that creative discoveries often use analogies from remote domains leaves us with an enigma: How are remote analogies noticed in the first place? Clearly, this is an important question for future studies on creative cognition.

Summary

Theoretical Implications

Memory obviously plays an important role in creative cognition. We began by considering the topic of insight and reviewed studies showing that success in solving insight problems depends on both the retrieval of prior knowledge related to the problem and a sudden, unanticipated restructuring of the problem. This restructuring indicates that memory mechanisms that are triggered in insight problems interact with those that are involved in exploring deeper structural relations and implications. Thus, whereas the previous chapter showed that creative cognition is highly structured, reflecting a person's knowledge and beliefs, these findings suggest that in some cases the initially retrieved structures must be modified or transformed, resulting in new, unexpected structures.

In terms of the Geneplore model, the retrieval of relevant knowledge relates to the generative stage, whereas the rapid cognitive restructuring that signals insight occurs during the exploratory stage. Thus, whereas memory can serve to structure initial creations, retrieval alone is not enough. New kinds of structures may need to be considered and then evaluated with respect to the requirements of the problem. This would normally involve repeated cycles of generating preinventive structures and evaluating their suitability. Eventually a structure could be discovered that provides the solution.

In view of these considerations, one might distinguish between two general types of insight: a global restructuring of a situation or problem, as in classical insight problems, or a new interpretation of an already-existing but ambiguous structure, as was the case in the creative invention and conceptualization tasks that were considered in chapters 4 and 5. New insights could arise from either discovering a new preinventive structure that affords a necessary interpretation or finding a new interpretation for a given preinventive structure.

Fixation can often impede creative cognition, as was shown in studies on interference, tip-of-the-tongue states, problem solving, and creative generation. In the Geneplore model, we regard fixation as relevant to both the generative and exploratory stages. One could end up generating items that contain useless or even detrimental features, as was shown particularly by studies on design fixation. Or fixation could operate in restricting the exploratory strategies that one might employ, an issue that we take up in chapter 8.

In chapter 3, we found that providing examples to subjects in experiments on generating creative patterns did not affect their performance. This might seem to contradict the findings on design fixation, which showed that features contained in the examples were often incorporated into a person's creations even when the person was explicitly instructed not to do so. However, in these earlier tasks, the parts that subjects could use in their creations were highly restricted, whereas in studies on design fixation, the subjects were free to use any parts or features they wished. What these studies show, in effect, is that although providing examples does not necessarily inspire one to be more or less creative, it can influence the content of the resulting products.

This chapter also considered the general topic of incubation. Cognitive mechanisms that possibly underlie incubation include spreading activation and recovery from interference. Although evidence that spreading activation leads to incubation is inconclusive, the recovery hypothesis is supported by studies on problem solving and reminiscence. These studies have implications not just for creative cognition but for traditional work on interference and memory retrieval as well.

Analogical transfer can yield new insights and can help one to solve problems, but it tends not to occur spontaneously and is context dependent. Context may also influence other types of generative and exploratory processes that contribute to creative cognition. For example, as we showed in chapter 4, exploring the possible functions of a preinventive form was often assisted by imagining shifts in context in which the object might be used. This is not to imply that creative thinking is necessarily domain specific; rather, such findings imply that the efficiency with which creative processes might be transferred from one situation to another may depend on the similarity between the situations.

Basic research in creative cognition is important not only because it can help to clarify the nature of creativity, in terms of specific cognitive structures and processes, but also because the findings can contribute back to traditional cognitive areas. For example, such studies could call attention to new ways in which insight and fixation might bear on standard memory and problem-solving tasks.

Practical Implications
People often become stuck when trying to solve a problem or come up with a new idea. The findings presented in this chapter offer some practical suggestions for how to overcome these mental blocks. For

example, one could deliberately engage in activities that interfere with or result in the decay of fixation. If one were trying to design a new video game, one might intentionally not think of other video games and concentrate on some other activity prior to engaging in the creative process. The classic example of coming up with great ideas while taking a shower may simply reflect the importance of releasing oneself from fixated retrieval processes.

Reinstating a creative context can also help. For example, one might try working on a problem in the same place where one had had previous creative insights in the past. Another technique is to pick a particular place that is isolated from everyday routines and to go there for the expressed purpose of generating creative ideas. These techniques would work to the extent that creative cognitive processes are reactivated in those same contexts.

On the other hand, fixation might become associated with certain contexts, in which case one might want to take one's ideas away from that context. Indeed, many of the anecdotal accounts of insightful discovery refer to cases in which the person was preoccupied with a problem and was thus thinking about it in many different situations. When one's immediate environment is stifling or uninspiring, a sudden shift in context might lead to new, creative insights.

There are also creative strategies for recalling lost information. For example, if you were trying to remember where you had misplaced a set of keys, you might search your memory to recall less obvious places, where you would not have noticed having left them. A related strategy concerns remembering places where you deliberately hid something. Winograd and Soloway (1986) found that when people hide things, they tend to select unusual locations, believing that these would be easy to remember. Such locations in fact tend to be more difficult to retrieve from memory. Thus, when trying to find something one has hidden, one might focus on thinking of unusual locations as opposed to retrieving the more obvious, easily recalled locations.

8

Creative Strategies for Problem Solving

Creative Reasoning and Exploration

In contrast to memory, a topic seldom linked to creativity, problem solving has often been the focus of previous cognitive approaches to creative thinking. In this chapter, we consider various types of creative strategies for problem solving. In view of the enormous literature on this subject, our considerations will be somewhat selective, and we concentrate on topics that are most relevant to creative cognition. In particular, we consider induction, the use of algorithms and heuristics, analogical mapping, metacognition, the use of mental models, suspension of expertise, and divergent thinking. We also address some of the additional exploratory processes specified in the Geneplore model, such as hypothesis testing and searching for limitations.

Types of Problems

Duncker (1945) defined a problem as a situation in which one has a goal but does not know how to reach it. As simple as this definition sounds, there is considerable ambiguity about what actually constitutes a problem. For example, even a simple sum can be difficult for a child who is just learning to do math, whereas for an adult, this involves little more than direct retrieval of the relevant information from memory. Thus, what is a problem for some may not be for others. This points to the importance of considering the types of cognitive processes that need to be employed in any given problem-solving situation.

Even if one has knowledge of the solution, a task can still constitute a problem if the relevant knowledge is temporarily inaccessible. Similarly the status of a problem may fluctuate; it may begin as a problem, become a nonproblem for a short while after it is initially solved, and then become a problem again if the task is reintroduced later. Even simple remembering can be ambiguous in terms of whether it constitutes a problem. For example, recalling one's activities on some particular date could be considered a problem if it involves generating contextual landmarks and zeroing in on the memory, whereas the activities could be remembered directly and automatically if the date were important to the individual. Thus, whether a task creates a problem depends not only on one's prior experience but also on the knowledge and strategies needed when the task is undertaken.

Attempts to specify whether something constitutes a "problem" in traditional problem solving studies, without considering the underlying cognitive processes, may be futile. Instead, one needs to examine the subject's background knowledge, how he or she represents the problem, and the cognitive strategies used to explore possible solutions. In creative cognition, we emphasize the importance of trying to identify the cognitive processes and structures that contribute to creative problem solving, as opposed to merely focusing on the nature or features of the problem itself.

Well-Defined Versus Ill-Defined Problems
According to Reitman (1965), a problem is classified as well defined if a starting state, a goal state, and a set of processes or operations that may be used to get from start to goal are completely specified. A multiplication problem, for example, is typically considered to be well defined because it meets each of these criteria.

Ill-defined problems, on the other hand, have no clearly specified goal state because there may be more than one satisfactory solution. In such problems, the cognitive operations needed to reach a goal state cannot be unambiguously specified, not only because there are many potential solutions but also because there may be more than one means for reaching a solution. Examples of well-defined and ill-defined problems are shown in Table 8.1. Creative problem-solving strategies are more relevant to ill-defined problems.

Table 8.1
Examples of Well-Defined and Ill-Defined Problems

Well-defined problems
    What is the sum of the internal angles in an octagon?
    What is the molecular weight of carbon dioxide?
    If some Morlans are Vaculins and all Vaculins are Rittlefins, then are some
        Morlans Rittlefins?

Ill-defined problems
    How can recycling be improved?
    What would cars of the future look like?
    How can creativity be enhanced?

Consider the problem of how recycling can be improved. Clearly there are no commonly agreed upon methods for solving this problem. It could be addressed from the perspective of what a person could do, what businesses could do, what a local city government could do, or what an entire country could do. The possible solutions might focus on how to make recycling more efficient, more convenient, more economical, or more widespread. Various types of creative strategies and approaches, including some of the exploratory processes described in the Geneplore model, could be used to create solutions for such ill-defined problems.

Insight Problems
In chapter 7, we considered several examples of traditional insight problems. In one sense, these problems are well defined: the form that the solution must take can be specified exactly. In another sense, however, these problems are ill defined: the method for arriving at the solution is often unclear, requiring a creative approach.

Such problems often lead to a sudden restructuring on the part of the problem solver, resulting in the discovery of a creative solution. However, it should be evident that sudden insight is not always necessary for solving these problems; sometimes one can draw on previous experience to discover a direct, immediate solution. Thus, whether a particular problem requires insight may depend on the type of knowledge or strategies applied to the problem.

Additional examples of traditional insight problems are presented in figure 8.1. Whether these problems actually involve insight depends on how the problem is initially represented and how the search for a solution proceeds. Typically, insightful discovery will result if the problem has to be restructured or if unusual approaches to the solution need to be considered. These can often be triggered by various hints, such as those presented in figure 8.2. However, the problems could also be solved without insight if the person had sufficient experience in solving related types of problems and recognized the connection between them (Perkins 1981; Weisberg 1986). This emphasizes that the focus of creative cognition should be on identifying the cognitive processes underlying attempts to solve a problem rather than on identifying characteristic features of the problem.

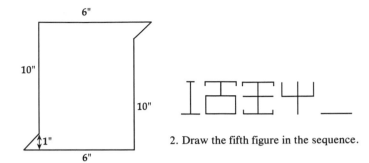

2. Draw the fifth figure in the sequence.

1. Determine the area of the figure.

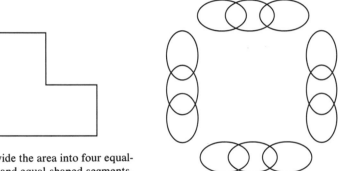

3. Divide the area into four equal-sized and equal-shaped segments.

4. Connect all the links in the chain by opening and closing only three links.

Figure 8.1
Four classic insight problems.

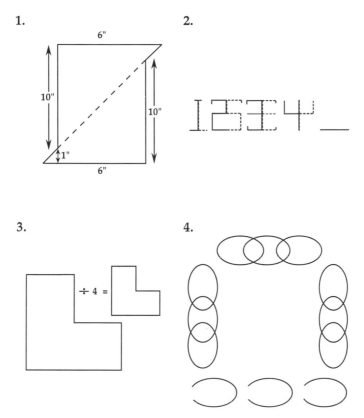

Figure 8.2
Hints for the insight problems shown in figure 8.1.

General Problem-Solving Strategies

Algorithms and Heuristics
Algorithms are step-by-step methods or formulas that essentially guarantee a correct solution of the problem. Examples are arithmetic rules, mathematical formulas, and production systems that mechanically produce a solution using a set of prescribed operations. *Heuristics* are general rules of thumb that provide useful shortcuts for solving problems. Experts at solving anagrams, for example, know what letter combinations and positions are most likely to produce a solution.

As an illustration, try to solve each of the anagrams shown in figure 8.3. The first anagram can be trivially solved by using the following algorithm: Rearrange the letters, generating every possible combination of the letters, and then check each letter string against a dictionary

1. EHT   2. REARPOOT   3. NEW DOOR

Rearrange the letters to make *one word* using
all of the original letters.

Figure 8.3
Examples of anagrams.

to see if it corresponds to a word. Although the second anagram can be solved with exactly the same algorithm, the number of possible letter strings makes such an approach highly impractical. In such cases, one tends to rely on heuristics to explore potential solutions. For example, it is likely that you would not have considered letter strings such as RRPTOOEA or AEOOPRRT because they contain highly unlikely letter combinations. Using various heuristics, such as knowing that words often end in "er" or "or," the solution can be discovered within a reasonable length of time.

But there is more to problem solving than simply applying algorithms and heuristics. The third anagram requires a novel approach—a creative solution. Once seen, the solution seems quite obvious, especially because it is underlined in the instructions. This demonstration shows the advantages and disadvantages of using known approaches to solving problems. Algorithms are simple and reliable. Heuristics are useful because of their relative efficiency. There are times, however, when established approaches will not suffice, and a novel, creative approach is necessary.

Another problem with relying on heuristics is that there are many cases where expert knowledge is applied inappropriately and thus interferes with successful problem solving. In the previous chapter, we considered instances where this occurred in the context of generating creative ideas and designs. It can also occur when one has to make critical judgments and evaluations.

One example of this type of heuristic is the *availability heuristic* (Tversky and Kahneman 1973). This refers to the rule that the more quickly and easily something comes to mind, the more frequent or probable it is likely to be. For example, one might judge dogs to be more common house pets than birds if instances of pet dogs are more easily recalled. The availability heuristic is generally useful because actual frequency typically does correlate with availability (Hintzman 1969). However, this is not always true. For example, when an examination is returned, students are more likely to notice cases in which they changed correct answers to incorrect ones than the reverse, although both changes are equally likely. Thus, in spite of considerable evidence to the contrary (Benjamin and Shallenberger 1985), most students believe that changing a test answer before handing it in is more likely to result in an error.

Because heuristics are typical rules of thumb, creative strategies for problem solving often require a suspension of one's expertise. For example, familiarity with dot-to-dot puzzles can implicitly suggest to those trying to solve the nine-dot problem (figure 7.1) that a correct solution would require that each segment must begin and end on a dot, which is not the case. Similarly, an expert dancer must suspend his or her expertise if he or she is portraying an ungraceful character in a ballet. However, even if experts are aware of the need for creative strategies that go beyond the heuristics they normally employ, there is still the problem of knowing when applying expertise is counter-productive and creative thinking is necessary. Thus, it is important not only to have expertise in a domain but also to be sensitive to situations that demand suspension of that expertise.

Induction

Holland et al. (1986) define *induction* as "all inferential processes that expand knowledge in the face of uncertainty" (p. 1). This definition extends beyond traditional concept learning, which focuses more on the determination of rules that encompass a given set of exemplars, and includes the use of mental models and analogical reasoning, both of which apply existing knowledge to novel uses in a target domain. Because induction involves systematic methods for discovering new knowledge, we view it as another general strategy for creative problem solving.

Some cognitive scientists have taken a computational approach to induction, proposing sets of rules to generate new ideas and solutions to problems (Newell, Shaw, and Simon 1962; Langley and Jones 1988; Schank 1988b). Such approaches may represent the ultimate in terms of demystifying creativity because all knowledge, rules, and opera-tions are completely specified in computational terms.

One computational model uses a program called BACON to dis-cover scientific laws from a set of observations (Langley et al. 1987). This program notices invariants, or characteristics of situations that tend to reoccur, and uses them to generate new rules. Kaplan and Simon (1990) found that this program could also be used for solving insight problems. Further support for the model was found by Qin and Simon (1990), who gave subjects data taken from observations about plane-tary orbits and asked them to find laws that summarized the data.

Several of the subjects were able to induce Kepler's laws by applying a similar heuristic of seeking out invariants.

In spite of these successes, other studies have shown that people often make fundamental errors during inductive reasoning. One such error is *confirmation bias*, a tendency to try to validate a hypothesis by finding confirming evidence rather than attempting to reject the hypothesis by finding disconfirming evidence. Confirmation bias has been demonstrated with a number of problems, such as the "2-4-6" problem, which requires that one determine the rule that generated the number sequence (Wason and Johnson-Laird 1972). Subjects given this task typically seek out confirming instances, supporting rules such as "any three even numbers increasing by two." Although the subjects are told to announce the rule only after they are sure they know what it is, few alternative hypotheses are considered, (such as "any three numbers increasing by two" or "any three numbers that sum to twelve"), and few of the subjects attempt to disconfirm their hypotheses. This finding is consistent with the common failure to recognize valid proofs and disproofs in conditional reasoning tasks (Johnson-Laird and Wason 1977).

These errors in inductive reasoning point to the importance of systematic and critical hypothesis testing in creative cognition. One needs to test carefully hypotheses that might relate to preinventive structures, so that the creative concepts that emerge are not self-deceiving. One can be creative in confirming one's biases, but this is neither a healthy nor a practical form of creativity. By deliberately seeking out disconfirming evidence in testing hypotheses, one reduces the likelihood of making these types of fallacies.

Related to this is the importance of searching for limitations, another exploratory process in the Geneplore model. Just as one can discover new conceptual interpretations, one can also discover limits on the kinds of possible interpretations. When exploring possible uses of a preinventive form, for example, it is often more important to know what will not work and why. Certain properties of the forms might not lend themselves to specific kinds of applications or inferences.

To return to the problem of how recycling could be improved, one might consider the kinds of solutions that would not work as a way of gaining insight into the possible solutions that would. Establishing a greater number of recycling centers, for example, and encouraging people to use them might have the limitation that people would still have to sort out the items to be recycled. It might be better simply to collect the items and hire others to do the sorting.

Searching for limitations is related to the idea of considering extreme possibilities in problem solving (Levine 1987). For example, consider the following problem: A 150-foot rope is hung between two flagpoles that are each 100 feet off the ground. At its lowest point, the rope is 25 feet off the ground. How far apart are the flagpoles? The solution to this problem can be quickly seen by considering the two extreme cases: that the flagpoles are as far apart as possible or are as close together as possible.

Using Mental Images
Another general strategy for solving problems is to seek out new relations by representing or restructuring the problem in the form of mental images. Expert problem solvers, for example, frequently report the use of visualization and visual analogies when attempting to solve difficult problems (Shepard 1978; Simon and Barenfeld 1969). Larkin and Simon (1987) found that experts tended to construct visual diagrams when given verbal descriptions of a problem; this facilitated searching for relevant information in the problem, recognizing important patterns and relations, and handling complexity. Similarly, Meyer (1989) found that using visual diagrams and illustrations helped people to answer hypothetical questions about how various types of inventions could be improved. Visual representations are also useful in attempting to solve problems involving analogies and ordered relations (Beveridge and Parkins 1987; Huttenlocher 1968). Visualizing a problem can therefore help in the exploration of possible new approaches and solutions.

One of the reasons that imagery can be so effective in problem solving is that in constructing visual representations of a problem, key features often emerge that reveal a simple or obvious solution. An example is the monk problem (McKim 1980), in which a monk ascends a mountain to meditate at the summit. He stays overnight on top of the mountain and then descends the following day along the same path. Was the monk ever at the same place on the path at exactly the same time of day on both days? The solution becomes obvious by visualizing the monk simultaneously ascending and descending the mountain. Since there must be a point at which he would "meet" himself, such a place must indeed exist.

In chapter 5, we considered how preinventive forms could serve as visual metaphors for representing abstract concepts; such forms could also be used in trying to solve problems. For example, in trying to solve the problem of how the solar system was formed, a scientist might generate preinventive forms to represent, metaphorically, possible mechanisms by which this process might have taken place. The forms could then be explored and evaluated to determine whether they might serve as plausible models for the formation of the solar system. Often the structural properties of a mental image can give rise to new insights about the structure of an unusual or difficult problem, which can then lead to solutions that might otherwise have been overlooked.

Exploring Mental Models

Constructing mental models can be especially useful for representing complex systems or events. Although mental models typically include images, they can be distinguished from mental images and from representations that are based only on formal syntactic rules (Collins and Quillian 1969) in that these models are inferential and are capable of representing a broad variety of problems, such as those involved in deductive reasoning (Johnson-Laird 1988b), inductive reasoning (Holland et al. 1986), and text comprehension (Garnham 1981). Mental images, by comparison, need not contain propositional, semantic, or logical information.

A mental model can specify a set of individuals, a collection of objects, a series of events, a group of relations, and a set of possible operations. In the recycling problem, a mental model could represent new ways in which a factory might reorganize its production in order to recycle a product or in which workers at the factory might cooperate to reduce the amount of wasted materials. Such models could thus represent events and operations in which the agents and objects interact in ways related to various components of the recycling process.

Some of the advantages of mental models in problem solving are that they can be updated, can integrate information from a variety of sources, and can allow for the discovery of novel and emergent ideas (Glenberg, Meyer, and Lindem 1987). Mental models are ideal for many aspects of creative exploration, such as making predictions about hypothetical solutions, examining recombinations of various elements, and considering extremes and limits of various situations. In addition, in cases where one cannot physically implement a solution or directly observe the consequences of solution attempts, mental models can be extremely valuable. A scientist might need to make remote-controlled adjustments in the functioning of an interplanetary spacecraft, where direct observation is not possible. Or one might want to explore various strategies for repairing a home appliance before implementing any actual repairs. By using mental models, the likely consequences of such actions can be anticipated.

Analogical Reasoning

Analogical reasoning involves the transfer or mapping of knowledge from one domain, called the *source*, to another domain, called the *target* (Gentner 1989). Analogies provide another means for creatively exploring solutions to problems, especially those that are ill defined. In chapter 7, we discussed whether a problem solver would spontaneously retrieve an analogy from memory. Presently, we deal with the process of mapping knowledge from one domain to another once the analogy is retrieved.

One promising approach to the use of analogies is provided by Gentner's structure-mapping theory (Gentner 1989). This theory distinguishes between first-order and second-order predicates in analogical mapping. First-order predicates relate objects on the basis of simple features, such as size, mass, or brightness. Second-order predicates involve higher-order relations, such as the idea that if X is brighter than Y, X may obscure Y. Although people tend to select analogies based on mappings of first-order predicates, such analogies are often superficial. Gentner recommends choosing analogies based on higher-order predicate mappings. For example, although both an atom and a microorganism are microscopic in size and both contain nuclei as well as other tiny bodies, a cellular model of the atom is not as useful as a planetary model. The latter preserves higher-order relations, such as a massive central body that attracts smaller ones, which are maintained in various orbits.

Gentner also distinguishes between two basic functions of analogical mapping: matching existing predicate structures and carryover, or importing new predicates. These clearly depend on the subject's state of knowledge. For example, having a thorough knowledge of source and target domains results in structural matching, whereas having knowledge of only the source domain leads to carryover.

In structural matching, the subject's attention is drawn to specific parts or aspects of existing knowledge, potentially resulting in new ways of understanding known material. Given the analogy "genetic material is like a hologram," someone familiar with holography and genetics can match predicates from the two domains, such as "each component piece contains information about the whole" and "information is distributed." Although it would not establish new predicates, such matching could lead to novel restructuring within either of the existing domains.

In carryover, new knowledge structures are created as predicates are transferred from the source to the target domain. Someone who is more familiar with genetics than holography may try to import new predicates from the known domain, such as speculating that holograms might be capable of being grafted or cloned, as can be done with living tissue. In general, most analogies represent a combination of these two processes.

These ideas tie in directly with the basic concepts in the Geneplore model. Carryover, a form of analogical transfer, would be considered a generative process, resulting in the creation of new preinventive structures. Structural mapping would involve the exploratory processes of attribute finding, conceptual interpretation, and possibly functional inference. Discovering the implications of an analogy would thus involve the coordinated use of these various processes.

An alternative to the structure-mapping theory is Holyoak's pragmatic model of analogical problem solving (Holyoak 1985). In this model, the goals of problem solving determine whether relations among domains constitute surface or structural similarities. Commonalities that are not relevant to possible problem solutions are considered surface similarities; those that are instrumental in solving the problem are considered structural similarities.

Although the pragmatic model is appealing in that it focuses on the goals of a problem more than the formal characteristics of predicates, it has some important limitations, especially for creative problem solving. Because the initial goals may change as one works on a problem, establishing a problem's goals in advance may not always be advisable. Reconceptualizations and redefinitions of problems often lead to important insights; thus, adherence to the original goals of a problem can block creative solutions. Gentner's approach seems more consistent with the general spirit of creative cognition, in which one searches for unanticipated attributes, structural relations, and conceptual interpretations.

A less formal approach to the role of analogical reasoning in creative problem solving is *synectics* (Gordon 1961), the general process of connecting different and apparently unrelated elements in the search for creative solutions to problems, mostly in the form of analogies that call attention to the unusual aspects of a problem or to alternative ways of thinking about a task.

Four types of analogy are considered useful in the synectics approach: personal analogy, direct analogy, symbolic analogy, and fantasy analogy. *Personal analogy* places the problem solver in a role-playing situation, imagining himself or herself as some entity that plays a part in the problem. In an engineering problem that required a rotating shaft to translate variable speeds into motion at a constant rate, problem solvers were successful when they imagined themselves momentarily to be the rotating shaft. *Direct analogy* refers to a straightforward mapping from one domain to another, often involving structures found in nature. One could try to design a glue dispenser that opened and closed cleanly by trying to relate it to how a tear duct functions. *Symbolic analogies* are poetic phrases generated in response to a problem. In creating a jack that would fold into a small space and unfold to hold a great weight, the symbolic phrase "Indian rope trick" helped lead engineers to a solution. Finally, the *fantasy analogy* suggests how a solution could occur if the impossible were suddenly made possible, such as trying to close a spacesuit by willing it to close.

The synectics method is particularly well suited for generating preinventive structures that can be creatively explored, leading one to discover new meanings, functions, and attributes.

Mental Blocks

Mental blocks, which prevent successful problem solving in cases where it ought to occur, must be distinguished from limitations such as the inability to use certain inferential processes or the lack of knowledge critical for solving a problem. In this regard, it is important to specify not only the processes that problem solvers must undertake and the knowledge they must possess but also the potential traps that can be recognized, avoided, and overcome. We next consider the different types of mental blocks that can prevent successful problem solving.

Mental set refers to a tendency to approach a problem or situation in some habitual way. Although mental sets are useful in many situations because they can make it easier to organize and understand new information (Bransford and Johnson 1972), they can sometimes lead to erroneous interpretations or misleading searches when one is confronted with a problem. In chapter 7, we saw how providing people with biasing clues and examples induced temporary mental sets that resulted in various types of fixation in problem solving, creative generation, and design. Introducing incubation periods and shifts in context provided useful techniques for overcoming these momentary blocks.

Other mental sets are more enduring, however. *Functional fixedness* is a tendency to think of an object only in terms of its typical functions (Duncker 1945). For instance, people tend to think of using pliers as a grasp extender, not as a weight for a pendulum, which prevents them from solving the classic two-string problem (Maier 1931). As another example, most people would suggest using a gasoline cap or an oil cap for temporarily plugging an automobile radiator rather than using a potato, an unusual but more effective solution. Unlike simple fixation, functional fixedness does not usually fade or decay; a typical use for a tool such as a pair of pliers will still be typical even if one has not recently used the tool. Rather, it may be necessary to apply categorical reduction, or to suspend one's expertise, in overcoming this type of mental block.

Adams (1974) identified other types of mental blocks, as well as methods for avoiding and overcoming them: *emotional blocks* (fear of thinking in unusual ways, fear of making mistakes, being excessively judgmental about creative ideas, and lacking motivation), *Cultural blocks* (the notions that fantasy, playfulness, and humor have no place in serious problem solving, that traditions are important to uphold, and that taboos are not to be considered), and *environmental blocks* (the lack of cooperation and support of colleagues and superiors, job distractions, and lack of resources). Although not strictly cognitive, these blocks can also create serious impediments to successful problem solving.

A type of block that is more directly related to creative cognition is searching the wrong domain for an analogy. The problem-solving context strongly influences one's expectations about the appropriate source domain, which in turn constrains the set of matching predicates that will be found in the target domain. As Gentner (1989) points out, this mental set can be helpful if one's initial conception of the problem is appropriate but devastating if it is not. Redefining goals in the course of working on a problem can thus lead to new, and often more appropriate, analogies, which can result in new insights for possible solutions.

As a general rule, unfounded assumptions and needless, self-imposed restrictions interfere with creative problem solving. Making a person aware of these assumptions and restrictions may be the first step in overcoming these mental blocks. For example, the notion that there is a single correct solution to the classic nine-dot problem is unfounded (Adams 1974). With sufficiently thick dots, one can angle each line diagonally through each row of dots, reducing the number of required lines to three. Or one could fold the paper or cut out the dots with scissors. Being aware of such possibilities would help people to transcend the kinds of restrictions that they tend to impose upon themselves.

Metacognition and Problem Solving

There has been a growing interest in the role that a person's awareness of his or her own cognitive processes plays in various cognitive tasks. This form of awareness, which has been called *metacognition*, will be considered with respect to creative problem solving. Under this heading, the usefulness of intuition in problem solving will be considered, as well as the value and limitations of protocol analysis.

Intuition

The term *intuition* means to know something without the use of rational thought or to become instantly aware of something without knowing the source of that knowledge or the means by which one attained it. Historically, intuition has had the unfortunate connotation of defying causal explanations, implying the operation of mysterious, unknown forces in giving rise to new insights and understandings. For this reason, the scientific community has largely avoided the concept.

But, nearly everyone has had the experience of suddenly knowing or recalling something without knowing why. For example, a meaningful word or image will often emerge into consciousness without any obvious intention or purpose (Reason and Lucas 1984). Traditional theories of memory and attention have had no problem accepting and providing accounts for such phenomena. Many theories, for example, have proposed the existence of "automatic" cognitive processes, which respond to meaningful stimuli, do not require attentional effort, and occur very rapidly (Shiffrin and Schneider 1977). Certain types of memories are thought to be retrieved by mechanisms that operate implicitly, outside one's knowledge (Tulving and Schacter 1989). In addition, most neural network or parallel distributed processing models describe cognition in terms that are essentially inaccessible to conscious awareness (McClelland and Rumelhart 1986). Thus, it seems reasonable that intuition could be examined using approaches similar to those that have already been applied in these and other cognitive domains.

Bowers et al. (1990) have taken this important step in trying to understand intuition. Instead of characterizing intuition as the sudden apprehension of knowledge, they proposed that intuitions are more like hunches that may or may not ultimately lead to correct insights or solutions. In this sense, intuition is similar to generating a hypothesis. The basic process by which intuitions arise is the automatic activation of semantic networks by various cues in a problem (Anderson 1983). When activation of information in memory reflects coherent relations, then intuitive leads or hunches may occur, directing problem solving toward appropriate solutions.

The basic paradigm Bowers et al. used was to have subjects attempt to solve remote associates problems and then to guess which of a pair of unsolved problems they had worked on was solvable, at least in principle. These pairs consisted of a problem that could actually be solved and one that had no clear solution, consisting of a random set of words. The subjects were more likely to choose the solvable over the unsolvable problems in each pair, and they were increasingly more likely to do so as they expressed higher confidence in their judgments. Bowers et al. concluded that people can be sensitive to the underlying coherence in a problem, even when they cannot actually solve the problem or identify the nature of that coherence.

Bowers et al. point out that their results may be limited, not only because the tasks used in their studies tended to focus attention on the ultimately relevant features of the problems but also because their methods disproportionately emphasized the hypothesis generation phase of problem solving, minimizing the hypothesis testing phase. The hypothesis testing phase, according to their view, is an explicit analytic period during which a hypothesis is validated or rejected and, as such, is not particularly relevant to intuition.

It is precisely this deficiency that may limit the usefulness of intuition in solving insight problems. In chapter 7, we noted that premonitions of insight were more likely to be predictive of impending failures than successes (Metcalfe 1986b). If such false premonitions reflect an implicit sensitivity to false coherence, then intuitive leads in such situations might systematically and unwittingly lead subjects down blind alleys, resulting in mental blocks. False coherence in problem solving may be related to perceptual processes that cause impossible figures to seem possible (Shepard 1990) or to illusions of knowing that make subjects feel that they understand incoherent explanations (Glenberg, Wilkinson, and Epstein 1982). Thus, classic insight problems may be exactly those for which intuitions are unlikely to lead to correct solutions.

Protocol Analysis
Another method for exploring the cognitive processes that contribute to problem solving is *protocol analysis* (Ericsson and Simon 1984). In this approach, subjects are required to try to say out loud what they are thinking as they go about trying to solve various types of problems. The recorded protocols are then analyzed to determine the subjects' *problem space* (their current mental representation of the problem) and the cognitive operations they used at various stages. Analyses of these protocols can reveal subgoals and heuristics that were useful in solving the problems. Protocols of expert problem solvers can lead to the development of "expert systems" that can apply these same subgoals and heuristics to new problems.

One potential limitation of protocol analysis is that it may give an inaccurate picture of the actual, underlying cognitive processes. For example, a limited ability to verbalize, or a reluctance to do so, might lead to protocols that do not fully represent the person's thinking. Even a subject who is a willing and able verbalizer may not be capable of describing certain mental operations. Finally, some aspects of cognition operate beyond awareness, such as implicit remembering and the intuitive detection of coherence in problems.

Another potential limitation of protocol analysis is that speaking aloud during some types of thinking may inadvertently affect the thought processes being measured. There is evidence, for example, that verbalization can interfere with visual recognition (Schooler and Engstler-Schooler 1990), as well as solving insight problems (Schooler, Ohlsson, and Brooks 1991). Other studies, however, have shown that verbalizing as one works on problems can often facilitate performance (Ahlum-Heath and Divesta 1986). Schooler, Ohlsson, and Brooks have suggested that such facilitation should occur only in step-by-step, noninsight problems, where it might force subjects to attend to the necessary steps throughout the problem.

Divergent Thinking

Two different types of thinking, divergent and convergent, have been distinguished as useful in creative and noncreative problem solving, respectively (Mednick 1962). In *convergent thinking,* one goes from an initial problem state through a series of prescribed operations in order to converge upon a single correct solution. Convergent thinking is ideal for well-defined problems for which there is only one allowable conclusion. *Divergent thinking,* on the other hand, allows one to explore in different directions from the initial problem state, in order to discover many possible ideas and idea combinations that may serve as solutions. In chapter 1, we discussed divergent thinking with regard to approaches to creativity that emphasized cognitive style. Here, we consider it as it relates specifically to creative strategies for problem solving.

Finding Alternative Uses

One test of divergent thinking is the alternate uses test, in which one lists as many different ways as possible to use a common object, such as a brick or a safety pin. Evidence for divergent thinking is provided by ideas that are unconventional or that span many different categories. Table 8.2 shows some examples of conventional and unusual ideas for alternate uses of a two-liter plastic bottle. Generating such possibilities can lead to novel solutions for a variety of ill-defined problems.

In the recycling problem, considering unusual uses for a plastic bottle could lead to new insights for how to improve recycling or make it more appealing. Realizing that a plastic bottle could be used to make

Table 8.2
Conventional and Unusual Uses for a Two-Liter Plastic Bottle

Conventional uses
Holding rainwater for plants
Mixing Kool-aid
Storing paper clips
Storing leftover spaghetti sauce
Mixing plant food
Carrying extra gasoline for road trips
Unusual uses
Toy bowling pins
Flotation buoys for a raft
Makeshift rolling pin
Melt and use as glue
A fish tank
An emergency log for a fireplace

glue, for instance, or could provide a source of heat could suggest new possibilities for how such an object could be reused in potentially important ways.

The discovery of alternate uses was explored to some degree in the creative invention studies in chapter 4. Recall that subjects generated preinventive object forms and then explored possible uses of the forms. The unusual nature of many of the forms made it relatively easy to find novel, creative uses. For more conventional objects, however, it was often necessary to overcome functional fixedness in exploring creative possibilities.

Remote Association
Divergent thinking can be considered an example of *remote association*, which refers to the general process of thinking of unusual associates rather than common ones (Mednick 1962). For example, if given the word *cat*, a common association would be "dog," whereas an unusual or remote association would be "sneeze." If associates to an item are rank ordered in a hierarchy of associative strengths, the slope of the associative hierarchy is related to the relative accessibility of the more unusual associates. The steeper the slope is, the more likely it is that only common associates will be generated, whereas a shallower slope indicates that remote associates are relatively more accessible.

Although the slope of an associative hierarchy may reflect the characteristics of a particular item, it can also relate to how one's attention is allocated (Martindale 1981). Narrowly focused attention steepens the gradient of the hierarchy, highlighting the strongest associates to the exclusion of weaker associates. Defocused attention, in contrast, makes remote associates more accessible (Martindale 1981). In addition, defocused attention may result from lowered arousal, which has long been thought to stimulate creative insight (Thurstone 1952).

This may help to explain why concentrating attention on the common uses of an object, as when one is under pressure to perform, might lead to increased functional fixedness and a reduced amount of divergent thinking. It may therefore be important to deliberately defocus one's attention when attempting to discover creative solutions to a problem.

Brainstorming

Brainstorming is a procedure used by groups of people to generate new ideas for solving problems (Osborn 1963). The primary principle in conducting a brainstorming session is deferred judgment; criticism, even of one's own ideas, is prohibited. This principle is based on the idea that although evaluative judgments are a necessary part of the creative process, ideas should be allowed to develop freely in the early stages of problem solving, before criticism can inhibit their growth. This was also an important principle in the Geneplore model; recall that in chapter 4, we had found that the likelihood of discovering a creative invention was greater when preinventive forms were initially generated without regard to their possible interpretations.

Besides deferring judgment and criticism, other guidelines in the brainstorming approach include encouraging one to generate as many ideas as possible, to try to be imaginative, and to look for novel combinations of ideas. There are also prescriptions regarding the composition and size of the groups for obtaining optimal results. Brainstorming has been applied in a variety of different settings, including businesses, universities, and hospitals.

Although Osborn (1963) and others have compiled numerous reports, mostly from industry, that brainstorming is a highly effective procedure, recent experimental studies on creative idea generation have suggested otherwise. For example, the phenomenon of *productivity loss*, which refers to the reduction of ideas produced by working in a group relative to working individually, has been well documented (Dennehy et al. 1991). This loss in productivity in group situations can be attributed to various factors, such as evaluation apprehension (worrying about the negative judgments of others), social loafing (working less when others share responsibility), and limitations of short-term memory while others in the group are stating their ideas (Diehl and Stroebe 1986).

We recommend a modified approach to brainstorming, in which ideas are initially generated in the absence of group influences but are then subjected to critical evaluation and exploration in group settings. In this way, one could avoid the inhibiting effects of the presence of others as ideas are being conceived, while benefiting from the diversity of interpretive possibilities that would be afforded by a group. It would also avoid the dangers of groupthink (Janis 1972). These recommendation are in the spirit of separating generative and exploratory processes, as in the Geneplore model.

Creative Expertise

Heuristics can often provide effective means for solving problems, particularly as they relate to one's area of expertise. They can also be applied to the detriment of creativity. In tasks requiring divergent thinking or other forms of open-ended, creative exploration, it is often advantageous to suspend one's expertise temporarily. The need for having expertise in efficient problem solving therefore seems at odds with the need to suspend that expertise in situations requiring creative thought.

We attempt to resolve this paradox by recommending the development of creative expertise. The various strategies for creative problem solving discussed in this chapter constitute a knowledge base that individuals could apply in the pursuit of creative solutions. In addition, one could strive to apply principles of creative cognition that were discussed in previous chapters to find new ways to think about a problem, generate new solution possibilities, and explore new implications of those potential solutions. What we are advocating, in effect, is the development of cognitive skills related to expert creative thinking in general. These skills would be founded on deeper understandings of the cognitive processes underlying creativity, particularly those that are involved in generating preinventive structures, combining existing concepts, and interpreting emergent properties. Such skills would be especially helpful in situations where the usual problem-solving rules and heuristics would not apply.

Summary

Theoretical Implications
In this chapter, we have considered findings on various types of strategies that could be used in creative problem solving. These findings were based on studies of insight, algorithms and heuristics, in-

duction, mental imagery, mental models, analogical reasoning, fixation and mental sets, metacognition, protocol analysis, and associative hierarchies. They have important implications not only for creative cognition but also for the field of problem solving in general.

Based on these studies, we draw the following conclusions about creative expertise in problem solving: First, the creative problem solver must be able to recognize and avoid habitual or conventional ways of thinking, especially when confronted with novel situations and problems. Second, the creative problem solver must be sensitive to mental blocks and other impediments to discovering the solutions to particular problems. These include implicit, self-imposed restrictions on one's creative explorations. Third, the creative problem solver must avoid confirmation bias in inductive reasoning. This can be achieved by learning to generate a variety of alternative hypotheses and then attempting to disconfirm them, rather than simply finding confirming evidence to support them.

Hypotheses can be generated and explored in many ways. One can draw on intuitive hunches, resulting from the activation of semantic networks that detect coherence in a structure, or explore the implications of mental models and creative analogies. These processes can be used for identifying the key attributes of a problem or for discovering the kinds of hypotheses that are likely to be relevant. We emphasize again, however, the importance of critically testing such hypotheses and searching for limitations in trying to develop creative approaches to solving a problem.

Practical Implications
There are a number of popular books on problem-solving techniques, many of which have discussed specific strategies for discovering insightful solutions to problems (Bransford and Stein 1984; Gardner 1978; Hayes 1981; Levine 1987; Polya 1957; Wickelgren 1974). The approach we have taken differs from most of these previous efforts in at least one important respect. In creative cognition, we are interested in combining theoretical and practical considerations. Our goal is not simply to list useful strategies or heuristics but also to try to identify some of the cognitive processes that are at work when these techniques are applied. In this regard, we believe that future research in creative cognition can lead to the development of new and potentially more effective strategies for approaching and solving problems.

9
General Implications and Applications

Summary of Theoretical Implications

We have explored various types of cognitive processes and structures that are relevant to the study of creative cognition, considering, in particular, the kinds of preinventive structures that can lead to creative insights, how those structures are formed, the properties of those structures that contribute to creative exploration and discovery, and effective strategies that could be employed to uncover additional creative possibilities. In addition, we have developed new experimental methods that help to identify these structures and processes under controlled laboratory conditions in which subjects are given the opportunity to make creative discoveries for themselves. Thus, not only have we provided a general framework for conducting research on creative cognition, we have also shown that these methods work.

The methods of creative cognition contribute to an understanding of the cognitive processes underlying many different aspects of creative thinking. In addition, these studies identify traditional areas in cognitive psychology and cognitive science that could be explored in a more creative way, such as mental imagery, concept formation, categorization, memory retrieval, analogical reasoning, and problem solving. We believe that research in creative cognition will continue to have implications for work in these more traditional cognitive areas and, similarly, that research in these areas will continue to influence future developments in creative cognition. Indeed, many researchers in traditional cognitive areas have been doing creative cognition research but without thinking about it as such.

The studies presented in this book reveal a number of general principles of creative cognition. For example, we find that preinventive structures are more likely to result in creative insights when interpretive constraints are withheld or suspended at the time the structures are conceived. The resulting structures tend to be less conventional and more ambiguous and display emergent features that can be utilized during creative exploration. We also find that the interpretive constraints should not be too general or too specific. For example, in attempting to conceive of a creative invention, it is better to constrain the object category or function rather than the basic object type. Other examples of principles that result from these studies are that imaginative concepts are structured in the same manner as familiar concepts, that incubation leads to release from fixated retrieval strategies, and that analogical transfer is facilitated by reinstating prior learning contexts. These general principles of creative cognition show that at least some creativity skills are universal and, thus, that creative expertise is not necessarily restricted to particular domains.

We have introduced a number of new concepts within the creative cognition approach, such as preinventive structures, structured imagination, design fixation, and exemplar generation. These concepts are not limited to creative cognition but are directly related to current work in other cognitive domains. For example, the study of preinventive structures and their properties ties in with contemporary studies on mental imagery, conceptual combinations, and metaphors. Again, we emphasize that creative cognition is an integrative field, both drawing from findings in other cognitive areas and generating new findings that feed back into those areas.

Finally, in developing new paradigms for studying creative cognition, we find that traditional measures such as speed and accuracy often do not apply. On the contrary, creative ideas can often be judged without regard to whether they constitute "correct" responses, and creative cognitive processes can often be identified without regard to the time needed to apply them. We thus avoid a reliance on chronometric and related methods in designing studies on creative cognition, although such methods may still be useful in some respects.

Implications of the Geneplore Model

One example of a general model of creative cognition is the Geneplore model, which, we believe, can account for many of the findings we reviewed and can provide a valuable theoretical framework for thinking about creative cognition. We do not claim that this is necessarily the ideal or most complete model of creative cognition or to have tested all of the implications of the model. Rather, we have tried to address our studies to the most important features of the model.

One advantage of the Geneplore model is that it considers generation and exploration as distinct though interactive processes. In forming creative ideas, one may initially generate structures that seem interesting or meaningful in a general sense and then consider their various implications during an exploratory phase. We have presented many examples of creative discoveries that follow this pattern; a preinventive structure is generated, and a creative discovery is then inspired by the structure. Moreover, certain properties of these structures, such as their ambiguity, emergence, and incongruity, contribute to creative exploration and discovery; these properties are explicitly addressed within the model as well.

Apart from its value in accounting for the findings of creative cognition experiments, the Geneplore model is useful in raising new empirical questions. For example, questions regarding some of the ways in which constraints on preinventive structures and interpretive categories might affect the likelihood of making a creative discovery are directly motivated by the model. In addition, the model suggests possible new experiments for exploring the properties of preinventive structures and for determining which types of exploratory strategies are most efficient in various creativity tasks. Such questions might never have been asked outside the context of the model. Thus, whether or not Geneplore turns out to be the right model, it nevertheless has considerable heuristic value.

The model also considers the potential importance of an alternative approach to invention and concept formation, the function-follows-form approach. This approach can complement the more usual form-follows-function approach and can often lead to enhanced creativity. In terms of the Geneplore model, whether one approach or the other should be used normally depends on how early in the creative process product constraints would need to be imposed.

The function-follows-form approach has implications not only for creative thinking but also for the utilization of cognitive changes that might occur during evolution. Consider, for example, the basic notion in evolutionary theory that creatures that could find practical uses for the physical structures that they happened to evolve would have a greater chance for survival. By analogy, one might expect that creatures capable of finding practical uses for novel types of mental structures that they happened to generate would also have an increased chance of survival (e.g., see Perkins, 1988). This would result in a distinct evolutionary advantage. One might erroneously infer, however, that a novel mental structure, like a novel physical structure, was necessarily created with a particular purpose in mind, whereas the purpose was in fact discovered after the creation.

The Geneplore model has a number of features in common with other contemporary cognitive models. For example, the concept specialization model uses generative and elaborative processes in constructing conceptual combinations (Cohen and Murphy 1984), which can be related to some of the generative and exploratory processes in the Geneplore model. The structure-mapping model of analogical reasoning (Gentner 1989) is based on information transfer and matching processes that are also related to the generative and exploratory processes we have considered. In addition, some models have proposed separate generative and interpretive processes in recalling information from memory (Anderson and Bower 1973). The features of the Geneplore model are therefore not unique, although the model has implications that go beyond other contemporary cognitive models.

Ecological Validity of Creative Cognition
There has been a growing sensitivity to the importance of ecological considerations in cognitive research. Inspired by the ecological approach to perception advocated by J. J. Gibson (1966, 1979), a number of cognitive researchers have emphasized the need for making cognitive experiments ecologically "valid" (Neisser 1976; Shepard 1984). They have criticized the typical reliance on highly artificial experimental paradigms in traditional studies, proposing instead that cognitive experiments should incorporate more of the features of natural, ecological conditions. In addition, they have advocated trying to uncover experimental findings that have important implications outside the laboratory.

We believe that experiments on creative cognition are generally in the spirit of this ecological approach. Although creative performance is often placed under certain constraints in these experiments, subjects nevertheless have considerable freedom to explore creative possibilities within the context of the experimental situation. Genuine discoveries are possible, many of which have useful implications for real-world situations and applications. This is illustrated, for example, by many of the objects that subjects created in studies on creative invention and exemplar generation.

With regard to ecological implications, it may also be possible to achieve perceptual learning during the exploratory phase of the Geneplore process, in that one may come to recognize the "affordances" of the preinventive structures (E. J. Gibson 1969; J. J. Gibson 1979). That is, the act of mentally exploring these structures and discovering their underlying meaning is analogous to the way a person actively explores a novel object and learns to "resonate" to its invariant properties. Although it might seem contradictory to claim that perceptual learning can occur in imagination, the presence of emergent features in preinventive structures would make this possible, at least in principle.

Creative Artificial Intelligence
Studies in creative cognition could lead to advances in artificial intelligence that might conceivably address criticisms that natural, human

creativity can never be captured in these approaches (Dreyfus 1972). Although sophisticated programs exist that can solve complex problems in mathematics, assist in engineering design and scientific discovery, and generate music and art (Boden 1991), these advances are still subject to the criticism that they are domain restricted. For example, a program that can generate music may have little in common with one that leads to the design of a new aircraft. To their credit, some recent AI approaches have attempted to account for general aspects of creative problem solving—for example, by developing programs that can induce rules from an arbitrary set of observations (Langley et al. 1987)—though such efforts have only just begun.

One of the advantages of the creative cognition approach is that the same principles can apply across many different domains. The same method of generating and interpreting preinventive structures, for example, could result in the invention of a new tool, the discovery of a new concept in physics, or the development of a new theme for a novel. Similarly, the same principles of structured imagination could apply to creative exemplars generated within many different conceptual categories, such as "imaginary creatures," "toys and games," and "possible solutions to a particular problem." We therefore believe it would be possible to incorporate many of these principles into current efforts to develop creative forms of artificial intelligence.

In programming a computer to generate new ideas for an invention, for example, one might have the computer first generate a preinventive structure, which could be done in such a way as to include as many of the structural properties as possible that typically lead to creative insights. Then the computer could systematically explore the structure, using various strategies to arrive at meaningful interpretations, such as searching for novel attributes, testing out possible functions, and varying the context in which the structure might be used. Methods for avoiding fixation effects could also be incorporated into the program. In this way, it might be possible to develop a form of artificial intelligence that could simulate human creativity in more than one domain.

Components of Creative Cognition
Although we have not systematically explored individual differences in creative cognition, this approach does provide for new ways of exploring these differences in terms of cognitive components that would contribute in various ways to creative performance. Componential approaches to individual differences have already been employed in many cognitive areas, such as mental imagery (Kosslyn 1987; Kosslyn et al. 1984), pattern recognition (Biederman 1987), an-

alogical reasoning (Sternberg 1977), and problem solving (Kaplan and Simon 1990). We believe it would also be possible to explore such differences in terms of the various components of the Geneplore model.

For instance, people are likely to differ in their ability to generate different kinds of preinventive structures and in the extent to which they can effectively employ various exploratory strategies. In addition, they may vary in how they are affected by different constraints on the creativity task, in the extent to which they incorporate features of previously seen examples in their creations, and in their ability to overcome fixation if creative thinking is blocked. These components could be measured independently and then used to predict performance differences on creativity tasks. The components could also be related to previous work on individual differences in cognitive style. In fact, such efforts could help to bring about an eventual convergence between current componential approaches in cognitive science and approaches to creativity based largely on the identification of personality traits.

Preconscious Processes in Creative Thinking
The findings of creative cognition research have implications for the general role that preconscious processes might play in creative thinking. Previous studies claim to have demonstrated the preconscious recognition of words (Marcel 1983), as well as the preconscious extraction of generative rules (Reber 1989). Although such findings have remained controversial, there appears to be sufficient evidence from other studies, such as those discussed in chapters 7 and 8, that some preconscious activity is involved in creative cognition. Whether it is regarded as incubation, insight, or intuition, this activity generally serves to guide or alert a person to new creative possibilities.

Creative cognition can help to demystify such notions by considering ways in which they can be described in terms of specific types of cognitive processes. Incubation, for example, can be considered as an instance of release from cognitive fixation, as opposed to the workings of an intelligent unconscious. Intuition can be described in terms of spreading activation that is initiated by the presence of distinctive cues or features of a problem, as opposed to the instantaneous apprehension of a basic truth.

We propose that these various types of preconscious processes work in conjunction with more directly accessible and consciously controlled forms of cognitive activity in bringing about creative insights and discoveries. In exploring possible interpretations of a preinventive structure, one might combine intuitive feelings with rational considerations about the kinds of possibilities that seem to be most feasible. It is in this sense that we regard creative exploration as an organized, "intelligent" activity, as opposed to an unstructured activity lying completely outside the domain of conscious control.

Limitations of Creative Cognition

In addition to these various implications, there are certain limitations of creative cognition that reflect limitations on cognitive processes in general. Such limitations apply to both noncreative and creative cognition.

Constraints on Reinterpretation

One limitation concerns the degree to which it is possible to reinterpret the structure of a mental representation. In chapter 3, we considered cases in which the structural goodness of a pattern generated in imagination limited how extensively the pattern could be reorganized and reinterpreted (Reed 1974). More recently, Chambers and Reisberg (1985) reported that classical ambiguous figures, such as the Necker cube and duck-rabbit, cannot be reversed in imagination, implying that mental images, unlike actual forms and patterns, can never be truly ambiguous.

These failures to reinterpret mental images have several possible explanations. One is that certain types of structures, such as classical ambiguous figures, may be too complex to be maintained all at once in an image, resulting in partial fading of the image and subsequent loss of reinterpretive opportunities (Finke, Pinker, and Farah 1989). A second explanation is that certain types of reinterpretations, such as those involving reconceptualizing or reparsing the individual features of an image, may be easier than those involving more global reconceptualizations, such as reversing figure and ground (Finke, Pinker, and Schwob 1989). Another explanation is that subjects are fixated by the initial interpretation they give to the image, which prevents them from recognizing alternative interpretations. In support of this explanation, Hyman and Neisser (1991) found that providing subjects with appropriate orientation cues enabled them to reinterpret their images of classical ambiguous figures—for example, informing them to think of the "front" of the form as the "back" of another possible form.

Related studies have shown that verbal labels given to an initial interpretation can influence the way one recalls an ambiguous figure. Carmichael, Hogan, and Walters (1932) found that when subjects were shown an ambiguous drawing and were given one of two possible labels identifying it, they remembered not the actual drawing but distortions of it that conformed with the label. Bartlett (1932) reported similar examples of how visual memories could be distorted over time by verbal labels. More recently, Hinton (1979) reported various demonstrations of how one's initial structural description of an imagined object could limit one's ability to recognize features of the object that were inconsistent with that description. Brandimonte, Hitch, and Bishop (in press) have since found that suppressing articulation increases the likelihood of detecting alternative interpretations of an image. In related work, Schooler and his colleagues have shown that verbalization can suppress both accurate recall of visual details (Schooler and Engstler-Schooler 1990) and successful performance on insight problems (Schooler, Ohlsson, and Brooks 1991).

These studies imply that verbal labels can diminish the opportunity for the subsequent reinterpretation of mental structures. However, even when a biasing interpretation or label is imposed, it may still be possible to recover some of the original information contained in the initially ambiguous structure. Chambers (1991), for example, found that when subjects were told the alternative interpretation of the duck-rabbit figure after having failed to reinterpret it, they were able to recover details of the figure that were consistent with the alternative interpretation. In an earlier, related study, Anderson and Pichert (1978) found that shifting one's perspective after having read a story from one character to another results in the recall of additional details that are consistent with the new perspective. This suggests that, at least temporarily, it may be possible to overcome one's initial biases and discover alternative interpretations of the structure. Nevertheless, the possibility for reinterpretation is likely to diminish over time in view of evidence that such biases can eventually lead to permanent changes in memory (Loftus 1979).

It may therefore not always be possible to reinterpret a preinventive structure for creative purposes. If there is a strong initial bias to interpret the structure in some particular way, other interpretations might not be discovered. And even in the absence of a strong initial bias, if the reinterpretation involves deeper levels of reorganization, such as changing figure-ground assignments or canonical orientation, the alternative interpretations might not be discovered without appropriate cues. These limitations, however, would probably not apply to the majority of cases in which preinventive structures lead to creative insights and discoveries, as implied by the results of the creative invention and conceptualization studies.

Constraints on Mental Transformation

The extent to which preinventive structures can be transformed when a person attempts to explore creative possibilities also remains to be determined. For example, subjects in the preinventive form studies in chapter 4 often reported that they imagined turning their forms around to different positions and then imagined how they might look from new perspectives, as a way of exploring possible new interpretations of the forms. What limitations might exist on these transformational and exploratory processes?

There has been an ongoing controversy over the way people come to recognize forms that are seen from entirely novel perspectives (see Pinker 1984). According to one position, people represent in memory the underlying three-dimensional structure of a form, which then enables them to recognize the form from any possible vantage point (Marr and Nishihara 1978). Presumably in this case people make use of a single, object-centered coordinate system that will work with any viewing perspective. According to a second position, people represent in memory the way a form looks from a single, canonical viewing perspective and then mentally transform the represented form to other viewing perspectives (Shepard and Cooper 1982). Here one is presumably using a single viewer-centered coordinate system to represent the form initially. According to a third position, people represent a form using multiple viewer-centered representations, each depicting how the form would look from a different viewing perspective, thereby eliminating the need for mental transformations (Rock and DiVita 1987; Rock, Wheeler, and Tudor 1989). Presumably, in this case recognition would be possible only from the previously seen vantage points.

Which of these accounts would best describe the way preinventive structures are represented and transformed? The current evidence suggests that each account is partly right. Tarr and Pinker (1989) found that people can form memory representations of how a form appears from a number of different, previously seen perspectives but that they can also mentally rotate the forms to orientations that they have never previously seen. How successfully this can be done usually depends on how familiar the forms are and how well they are organized.

Although the preinventive structures that subjects use in creative cognition experiments are often ambiguous, they also tend to be meaningful and well organized. For this reason, we would expect that these structures could normally be transformed with little difficulty. In cases where a preinventive form was poorly organized, however, it might be difficult to explore creative possibilities of the form from new perspectives. The extent to which such limitations would arise in actual practice is a topic for future research.

Another possible limitation on the transformation of preinventive structures concerns inherent constraints on the transformational processes themselves. Parsons (1987) has shown that mental transformations incorporate many of the natural, biomechanical constraints on physical motions. For instance, it is easier to imagine turning your hand in a natural direction than to imagine a physically impossible hand motion. Such constraints may limit the extent to which creative possibilities can be explored that violate natural directions of motion.

General Capacity Limitations

Creative cognition would be limited by general capacity restrictions on human cognition as well. For example, studies on attention have revealed that only a certain amount of information can be actively searched or processed at once (Schneider and Shiffrin 1977). Similarly, studies on mental imagery have revealed general limitations on the amount of information that can be actively depicted in an image (Kosslyn 1975). We could expect these same limitations to affect the amount of information that could be effectively handled in the generative and exploratory processes used in creative cognition.

Recommendations for Creativity Training

Some writers have offered a variety of recommendations for how to stimulate creative thinking. Perkins (1981), for example, suggested that in attempting to come up with new ideas, a person should strive to be original, take a problem-finding attitude, strive for objectivity, strive for quality, notice new possibilities, change the problem when one gets stuck, make one's thoughts concrete, focus on particular contexts, and consider unusual objects or possibilities. Others have made numerous practical recommendations for how to generate creative ideas and solutions to problems (Bransford and Stein 1984; Davis 1973; Gordon 1961; Levine 1987; Osborn 1953; Wickelgren 1974).

Applying the Principles of Creative Cognition

The findings of studies on creative cognition lead to additional suggestions for how to generate creative ideas. We recommend, for example, that a person who wants to become more creative should practice generating preinventive structures and exploring novel interpretations of them, using the techniques we have described in this book. For instance, one might imagine preinventive object forms and then consider various ways in which the forms could be seen as representing new types of inventions or possible new concepts. Similarly, one could imagine putting together words or phrases in interesting combinations and then exploring some of their semantic or metaphorical implications.

We recommend trying to generate preinventive structures that are rich in the kinds of properties that increase the likelihood of having a creative insight—in particular, preinventive structures that are novel and ambiguous, have emergent features, appear meaningful, display apparent incongruities among the features, and have the potential for a high level of divergence. We think it should be possible, at least in principle, to train people to incorporate these features into their mental constructions.

In practicing these methods, we recommend keeping creativity notebooks in which to record preinventive structures so that one can return to them later for further exploration and evaluation. Often a preinventive structure may at first seem intriguing and meaningful in some abstract sense but may not immediately lead to a specific, insightful interpretation. Later, a context may arise in which the structure suddenly inspires a variety of new insights. Recording one's preinventive structures allows for extended opportunities to explore the creative possibilities that they might afford.

Another recommendation is to practice imagining creative exemplars that pertain to hypothetical categories or situations and then exploring their implications—for example, imagining how people might behave differently if the world were suddenly changed in certain respects. If gasoline did not exist, how would this affect the way we live today? If ears had not evolved, how would human sensory systems be different?

Practicing the technique of having imaginary "conversations" can also lead to new insights, in that one may discover unexpected things in the course of mentally carrying out the conversation. A scientist might come to a new insight about a theory in physics by imagining that he or she was talking with Einstein. What would Einstein have thought of that idea? A person might discover something important about an interpersonal relationship by imagining talking with a counselor or a friend. This technique would be effective to the extent that one could discover new and potentially meaningful emergent properties in the imagined conversation.

Adopting Attitudes Conducive to Creativity
In considering the most important attitudes to have when trying to think creatively, we refer to Maslow's (1968) characterization of highly creative, self-actualized people. Maslow called attention to how such

people tried to explore creative possibilities in all of their activities, how they were often spontaneous in generating creative ideas, and how they tended not to fear their own creative thoughts or the evaluations of others. Maslow characterized real creativity as something that is radiated, like sunshine, touching and inspiring others.

We believe that an important part of training oneself to think more creatively is to learn not to fear creativity. In our experiments, subjects often expressed initial apprehension at having to generate something creative. Once they became accustomed to doing so, however, this apprehension usually faded, and they became interested in, and even excited by creative possibilities.

Developing an exploratory attitude is also important in learning to become more creative. As we have seen, there are numerous ways in which a person can become fixated on a single interpretation or approach. This stifles creativity. In overcoming functional fixedness and related tendencies, we recommend getting into the habit of looking beyond conventional ideas, perhaps by using categorical reduction in order to reduce strong, initial conceptualizations, shifting context in order to gain access to more remote associations, and searching for new or unusual attributes in order to discover novel uses or applications.

Creativity versus Competence
We need to distinguish between creativity and competence in developing a creativity training program. Spending a lot of time on something often makes one competent but not necessarily creative. A person could spend years mastering the techniques of musical theory and composition yet be unable to create anything of real value. Applying the principles of creative cognition can complement expertise, allowing one to explore creative possibilities in such a way as to transcend mere competence.

At the same time, practicing creativity techniques alone will not necessarily lead to creative outcomes. Without having some expertise, there would be little opportunity for an individual to appreciate the appropriateness of a new idea, to comprehend key problems, or even to express solutions in meaningful ways. It is in this sense that we are in agreement with previous arguments for the role that expert knowledge plays in creativity (Perkins 1981; Weisberg 1986).

Creativity Training in the Sciences
Can the methods of creative cognition be truly helpful in the attempt to think more creatively in highly specialized professional fields, such as the physical sciences? Consider, for example, the potential criticism

that cognitive psychology could not possibly have anything important to say about how a physicist might learn to generate new concepts in physics. As one might argue, recognizing and using such concepts requires a profound understanding of the principles of physics, not psychology.

On the contrary, we believe that creative cognition has much to say about how to go about making creative discoveries in the sciences. Again, we need to make the distinction between being competent and being creative. A person becomes competent by virtue of having acquired expertise in a particular field. Creative cognition is not primarily concerned with how one acquires this expert knowledge. From the standpoint of creative cognition, what is important is learning how to use that expertise in original and insightful ways.

Unfortunately, creativity is seldom emphasized in training people to become scientists. Many creative insights in physics have resulted from so-called Gedanken, or "thought" experiments (in which one envisions a hypothetical, often paradoxical situation and considers its consequences), yet physics students are rarely taught how to do this. Creative cognition could have important implications for teaching people how to think in scientifically creative ways. To the extent that the human mind is capable of conceiving of new conceptual structures, the methods of creative cognition can help one to generate and explore these structures, thereby improving one's chances for making scientific discoveries. We therefore recommend that scientists practice generating preinventive structures and then attempt to interpret the structures in ways that might be theoretically significant.

General Applications

Product Development
The methods of creative cognition could have enormous implications for the development of innovative products. In our experiments, we have found that inventions and other designs that result from novel interpretations of preinventive forms often have an intrinsic fascination and appeal. These qualities would very likely enhance the marketability of the resulting products. In fact, when people see examples of objects that were rated as highly creative inventions in these experiments, they often comment that they wish they had thought of the idea and express a desire to own such a product.

The creative cognition approach lends itself naturally to other considerations in product development. For example, one might wish to consider how creative a new product should be compared with those already on the market. If a product were too original, it might not be as marketable. The methods of creative cognition could be employed to vary the extent to which the features of newly conceived products depart from those of products that already exist. In addition, these methods could be used to help one determine which attributes to keep and which to eliminate in modifying an existing design.

Creative cognition can also help to identify the kinds of cognitive processes that guide or limit the way designers think. We have found that new products developed by both experimental subjects and professional engineers are heavily influenced by existing knowledge structures. By examining how categories, schemas, implicit theories, and mental models function to retain old features in new products, the full weight of cognitive science can be brought to bear on the important task of understanding and enhancing the development of new products.

Architecture
Architecture represents an interesting balance between aesthetics and practical considerations. Indoor and outdoor spaces, for example, should be pleasing but also functional; buildings should be attractive and also safe. The ideas and techniques of creative cognition can contribute to this sense of balance in architectural design. For example, the aesthetic quality of a design could be the primary consideration in initially generating a preinventive structure, whereas its functional properties could then be assessed during the exploratory phase. In addition, with the advent of computer-assisted design programs, the designer's ability to explore many different combinations and to see their consequences quickly is enhanced.

Human-Computer Interaction
By handling mundane tasks, a computer can allow a person to devote more effort to creative endeavors. In addition, its capacity for combining large amounts of information makes it an ideal device for facilitating creative cognition, especially in cases where the information would overload a person's cognitive capacity.

Research on creative cognition can have implications for the design of new types of software. A traditional approach to software development is to think of a programming task in terms of input, processing, and output; however, it is often necessary to consider major reorganizations of a program in order to get it to function properly. These and other kinds of structural transformations could be generated and tested as part of creative strategies for developing better programs.

Education

One obvious application of the creative cognition approach is to foster the development of creativity in our educational system. Although various procedures have already been used by educational psychologists to try to enhance creative thinking in schools (McLeod and Cropley 1989; Torrance and Myers 1970), the novel experimental tasks used in studies on creative cognition could lead to the development of new, effective teaching methods and the construction of new measures of creative aptitude.

Psychotherapy

An important part of most approaches to psychotherapy is helping clients achieve new therapeutic insights. This process could be facilitated through the use of preinventive structures. For example, a client could be encouraged to generate and explore preinventive structures as a vehicle for discovering new insights related to a particular problem or situation. Interpreting preinventive structures could also have value as a projective technique. Given that these structures often exhibit a deep sense of meaningfulness, they should be more effective in eliciting projective interpretations than traditional methods, such as using Rorschach inkblots.

One particular technique, developed mainly through the work of Milton Erickson, focuses on the utilization of a patient's natural responses in structuring therapeutic intervention (Haley 1973). The therapist accepts whatever a person says or does, and then tries to incorporate it into the treatment procedure in creative ways. This technique is related to the Geneplore concept that creativity is enhanced when one is allowed to generate preinventive structures naturally, without interpretive constraints, and then to explore their creative implications after the constraints are imposed.

Creative Writing

There are essentially two contrasting approaches to creative writing: develop the ideas as clearly as possible before writing them down, or write down ideas as they arise and then explore possible ways of developing them. In the latter case, the very act of writing leads to new discoveries and sometimes the realization that one's initial beliefs were entirely mistaken (Elbow 1981).

This alternative approach to creative writing has much in common with the function-follows-form strategy. Recall times when you started writing on a topic but then ended up shifting to another one as you discovered new conceptual possibilities. This is analogous to the way preinventive structures can come to be interpreted in unexpected ways. Recall, too, how it often helps to put down a manuscript and then come back to it later. This is reminiscent of the advantages of separating generative and exploratory processes and of suspending expertise. Writers should not necessarily draw upon all of their knowledge when writing an initial draft. By coming back to it later, they can often discover new possibilities and interpretations that they initially overlooked.

In chapter 5, we provided an example of how a preinventive object form might be interpreted as representing a new strategy for writing a story. In fact, there are many ways in which a writer might use preinventive forms as catalysts for new literary ideas—for example, by trying to interpret a preinventive form as representing a general theme for a novel, relationships among the characters, or potential sources of conflict within the plot. Both visual and verbal types of preinventive structures could be used to search for creative possibilities in one's writing.

The work on structured imagination discussed in chapter 6 is also relevant to creative writing. How do people think of possible new characters or scenes to begin with? To what extent are these creations influenced by the characteristics of one's existing knowledge structures? Can a writer become more creative by deliberately creating characters and scenes that violate his or her implicit assumptions?

Predicting Future Trends

A critical task for government and industry is to be able to foresee future needs and develop the capacity to meet those needs. Although we have claimed that creative cognition has widespread implications, we do not purport to understand the discipline of predicting future trends any more than we purport to understand other scientific disciplines. What we do suggest, however, is that understanding the cognitive processes involved in creativity can contribute to more accurate predictions regarding the future.

One of the most important contributions would be in encouraging planners to assess carefully any implicit assumptions that carry over from their conceptions of the world of today. Predicting the future is basically a task of imagination, but just as designers might retain unnecesary features in trying to come up with innovative designs, futurologists might retain inappropriate assumptions that will not hold in the world of the future.

Additional Applications

There are many other potential applications of creative cognition. It might be possible to explore creative performance in athletics using these methods. For instance, one might explore the generation of creative movements in gymnastics or figure skating and how those movements could then be developed or refined.

The principles of creative cognition could also help one to improve one's interpersonal relations. In applying these principles to developing a new relationship, one might want the relationship to start out ambiguously and to avoid defining it prematurely. The person might then end up discovering emergent, shared features of the relationship that would make original expectations and criteria obsolete.

Future Directions

Our main goal in this book has been to lay down a foundation for the field of creative cognition. There is much more work to be done, and we conclude by considering some possible directions that future work in this field might take.

For example, people often claim that their creativity is inspired by listening to great music or exploring great works of art. What gives rise to these experiences of creative synesthesia? In terms of creative cognition, we might suspect that great music and art express potentially meaningful preinventive structures, which can lead to creative inspiration, but other factors are no doubt involved as well.

How exactly do the properties of preinventive structures map onto the final creative products? We would expect, for example, that a preinventive structure with a high degree of novelty, ambiguity, and emergence would result in a final product that was highly creative, but we have yet to understand precisely how this occurs.

Finally, is there anything beyond creativity that might constitute an even higher form of human expression? We have said that perhaps the most important thing a person can do is to be creative, and perhaps the most important work a cognitive scientist can do is to explore the nature of creativity. But what lies beyond this? Once a person's creative potential is realized, what is the next cognitive frontier?

References

Adams, J. L. (1974). *Conceptual blockbusting.* Stanford, CA: Stanford Alumni Association.

Ahlum-Heath, M. E., and DiVesta, F. J. (1986). The effect of conscious controlled verbalization of a cognitive strategy on transfer in problem solving. *Memory and Cognition,* 14, 281–285.

Allen, M. S. (1962). *Morphological creativity.* Englewood Cliffs, NJ: Prentice-Hall.

Amabile, T. M. (1983). *The social psychology of creativity.* New York: Springer-Verlag.

Anderson, B. F. (1975). *Cognitive psychology.* New York: Academic Press.

Anderson, J. R. (1978). Arguments concerning representations for mental imagery. *Psychological Review,* 85, 249–277.

Anderson, J. R. (1983). *The architecture of cognition.* Cambridge, MA: Harvard University Press.

Anderson, J. R. (1990). *Cognitive psychology and its implications.* New York: Freeman.

Anderson, J. R., and Bower, G. H. (1973). *Human associative memory.* New York: Wiley.

Anderson, R. C., and Pichert, J. W. (1978). Recall of previously unrecallable information following a shift in perspective. *Journal of Verbal Learning and Verbal Behavior,* 17, 1–12.

Anderson, R. E., and Helstrup, T. (1991). Composition and decomposition in mind and paper. Manuscript submitted for publication.

Arnheim, R. (1969). *Visual thinking.* Berkeley: University of California Press.

Attneave, F. (1971). Multistability in perception. *Scientific American,* 225, 62–71.

Barnes, J. M., and Underwood, B. J. (1959). "Fate" of first-list associations in transfer theory. *Journal of Experimental Psychology,* 58, 97–105.

Barron, F. (1969). *Creative person and creative process.* New York: Holt, Rinehart and Winston.

Barsalou, L. W. (1983). Ad hoc categories. *Memory and Cognition,* 11, 211–227.

Barsalou, L. W. (1987). The instability of graded structure: Implications for the nature of concepts. In U. Neisser (Ed.), *Concepts and conceptual development: Ecological and intellectual factors in categorization* (pp. 101–140). Cambridge: Cambridge University Press.

Bartlett, F. C. (1932). *Remembering.* Cambridge: Cambridge University Press.

Bateson, G. (1979). *Mind and nature.* London: Wildwood House.

Bell, E. T. (1965). *Men of mathematics.* New York: Simon and Schuster.

Benjamin, L. T., and Shallenberger, W. R. (1985). Staying with initial answers of objective tests: Is it a myth? *Teaching of Psychology,* 11, 133–141.

Bethell-Fox, C. E., and Shepard, R. N. (1988). Mental rotation: Effects of stimulus complexity and familiarity. *Journal of Experimental Psychology: Human Perception and Performance,* 14, 12–23.

Beveridge, M., and Parkins, E. (1987). Visual representation in analogue problem solving. *Memory and Cognition,* 15, 230–237.

Biederman, I. (1987). Recognition-by-components: A theory of human image under-standing. *Psychological Review*, 94, 115–147.

Birch, H. (1975). The relation of previous experience to insightful problem solving. *Journal of Comparative Psychology*, 38, 367–383.

Bjork, R. A. (1989). Retrieval inhibition as an adaptive mechanism in human memory. In H. L. Roediger III and F. I. M. Craik (Eds.), *Varieties of memory and consciousness: Essays in honor of Endel Tulving* (pp. 309–330). Hillsdale, NJ: Erlbaum.

Blaxton, T. A. (1989). Investigating dissociations among memory measures: Support for a transfer-appropriate processing framework. *Journal of Experimental Psychology: Learning, Memory, and Cognition*, 15, 657–688.

Boden, M. (1991). *The creative mind: Myths and mechanisms.* New York: Basic Books.

Bower, G. H., and Glass, A. L. (1976). Structural units and the redintegrative power of picture fragments. *Journal of Experimental Psychology: Human Learning and Memory*, 2, 456–466.

Bower, G. H., Karlin, M. B., and Dueck, A. (1975). Comprehension and memory for pictures. *Memory and Cognition*, 3, 216–220.

Bowers, K. S., Regehr, G., Balthazard, C., and Parker, K. (1990). Intuition in the context of discovery. *Cognitive Psychology*, 22, 72–109.

Brandimonte, M. A., Hitch, G. J., and Bishop, D. V. M. (in press). Influence of short-term memory codes on visual image processing: Evidence from image transfor-mation tasks. *Journal of Experimental Psychology: Learning, Memory, and Cognition.*

Bransford, J. D., and Johnson, M. K. (1972). Contextual prerequisites for understanding: Some investigations of comprehension and recall. *Journal of Verbal Learning and Verbal Behavior*, 11, 717–721.

Bransford, J. D., and Stein, B. S. (1984). *The ideal problem solver.* New York: Freeman.

Briggs, G. E. (1954). Acquisition, extinction and recovery functions in retroactive inhi-bition. *Journal of Experimental Psychology*, 47, 285–293.

Brooks, L. R. (1968). Spatial and verbal components of the act of recall. *Canadian Journal of Psychology*, 22, 349–368.

Brown, A. S. (1976). Spontaneous recovery in human learning. *Psychological Bulletin*, 83, 321–338.

Brown, A. S. (1981). Inhibition in cued retrieval. *Journal of Experimental Psychology: Human Learning and Memory*, 7, 204–215.

Brown, R., and McNeill, D. (1986). The "tip-of-the-tongue" phenomenon. *Journal of Verbal Learning and Verbal Behavior*, 5, 325–337.

Bundesen, C., and Larsen, A. (1975). Visual transformation of size. *Journal of Experi-mental Psychology: Human Perception and Performance*, 1, 214–220.

Campbell, D. (1960). Blind variation and selective attention in creative thought as in other knowledge processes. *Psychological Review*, 67, 380–400.

Carmichael, L., Hogan, H. P., and Walter, A. A. (1932). An experimental study of the effect of language on the reproduction of visually perceived form. *Journal of Exper-imental Psychology*, 15, 73–86.

Chambers, D. (1991). *What an image includes depends on what an image means.* Paper presented at the Vanderbilt Conference on Imagery, Creativity, and Discovery, Nashville, TN.

Chambers, D., and Reisberg, D. (1985). Can mental images be ambiguous? *Journal of Experimental Psychology: Human Perception and Performance*, 11, 317–328.

Clement, J. (1988). Observed methods for generating analogies in scientific problem solving. *Cognitive Science*, 12, 563–586.

Clement, J. (1989). Learning via model construction and criticism: Protocol evidence on sources of creativity in science. In G. Glover, R. Ronning, and C. Reynolds (Eds.),

Handbook of creativity: Assessment, theory and research (pp. 341–381). New York: Plenum.

Cohen, B., and Murphy, G. L. (1984). Models of concepts. *Cognitive Science, 8*, 27–58.

Collins, A. M., and Quillian, M. R. (1969). Retrieval time from semantic memory. *Journal of Verbal Learning and Verbal Behavior, 8*, 240–247.

Connor, L. T., Balota, D. A., and Neely, J. H. (1990). *Activation and metacognition of inaccessible information: A further examination.* Paper presented at the meeting of the Midwest Psychological Association, Chicago.

Cooper, L. A. (1976). Demonstration of a mental analog of an external rotation. *Perception and Psychophysics, 19*, 296–302.

Cooper, L. A. (1990). Mental representation of three-dimensional objects in visual problem solving and recognition. *Journal of Experimental Psychology: Learning, Memory, and Cognition, 16*, 1097–1106.

Cooper, L. A., and Podgorny, P. (1976). Mental transformations and visual comparison processes: Effects of complexity and similarity. *Journal of Experimental Psychology: Human Perception and Performance, 2*, 503–514.

Cooper, L. A., and Shepard, R. N. (1973). The time required to prepare for a rotated stimulus. *Memory and Cognition, 1*, 246–250.

Corballis, M. C. (1988). Recognition of disoriented shapes. *Psychological Review, 95*, 115–123.

Crawford, R. P. (1954). *Techniques of creative thinking.* New York: Hawthorn.

Cropley, A. (1967). *Creativity.* London: Longmans.

Csikzentmihalyi, M. (1988). Society, culture, and person: A systems view of creativity. In R. J. Sternberg (Ed.), *The nature of creativity: Contemporary psychological perspectives* (pp. 325–339). Cambridge: Cambridge University Press.

Davidson, J. E. (1986). The role of insight in giftedness. In R. J. Sternberg and J. E. Davidson (Eds.), *Conceptions of giftedness* (pp. 201–222). New York: Cambridge University Press.

Davis, G. A. (1973). *Psychology of problem solving: Theory and practice.* New York: Basic Books.

Day, C. S. (1921). *This simian world.* New York: Knopf.

de Bono, E. (1975). *New think: The use of lateral thinking in the generation of new ideas.* New York: Basic Books.

Dennehy, E. B., Bulow, P., Wong, F. Y., Smith, S. M., and Aronoff, J. B. (1991). A test of cognitive fixation in brainstorming groups. Unpublished manuscript.

Diehl, M., and Stroebe, W. (1986). Productivity loss in brainstorming: Toward the solution of a riddle. *Journal of Personality and Social Psychology, 53*, 497–509.

Dominowski, R. L. (1981). Comment on "An examination of the alleged role of 'fixation' in the solution of several 'insight' problems" by Weisberg and Alba. *Journal of Experimental Psychology: General, 110*, 193–198.

Dreyfus, H. (1972). *What computers can't do: A critique of artificial reason.* New York: Harper & Row.

Duncker, K. (1945). On problem solving. *Psychological Monographs, 58*, no. 270.

Eich, J. E. (1980). The cue-dependent nature of state-dependent retrieval. *Memory and Cognition, 8*, 157–173.

Elbow, P. (1981). *Writing without teachers.* London: Oxford University Press.

Ellen, P. (1982). Problem solving is not like perception: More on Gestalt theory. *Journal of Experimental Psychology: General, 111*, 316–325.

Ericsson, K. A., and Simon, H. A. (1984). *Protocol analysis.* Cambridge, MA: MIT Press.

Farah, M. J. (1985). Psychophysical evidence for a shared representational medium for mental images and percepts. *Journal of Experimental Psychology: General, 114*, 91–103.

Farah, M. J. (1988). Is visual imagery really visual? Overlooked evidence from neuro-psychology. *Psychological Review*, 95, 307–317.

Ferguson, E. S. (1977). The mind's eye: Nonverbal thought in technology. *Science*, 197, 827–836.

Findlay, C. S., and Lumsden, C. J. (1988). The creative mind: Toward an evolutionary theory of discovery and invention. *Journal of Social and Biological Structures*, 11, 3–55.

Finke, R. A. (1979). The functional equivalence of mental images and errors of movement. *Cognitive Psychology*, 11, 235–264.

Finke, R. A. (1980). Levels of equivalence in imagery and perception. *Psychological Review*, 87, 113–132.

Finke, R. A. (1986). Mental imagery and the visual system. *Scientific American*, 254, 88–95.

Finke, R. A. (1989). *Principles of mental imagery.* Cambridge, MA: MIT Press.

Finke, R. A. (1990). *Creative imagery: Discoveries and inventions in visualization.* Hillsdale, NJ: Erlbaum.

Finke, R. A. (1991a). Emergent features in imagery and perception. Manuscript submitted for publication.

Finke, R. A. (1991b). *Mental imagery and creative invention.* Paper presented at the Vanderbilt Conference on Imagery, Creativity, and Discovery, Nashville, TN.

Finke, R. A. (in press). Beyond preinventive forms. *Creativity Research Journal.*

Finke, R. A., and Kurtzman, H. S. (1981). Mapping the visual field in mental imagery. *Journal of Experimental Psychology: General*, 110, 501–517.

Finke, R. A., and Pinker, S. (1982). Spontaneous imagery scanning in mental extrapolation. *Journal of Experimental Psychology: Learning, Memory, and Cognition*, 8, 142–147.

Finke, R. A., Pinker, S., and Farah, M. J. (1989). Reinterpreting visual patterns in mental imagery. *Cognitive Science*, 13, 51–78.

Finke, R. A., Pinker, S., and Schwob, S. L. (1989). Levels of reinterpretation in mental imagery. Unpublished manuscript.

Finke, R. A., and Shepard, R. N. (1986). Visual functions of mental imagery. In K. R. Boff, L. Kaufman, and J. Thomas (Eds.), *Handbook of perception and human performance* (Vol. 2). New York: Wiley-Interscience.

Finke, R. A., and Shyi, G. C.-W. (1988). Mental extrapolation and representational momentum for complex implied motions. *Journal of Experimental Psychology: Learning, Memory, and Cognition*, 14, 112–120.

Finke, R. A., and Slayton, K. (1988). Explorations of creative visual synthesis in mental imagery. *Memory and Cognition*, 16, 252–257.

Finke, R. A., and Smith, S. M. (1989). Creative inspiration in mental synthesis. Unpublished manuscript.

Finke, R. A., and Ward, T. B. (1991). Creative refinement of common objects. Manuscript in preparation.

Freud, S. (1916). *Leonardo da Vinci: A study in sexuality.* New York: Brill.

Freyd, J. J. (1983). Representing the dynamics of a static form. *Memory and Cognition*, 11, 342–346.

Freyd, J. J. (1987). Dynamic mental representations. *Psychological Review*, 94, 427–438.

Freyd, J. J., and Finke, R. A. (1984). Representational momentum. *Journal of Experimental Psychology: Learning, Memory, and Cognition*, 10, 126–132.

Freyd, J. J., and Johnson, J. Q. (1987). Probing the time course of representational momentum. *Journal of Experimental Psychology: Learning, Memory, and Cognition*, 13, 259–268.

Gardner, H. (1982). *Art, mind, and brain: A cognitive approach to creativity.* New York: Basic Books.

Gardner, M. (1964). *The ambidextrous universe.* New York: Basic Books.

Gardner, M. (1978). *Aha! Insight.* New York: Freeman.

Garnham, A. (1981). Mental models as representations of text. *Memory and Cognition, 9,* 560–565.

Gentner, D. (1989). The mechanisms of analogical learning. In S. Vosniadou and A. Ortony (Eds.), *Similarity and analogical reasoning.* Cambridge: Cambridge University Press.

Gentner, D., and Stevens, A. L. (1983). *Mental models.* Hillsdale, NJ: Erlbaum.

Getzels, J. W., and Csikszentmihalyi, M. (1976). *The creative vision: A longitudinal study of problem finding in art.* New York: Wiley.

Ghiselin, B. (1952). *The creative process.* Berkeley: University of California Press.

Gibson, E. J. (1969). *Perceptual learning and development.* New York: Appleton-Century-Crofts.

Gibson, J. J. (1966). *The senses considered as perceptual systems.* Boston: Houghton Mifflin.

Gibson, J. J. (1979). *The ecological approach to visual perception.* Boston: Houghton Mifflin.

Gick, M. L., and Holyoak, K. J. (1980). Analogical problem solving. *Cognitive Psychology, 12,* 306–355.

Glass, A. L., and Holyoak, K. J. (1986). *Cognition.* New York: Random House.

Glenberg, A. M., Meyer, M., and Lindem, K. (1987). Mental models contribute to foregrounding during text comprehension. *Journal of Memory and Language, 26,* 69–83.

Glenberg, A. M., Wilkinson, A. C., and Epstein, W. (1982). The illusion of knowing: Failure in the self-assessment of comprehension. *Memory and Cognition, 10,* 597–602.

Gluck, M. A., and Bower, G. H. (1988). From conditioning to category learning: An adaptive network model. *Journal of Experimental Psychology: General, 117,* 225–244.

Glucksberg, S. (1991). Beyond literal meanings: The psychology of allusion. *Psychological Science, 2,* 146–152.

Glucksberg, S., Gildea, P., and Bookin, H. B. (1982). On understanding nonliteral speech: Can people ignore metaphors? *Journal of Verbal Learning and Verbal Behavior, 21,* 85–98.

Glucksberg, S., and Keyser, B. (1990). Understanding metaphorical comparisons: Beyond similarity. *Psychological Review, 97,* 3–18.

Glushko, R. J., and Cooper, L. A. (1978). Spatial comprehension and comparison processes in verification tasks. *Cognitive Psychology, 10,* 391–421.

Goldschmidt, G. (in press). Farewell to "form follows function." *Creativity Ressearch Journal.*

Gordon, W. (1961). *Synectics: The development of creative capacity.* New York: Harper & Row.

Gruber, H. E., and Barrett, P. H. (1974). *Darwin on man: A psychological study of scientific creativity.* New York: Dutton.

Guilford, J. P. (1950). Creativity. *American Psychologist, 5,* 444–454.

Guilford, J. P. (1956). The structure of intellect. *Psychological Bulletin, 53,* 267–293.

Guilford, J. P. (1968). *Intelligence, creativity, and their educational implications.* San Diego: Knapp.

Haley, J. (1973). *Uncommon therapy: The psychiatric techniques of Milton H. Erickson, M.D.* New York: Norton.

Hampton, J. A. (1987). Inheritance of attributes in natural concept conjunctions. *Memory and Cognition, 15,* 55–71.

Hausman, C. R. (1984). *A discourse on novelty and creation*. Albany: State University of New York Press.

Hayes, J. R. (1981). *The complete problem solver*. Philadelphia: Franklin Institute Press.

Hayes, J. R. (1989). Cognitive processes in creativity. In G. Glover, R. Ronning, and C. Reynolds (Eds.), *Handbook of creativity: Assessment, theory and research*. New York: Plenum.

Hayes-Roth, B., and Hayes-Roth, F. (1977). Concept learning and the recognition and classification of exemplars. *Journal of Verbal Learning and Verbal Behavior*, 16, 321–338.

Hershman, D. J., and Lieb, J. (1988). *The key to genius*. Buffalo, NY: Prometheus.

Hilgard, E. R. (1968). Creativity: Slogan and substance. *Centennial Review*, 12, 40–58.

Hilgard, E. R. (1977). *Divided consciousness: Multiple controls in human thought and action*. New York: Wiley-Interscience.

Hilgard, J. R. (1970). *Personality and hypnosis: A study of imaginative involvement*. Chicago: University of Chicago Press.

Hinton, G. (1979). Some demonstrations of the effects of structural descriptions in mental imagery. *Cognitive Science*, 3, 231–250.

Hintzman, D. L. (1969). Apparent frequency as a function of frequency and the spacing of repetitions. *Journal of Experimental Psychology*, 80, 139–145.

Hintzman, D. L. (1986). "Schema abstraction" in a multiple-trace memory model. *Psychological Review*, 93, 411–428.

Hocevar, D., and Bachelor, P. (1989). A taxonomy and critique of measurements used in the study of creativity. In G. Glover, R. Ronning, and C. Reynolds (Eds.), *Handbook of creativity: Assessment, theory and research*. New York: Plenum.

Holland, J. H., Holyoak, K. J., Nisbett, R. E., and Thagard, P. R. (1986). *Induction: Processes of inference, learning, and discovery*. Cambridge, MA: MIT Press.

Holyoak, K. J. (1985). The pragmatics of analogical transfer. In G. H. Bower (Ed.), *The psychology of learning and motivation* (Vol. 19, pp. 59–87). New York: Academic Press.

Huttenlocher, J. (1968). Constructing spatial images: A strategy in reasoning. *Psychological Review*, 4, 277–299.

Hyman, I. E., and Neisser, U. (1991). Reconstruing mental images: Problems of method. Manuscript submitted for publication.

Intons-Peterson, M. J. (1983). Imagery paradigms: How vulnerable are they to experimenters' expectations? *Journal of Experimental Psychology: Human Perception and Performance*, 9, 394–412.

Janis, I. L. (1972). *Victims of groupthink*. Boston: Houghton Mifflin.

Jansson, D. G., and Smith, S. M. (1991). Design fixation. *Design Studies*, 12, 3–11.

Johnson-Laird, P. N. (1983). *Mental models: Towards a cognitive science of language, inference, and consciousness*. Cambridge: Cambridge University Press.

Johnson-Laird, P. N. (1988a). *The computer and the mind: An introduction to cognitive science*. Cambridge, MA: Harvard University Press.

Johnson-Laird, P. N. (1988b). Freedom and constraint in creativity. In R. J. Sternberg (Ed.), *The nature of creativity: Contemporary psychological perspectives* (pp. 202–249). Cambridge: Cambridge University Press.

Johnson-Laird, P. N., and Wason, P. C. (1977). A theoretical analysis of insight into a reasoning task, and postscript. In P. N. Johnson-Laird and P. C. Wason (Eds.), *Thinking: Readings in cognitive science* (pp. 143–157). Cambridge: Cambridge University Press.

Jones, G. V. (1989). Back to Woodworth: Role of interlopers in the tip-of-the-tongue phenomenon. *Memory and Cognition*, 17, 69–76.

Jones, G. V., and Langford, S. (1987). Phonological blocking in the tip of the tongue state. *Cognition*, 26, 115–122.

Kaplan, C. A., and Simon, H. A. (1990). In search of insight. *Cognitive Psychology*, 22, 374–419.

Keil, F. C. (1989). *Concepts, kinds, and cognitive development*. Cambridge, MA: MIT Press.

Kelly, M. H., and Keil, F. C. (1985). The more things change . . . : Metamorphoses and conceptual structure. *Cognitive Science*, 9, 403–416.

Kelly, M. H., and Keil, F. C. (1987). Metaphor comprehension and knowledge of semantic domains. *Metaphor and Symbolic Activity*, 2, 33–51.

Kneller, G. F. (1965). *The art and science of creativity*. New York: Holt, Rinehart, and Winston.

Koberg, D., and Bagnall, J. (1974). *The universal traveler. A soft-systems guidebook to: Creativity, problem solving, and the process of design*. Los Altos, CA: Kaufmann.

Koestler, A. (1964). *The act of creation*. New York: Macmillan.

Kohler, W. (1927). *The mentality of apes*. New York: Liveright.

Kosslyn, S. M. (1975). Information representation in visual images. *Cognitive Psychology*, 7, 341–370.

Kosslyn, S. M. (1980). *Image and mind*. Cambridge, MA: Harvard University Press.

Kosslyn, S. M. (1987). Seeing and imagining in the cerebral hemispheres: A computational approach. *Psychological Review*, 94, 148–175.

Kosslyn, S. M., Ball, T., and Reiser, B. J. (1978). Visual images preserve metric spatial information: Evidence from studies of image scanning. *Journal of Experimental Psychology: Human Perception and Performance*, 4, 47–60.

Kosslyn, S. M., Brunn, J. L., Cave, C. B., and Wallach, R. W. (1984). Individual differences in mental imagery ability: A computational analysis. *Cognition*, 18, 195–244.

Kosslyn, S. M., Pinker, S., Smith, G., and Shwartz, S. P. (1979). On the de-mystification of mental imagery. *Behavioral and Brain Sciences*, 2, 535–581.

Kosslyn, S. M., and Pomerantz, J. R. (1977). Imagery, propositions, and the form of internal representations. *Cognitive Psychology*, 9, 52–76.

Kosslyn, S. M., Reiser, B. J., Farah, M. J., and Fliegel, S. L. (1983). Generating visual images: Units and relations. *Journal of Experimental Psychology: General*, 112, 278–303.

Kubie, L. S. (1958). *Neurotic distortion of the creative process*. Lawrence: University of Kansas Press.

Kuhn, T. S. (1962). *The structure of scientific revolutions*. Chicago: University of Chicago Press.

Landau, B., Smith, L. B., and Jones, S. S. (1988). The importance of shape in early lexical learning. *Cognitive Development*, 3, 299–321.

Langer, E. J. (1989). *Mindfulness*. Reading, MA: Addison-Wesley.

Langley, P., and Jones, R. (1988). A computational model of scientific insight. In R. J. Sternberg (Ed.), *The nature of creativity: Contemporary psychological perspectives*. Cambridge: Cambridge University Press.

Langley, P., Simon, H., Bradshaw, G. L., and Zytkow, J. M. (1987). *Scientific discovery*. Cambridge, MA: MIT Press.

Larkin, J. H., and Simon, H. A. (1987). Why a diagram is (sometimes) worth ten thousand words. *Cognitive Science*, 11, 65–99.

Lassaline, M. E., Wisniewski, E. J., and Medin, D. L. (in press). Basic levels in artificial and natural categories: Are all basic levels created equal? In B. Burns (Ed.), *Percepts, concepts and categories: The representation and processing of information*. Amsterdam: Elsevier.

Levine, M. (1987). *Effective problem solving.* Englewood Cliffs, NJ: Prentice-Hall.

Lieberman, J. N. (1977). *Playfulness: Its relationship to imagination and creativity.* New York: Academic Press.

Loftus, E. F. (1979). *Eyewitness testimony.* Cambridge, MA: Harvard University Press.

Lorenz, K. (1974). Analogy as a source of knowledge. *Science, 185,* 229–234.

Luchins, A. S., and Luchins, E. H. (1959). *Rigidity of behavior.* Eugene: University of Oregon Press.

McClelland, J. L., and Rumelhart, D. E. (1986). *Parallel distributed processing: Explorations in the microstructure of cognition.* Cambridge, MA: MIT Press.

McGeoch, J. A., and Irion, A. L. (1952). *The psychology of human learning.* New York: Longmans.

McKellar, P. (1957). *Imagination and thinking.* New York: Basic Books.

McKim, R. H. (1980). *Experiences in visual thinking.* Monterey, CA: Brooks/Cole.

McLeod, J., and Cropley, A. (1989). *Fostering academic excellence.* New York: Pergamon.

Maier, N. R. F. (1931). Reasoning in humans: II. The solution of a problem, and its appearance in consciousness. *Journal of Comparative Psychology, 12,* 181–194.

Malmstrom, F. V., and Coffman, R. M. (1979). Humanoids reported in UFOs, religion, and folktales: Human bias toward human life forms? In R. F. Haines (Ed.), *UFO phenomena and the behavioral scientist* (pp. 60–85). Metuchen, NJ: Scarecrow Press.

Mandler, J. M. (1984). *Stories, scripts, and scenes: Aspects of schema theory.* Hillsdale, NJ: Erlbaum.

Marcel, A. J. (1980). Conscious and preconscious recognition of polysemous words: Locating the selective effects of prior verbal context. In R. S. Nickerson (Ed.), *Attention and performance VIII.* Hillsdale, NJ: Erlbaum.

Marcel, A. J. (1983). Conscious and unconscious perception: Experiments on visual masking and word recognition. *Cognitive Psychology, 15,* 197–237.

Marr, D., and Nishihara, H. K. (1978). Representation and recognition of the spatial organization of three-dimensional shapes. *Proceedings of the Royal Society of London, 200,* 269–294.

Martindale, C. (1981). *Cognition and consciousness.* Homewood, IL: Dorsey Press.

Maslow, A. H. (1968). *Toward a psychology of being.* New York: Harcourt Brace Jovanovich.

Maylor, E. A. (1990). Recognizing and naming faces: Aging, memory retrieval, and the tip of the tongue state. *Journal of Gerontology, 45,* 215–226.

Medin, D. L., Altom, M. W., Edelson, S. M., and Freko, D. (1982). Correlated symptoms and simulated medical classification. *Journal of Experimental Psychology: Learning, Memory, and Cognition, 8,* 37–50.

Medin, D. L., and Schaffer, M. M. (1978). Context theory of classification. *Psychological Review, 85,* 207–238.

Medin, D. L., and Shoben, E. J. (1988). Context and structure in conceptual combination. *Cognitive Psychology, 20,* 158–190.

Mednick, S. A. (1962). The associative basis of the creative process. *Psychological Review, 69,* 220–232.

Mensink, G., and Raaijmakers, J. G. W. (1989). A model for interference and forgetting. *Psychological Review, 95,* 434–455.

Metcalfe, J. (1986a). Feelings of knowing in memory and problem solving. *Journal of Experimental Psychology: Learning, Memory, and Cognition, 12,* 288–294.

Metcalfe, J. (1986b). Premonitions of insight predict impending error. *Journal of Experimental Psychology: Learning, Memory, and Cognition, 12,* 623–634.

Metcalfe, J., and Wiebe, D. (1987). Intuition in insight and non-insight problem solving. *Memory and Cognition, 15,* 238–246.

Meyer, R. E. (1989). Systematic thinking fostered by illustrations in scientific text. *Journal of Educational Psychology, 81*, 240–246.

Miller, A. I. (1984). *Imagery in scientific thought.* Cambridge, MA: MIT Press.

Murphy, G. L. (1988). Comprehending complex concepts. *Cognitive Science, 12*, 529–562.

Murphy, G. L., and Medin, D. L. (1985). The role of theories in conceptual coherence. *Psychological Review, 92*, 289–316.

Murray, E. L. (1986). *Imaginative thinking and human experience.* Pittsburgh, PA: Duquesne University Press.

Neblett, D. R., Finke, R. A., and Ginsburg, H. (1989). Creative visual discoveries in physical and mental synthesis. Unpublished manuscript.

Needham, D. R., and Begg, I. M. (1991). Problem-oriented training promotes spontaneous analogical transfer: Memory-oriented training promotes memory for training. *Memory and Cognition, 19*, 6.

Neisser, U. (1967). *Cognitive psychology.* Englewood Cliffs, NJ: Prentice-Hall.

Neisser, U. (1976). *Cognition and reality.* San Francisco: W. H. Freeman.

Newell, A., Shaw, J. C., and Simon, H. A. (1962). The process of creative thinking. In H. E. Gruber, G. Terrell, and M. Wertheimer (Eds.), *Contemporary approaches to creative thinking.* New York: Atherton Press.

Newell, A., and Simon, H. (1972). *Human problem solving.* Englewood Cliffs, NJ: Prentice-Hall.

Novick, L. (1988). Analogical transfer, problem similarity, and expertise. *Journal of Experimental Psychology: Learning, Memory, and Cognition, 14*, 510–520.

Olton, R. M. (1979). Experimental studies of incubation: Searching for the elusive. *Journal of Creative Behavior, 13*, 9–22.

Orne, M. T. (1962). On the social psychology of the psychology experiment: With particular reference to demand characteristics and their implications. *American Psychologist, 17*, 776–783.

Ortony, A. (1979). Beyond literal similarity. *Psychological Review, 86*, 161–180.

Osborn, A. (1953). *Applied imagination.* New York: Charles Scribner's Sons.

Palmer, S. E. (1977). Hierarchical structure in perceptual representation. *Cognitive Psychology, 9*, 441–474.

Parsons, L. M. (1987). Imagined spatial transformations of one's hands and feet. *Cognitive Psychology, 19*, 178–241.

Perfetto, G. A., Bransford, J. D., and Franks, J. J. (1983). Constraints on access in a problem solving context. *Memory and Cognition, 11*, 24–31.

Perkins, D. N. (1981). *The mind's best work.* Cambridge, MA: Harvard University Press.

Perkins, D. N. (1988). The possibility of invention. In R. J. Sternberg (Ed.), *The nature of creativity: Contemporary psychological perspectives* (pp. 362–385). Cambridge: Cambridge University Press.

Pinker, S. (1980). Mental imagery and the third dimension. *Journal of Experimental Psychology: General, 109*, 354–371.

Pinker, S. (1984). Visual cognition: An introduction. *Cognition, 18*, 1–63.

Pinker, S., and Finke, R. A. (1980). Emergent two-dimensional patterns in images rotated in depth. *Journal of Experimental Psychology: Human Perception and Performance, 6*, 244–264.

Pittenger, J. B. (1990). Body proportions as information for age and cuteness: Animals in illustrated children's books. *Perception and Psychophysics, 48*, 124–130.

Podgorny, P., and Shepard, R. N. (1978). Functional representations common to visual perception and imagination. *Journal of Experimental Psychology: Human Perception and Performance, 4*, 21–35.

Polya, G. (1957). *How to solve it*. Garden City, NY: Doubleday/Anchor.

Posner, M. I. (1973). *Cognition: An introduction*. Glenview, IL: Scott, Foresman.

Posner, M. I. (1978). *Chronometric explorations of mind*. Hillsdale, NJ: Erlbaum.

Posner, M. I., and Keele, S. (1968). On the genesis of abstract ideas. *Journal of Experimental Psychology, 77*, 353–363.

Pylyshyn, Z. W. (1973). What the mind's eye tells the mind's brain: A critique of mental imagery. *Psychological Bulletin, 80*, 1–24.

Pylyshyn, Z. W. (1984). *Computation and cognition: Toward a foundation for cognitive science*. Cambridge, MA: MIT Press.

Qin, Y., and Simon, H. A. (1990). Laboratory replication of scientific discovery processes. *Cognitive Science, 20*, 931–938.

Reason, J. T., and Lucas, D. (1984). Using cognitive diaries to investigate naturally occurring memory blocks. In J. Harris and P. E. Morris (Eds.), *Everyday memory, actions, and absent mindedness* (pp. 53–70). New York: Academic Press.

Reber, A. S. (1976). Implicit learning of synthetic languages: The role of instructional set. *Journal of Experimental Psychology: Human Learning and Memory, 2*, 88–94.

Reber, A. S. (1989). Implicit learning and tacit knowledge. *Journal of Experimental Psychology: General, 118*, 219–235.

Reed, S. K. (1972). Pattern recognition and categorization. *Cognitive Psychology, 3*, 382–407.

Reed, S. K. (1974). Structural descriptions and the limitations of visual images. *Memory and Cognition, 2*, 329–336.

Reed, S. K. (1982). *Cognition: Theory and applications*. Monterey, CA: Brooks/Cole.

Reitman, W. R. (1965). *Cognitive and thought: An information processing approach*. New York: Wiley.

Richardson-Klavehn, A., and Bjork, R. A. (1988). Measures of memory. *Annual Review of Psychology, 39*, 475–543.

Rock, I. (1973). *Orientation and form*. New York: Academic Press.

Rock, I., and DiVita, J. (1987). A case of viewer-centered object perception. *Cognitive Psychology, 19*, 280–293.

Rock, I., Wheeler, D., and Tudor, L. (1989). Can we imagine how objects look from other viewpoints? *Cognitive Psychology, 21*, 185–210.

Roediger, H. L., III, and Thorpe, L. A. (1978). The role of recall time in producing hypermnesia. *Memory and Cognition, 6*, 296–305.

Rosch, E. (1978). Principles of categorization. In E. Rosch and B. Lloyd (Eds.), *Cognition and categorization* (pp. 28–46). Hillsdale, NJ: Erlbaum.

Rosch, E., and Mervis, C. B. (1975). Family resemblances: Studies in the internal structure of categories. *Cognitive Psychology, 7*, 573–605.

Rosch, E., Mervis, C. B., Gray, W. D., Johnson, D. M., and Boyes-Braem, P. (1976). Basic objects in natural categories. *Cognitive Psychology, 8*, 382–439.

Rosenthal, R. (1976). *Experimenter effects in behavioral research*. New York: Halsted Press.

Roskos-Ewoldsen, B. (1991). *Recognizing emergent properties of images*. Paper presented at the Vanderbilt Conference on Imagery, Creativity, and Discovery, Nashville, TN.

Rothenberg, A. (1990). *Creativity and madness*. Baltimore: Johns Hopkins University Press.

Runco, M. A. (1990). Implicit theories and ideational creativity. In M. A. Runco and R. S. Albert (Eds.), *Theories of creativity* (pp. 234–252). Newbury Park, CA: Sage.

Runco, M. A. (in press). Cognitive and psychometric issues in creativity research. In S. G. Isaksen, M. C. Murdock, R. L. Firestein, and D. J. Treffinger (Ed.), *Understanding and recognizing creativity*. Norwood, NJ: Ablex.

Runco, M. A., and Albert, R. S. (1986). The threshold hypothesis regarding creativity and intelligence: An empirical test with gifted and nongifted children. *Creative Child and Adult Quarterly*, 11, 212–218.

Rundus, D. (1973). Negative effects of using list items as recall cues. *Journal of Verbal Learning and Verbal Behavior*, 12, 43–50.

Schacter, D. L. (1987). Implicit memory: History and current status. *Journal of Experimental Psychology: Learning, Memory, and Cognition*, 13, 501–518.

Schank, R. C. (1988a). *The creative attitude: Learning to ask and answer the right questions*. New York: Macmillan.

Schank, R. C. (1988b). Creativity as a mechanical process. In R. J. Sternberg (Ed.), *The nature of creativity: Contemporary psychological perspectives* (pp. 220–238). Cambridge: Cambridge University Press.

Schank, R. C., and Abelson, R. (1977). *Scripts, plans, goals, and understanding*. Hillsdale, NJ: Erlbaum.

Schneider, W., and Shiffrin, R. M. (1977). Controlled and automatic human information processing: Detection, search, and attention. *Psychological Review*, 84, 1–66.

Schooler, J. W., and Engstler-Schooler, T. Y. (1990). Verbal overshadowing: Some things are better left unsaid. *Cognitive Psychology*, 22, 36–71.

Schooler, J. W., Ohlsson, S., and Brooks, K. (1991). Thoughts beyond words: When language overshadows insight. Manuscript submitted for publication.

Segal, S. J., and Fusella, V. (1970). Influences of imaged pictures and sounds on detection of visual and auditory signals. *Journal of Experimental Psychology*, 83, 458–464.

Shepard, R. N. (1978). Externalization of mental images and the act of creation. In B. S. Randhawa and W. E. Coffman (Eds.), *Visual learning, thinking, and communication*. New York: Academic Press.

Shepard, R. N. (1984). Ecological constraints on internal representation: Resonant kinematics of perceiving, imagining, thinking, and dreaming. *Psychological Review*, 91, 417–447.

Shepard, R. N. (1988). The imagination of the scientist. In K. Egan and D. Nadaner (Eds.), *Imagination and education*. New York: Teachers College Press.

Shepard, R. N. (1990). *Mind sights*. New York: Freeman.

Shepard, R. N., and Cermak, G. W. (1973). Perceptual-cognitive explorations of a toroidal set of free-form stimuli. *Cognitive Psychology*, 4, 351–377.

Shepard, R. N., and Cooper, L. A. (1982). *Mental images and their transformations*. Cambridge, MA: MIT Press.

Shepard, R. N., and Feng, C. (1972). A chronometric study of mental paper folding. *Cognitive Psychology*, 3, 228–243.

Shepard, R. N., and Metzler, J. (1971). Mental rotation of three-dimensional objects. *Science*, 171, 701–703.

Shiffrin, R. M. (1970). Memory search. In D. A. Norman (Ed.), *Models of human memory* (pp. 375–447). New York: Academic Press.

Shiffrin, R. M., and Schneider, W. (1977). Controlled and automatic information processing: II. Perceptual learning, automatic attending, and a general theory. *Psychological Review*, 84, 127–190.

Shoben, E. J. (1991). *Comprehending conceptual combinations that contain non-predicating adjectives*. Paper presented at the conference on Categorization and Category Learning by Humans and Machines, Lubbock, TX.

Shouksmith, G. (1970). *Intelligence, creativity, and cognitive style*. New York: Wiley-Interscience.

Simon, H. A., and Barenfeld, M. (1969). Information processing analysis of perceptual processes in problem solving. *Psychological Review*, 76, 473–483.

Simonton, D. K. (1984). *Genius, creativity, and leadership.* Cambridge, MA: Harvard University Press.

Simonton, D. K. (1988). *Scientific genius.* Cambridge: Cambridge University Press.

Simonton, D. K. (1990). *Psychology, science, and history: An introduction to historiometry.* New Haven, CT: Yale University Press.

Slamecka, N. J. (1968). An examination of trace storage in free recall. *Journal of Experimental Psychology, 76,* 504–513.

Smith, E. E., and Medin, D. L. (1981). *Categories and concepts.* Cambridge, MA: Harvard University Press.

Smith, E. E., and Osherson, D. N. (1984). Conceptual combination with prototype concepts. *Cognitive Science, 8,* 337–361.

Smith, E. E., Osherson, D. N., Rips, L. J., and Keane, M. (1988). Combining prototypes: A modification model. *Cognitive Science, 12,* 485–528.

Smith, E. E., Shoben, E. J., and Rips, L. J. (1974). Structure and process in semantic memory: A featural model for semantic decisions. *Psychological Review, 81,* 214–241.

Smith, S. M. (1979). Remembering in and out of context. *Journal of Experimental Psychology: Human Learning and Memory, 5,* 460–471.

Smith, S. M. (1985). Background music and context-dependent memory. *American Journal of Psychology, 98,* 591–603.

Smith, S. M. (1988). Environmental context-dependent memory. In G. Davies and D. Thomson (Eds.), *Memory in context: Context in memory* (pp. 13–33). New York: Wiley.

Smith, S. M. (1991). *The TOTimals method: Effects of acquisition and retention factors on tip-of-the-tongue experiences.* Paper presented at the International Conference on Memory, Lancaster, England.

Smith, S. M., and Blankenship, S. E. (1989). Incubation effects. *Bulletin of the Psychonomic Society, 27,* 311–314.

Smith, S. M., and Blankenship, S. E. (1991). Incubation and the persistence of fixation in problem solving. *American Journal of Psychology, 104,* 61–87.

Smith, S. M., and Vela, E. (1991). Incubated reminiscence effects. *Memory and Cognition, 19,* 168–176.

Smith, S. M., Vela, E., and Heath, F. R. (1990). Environmental context-dependent homophone spelling. *American Journal of Psychology, 103,* 229–242.

Smith, S. M., Ward, T. B., and Schumacher, J. S. (1991). *Constraining effects of examples in a creative generation task.* Paper presented at the Texas Cognition Conference, College Station, TX.

Spencer, R. M., and Weisberg, R. W. (1986). Is analogy sufficient to facilitate transfer during problem solving? *Memory and Cognition, 14,* 442–449.

Stein, B. S. (1989). Memory and creativity. In G. Glover, R. Ronning, and C. Reynolds (Eds.), *Handbook of creativity: Assessment, theory and research* (pp. 341–381). New York: Plenum.

Sternberg, R. J. (1977). *Intelligence, information processing and analogical reasoning: The componential analysis of human abilities.* Hillsdale, NJ: Erlbaum.

Sternberg, R. J. (1985). *Beyond IQ: A triarchic theory of intelligence.* Cambridge: Cambridge University Press.

Sternberg, R. J., and Lubart, T. I. (1991). An investment theory of creativity and its development. *Human Development, 34,* 1–31.

Tarr, M. J., and Pinker, S. (1989). Mental rotation and orientation-dependence in shape recognition. *Cognitive Psychology, 21,* 233–282.

Thompson, A. L., and Klatzky, R. L. (1978). Studies of visual synthesis: Integration of fragments into forms. *Journal of Experimental Psychology: Human Perception and Performance, 4,* 244–263.

Thorndike, E. L. (1898). *Animal intelligence*. New York: Macmillan.

Thurstone, L. L. (1952). *The nature of creative thinking*. New York: New York University Press.

Torrance, E. P. (1974). *The Torrance tests of creative thinking: Norms-technical manual*. Bensenville, IL: Scholastic Testing Service.

Torrance, E. P., and Myers, R. E. (1970). *Creative learning and teaching*. New York: Dodd, Mead.

Tourangeau, R., and Rips, L. (1991). Interpreting and evaluating metaphors. *Journal of Memory and Language*, 30, 452–472.

Tourangeau, R., and Sternberg, R. J. (1982). Understanding and appreciating metaphors. *Cognition*, 11, 203–244.

Tulving, E., and Schacter, D. L. (1989). Priming and human memory systems. *Science*, 247, 301–306.

Tulving, E., and Thomson, D. M. (1973). Encoding specificity and retrieval processes in episodic memory. *Psychological Review*, 80, 352–373.

Tversky, A., and Kahneman, D. (1973). Availability: A heuristic for judging frequency and probability. *Cognitive Psychology*, 5, 207–232.

Tversky, B., and Hemenway, K. (1984). Objects, parts, and categories. *Journal of Experimental Psychology: General*, 113, 169–193.

Vela, E. (1991). *Environmental context-dependent memory: A cue-competition interpretation*. Paper presented at the meeting of the Midwest Psychological Association, Chicago.

Wallace, D. B., and Gruber, H. E. (Ed.) (1989). *Creative people at work: Twelve cognitive case studies*. New York: Oxford.

Wallas, G. (1926). *The art of thought*. New York: Harcourt, Brace, and World.

Ward, T. B. (1991a). *Structured imagination: The role of conceptual structure in exemplar generation*. Paper presented at the meeting of the Psychonomic Society, San Francisco.

Ward, T. B. (1991b). Structured imagination in film: The case of "Star Wars." Unpublished manuscript.

Ward, T. B., and Becker, A. H. (1991). Conceptual combination, metaphor, and creativity. Unpublished manuscript.

Ward, T. B., and Scott, J. (1987). Analytic and holistic modes of learning family-resemblance concepts. *Memory and Cognition*, 15, 42–54.

Ward, T. B., Vela, E., Peery, M. L., Lewis, S., Bauer, N. K., and Klint, K. (1989). What makes a vibble a vibble: A developmental study of category generalization. *Child Development*, 60, 214–224.

Wason, P. C., and Johnson-Laird, P. N. (1972). *Psychology of reasoning: Structure and content*. Cambridge, MA: Harvard University Press.

Wattenmaker, W. D., Dewey, G. I., Murphy, T. D., and Medin, D. L. (1986). Linear separability and concept learning: Context, relational properties, and concept naturalness. *Cognitive Psychology*, 18, 158–194.

Weber, R. J., and Dixon, S. (1989). Invention and gain analysis. *Cognitive Psychology*, 21, 283–302.

Weisberg, R. W. (1986). *Creativity, genius and other myths*. New York: Freeman.

Weisberg, R. W., and Alba, J. W. (1981). An examination of the alleged role of "fixation" in the solution of several "insight" problems. *Journal of Experimental Psychology: General*, 110, 169–192.

Weisberg, R. W., and Alba, J. W. (1982). Gestalt theory, insight, and past experience: Reply to Dominowski. *Journal of Experimental Psychology: General*, 111, 199–203.

Wertheimer, M. (1959). *Productive thinking*. New York: Harper & Row.

Wickelgren, W. A. (1974). *How to solve problems*. San Francisco: Freeman.

Winograd, E., and Soloway, R. M. (1986). On forgetting the location of things stored in special places. *Journal of Experimental Psychology: General*, 115, 366–372.

Wisniewski, E. J. (1991). *Modeling conceptual combination*. Paper presented at the conference on Categorization and Category Learning by Humans and Machines, Lubbock, TX.

Wisniewski, E. J., and Gentner, D. (1991). On the combinatorial semantics of noun pairs: Minor and major disturbances to meaning. In G. B. Simpson (Ed.), *Understanding word and sentence*. Amsterdam: Elsevier.

Wisniewski, E. J., and Medin, D. L. (in press). Harpoons and long sticks: The interaction of theory and similarity in rule induction. In D. Fisher and M. Pazzani (Eds.), *Computational approaches to concept formation*. San Mateo, CA: Kaufmann.

Woodworth, R. S., and Schlosberg, H. (1954). *Experimental psychology*. New York: Holt, Rinehart, and Winston.

Yaniv, I., and Meyer, D. E. (1987). Activation and metacognition of inaccessible stored information: Potential bases for incubation effects in problem solving. *Journal of Experimental Psychology: Learning, Memory, and Cognition*, 13, 187–205.

Younger, B. A., and Cohen, L. B. (1986). Developmental changes in infants' perception of correlation among attributes. *Child Development*, 57, 803–815.

Zwicky, F. (1957). *Morphological astronomy*. Berlin: Springer-Verlag.

Author Index

Subject Index

Adaptation, 47, 136, 160, 162
Affordances, 192
Algorithms, 3, 7, 105–151, 167, 171–172.
  See also Problem solving
Alternate Uses Test, 10, 183
Ambiguity, 11, 23, 50, 59, 75, 77, 91,
  97–98, 104–105, 108–109, 111, 119,
  164, 167–168, 189, 191, 195–197, 199,
  205
Ambiguous figures, 23–24, 59, 195–196.
  See also Impossible figures
Anagrams, 171–172
Analogies. *See also* Analogical transfer;
  Mental models; Metaphors; Problem
  solving; Reasoning, analogical;
  Synectics
  direct, 178
  discovery of, 10, 13, 34, 178–179
  fantasy, 179
  perceptual characteristics of, 162, 177
  personal, 13, 178
  remote, 164
  scientific, 21, 34
  searching wrong domains for, 180
  selection of, 161–164
  spatial, 22
  structural features of, 177–178
  surface features of, 162, 178
  symbolic, 178
  wish fulfillment in, 13
Analogical transfer. *See also* Analogies;
  Reasoning, analogical
  carryover in, 177–178
  in conceptual combination, 98, 103
  contextual effects in, 162–165, 180,
  190
  cues for, 162

features in, 177
as indirect measure of memory, 163
knowledge structures in, 21, 176–177
limitations of, 178
mapping in, 103, 162, 167, 176, 178
matching structures in, 177, 180, 192
predicates in, 177–178
problem representation in, 161–162
procedure adaptation in, 162
recency effects in, 162
relations in, 177
from remote domains, 163–164
restructuring in, 177
retrieval in, 162
similarity in, 162–163, 165, 178
source in, 176
spontaneity of, 161–163, 165, 177
target in, 177, 180
theories of, 162, 177–178
transfer-appropriate processing in,
  162–163
Anecdotes. *See* Discovery, creative
Archeology, 78
Architecture, 46, 62, 202
Art, visual. *See* Creativity, artistic
Artificial intelligence. *See also*
  Computers; Creativity,
  computational approaches to;
  Induction, computational
  approaches to
  applications of, 14
  avoiding fixation in, 193
  creative exploration in, 14, 193
  creative interpretation in, 14, 193
  criticisms of, 192–193
  domain restrictions in, 14, 193
  limitations of, 36–37